Curiosities Series

Pennsylvania
CURIOSITIES

Quirky characters,
roadside oddities, &
other offbeat stuff

3rd Edition

Clark DeLeon

Guilford, Connecticut

To my daughter, Molly Douglas DeLeon, who has always been good company, from Pittsburgh to Punxsutawney.

To buy books in quantity for corporate use or incentives, call **(800) 962–0973** or e-mail **premiums@GlobePequot.com.**

Photos by Clark DeLeon

Text design by Bret Kerr

Maps © Morris Book Publishing, LLC

LIbrary of Congress Cataloging-in-Publication Data is available on file.

ISBN 978-0-7627-4588-3

Printed in the United States of America

10 9 8 7 6 5 4 3 2

Pennsylvania CURIOSITIES

acknowledgments

America has been at war almost since the day the first edition of *Pennsylvania Curiosities* was published. On the evening of September 11, 2001, I was scheduled to appear at a book signing at Robin's Bookstore on Thirteenth Street in Philadelphia to promote my new book, with its full title, *Pennsylvania Curiosities: Quirky Characters, Roadside Oddities, & Other Offbeat Stuff.* Little did I know this would be the same day that America had not only been attacked but had mounted its first counterattack in the war on terrorism when the passengers of Flight 93 rushed the cabin of a hijacked aircraft bound for Washington, D.C., forcing it to crash on a grassy hillside scab covering an exhausted strip mine in western Pennsylvania.

By midday 9/11 Philadelphia was a ghost town. The fear was almost palpable, bordering on giddy. We had never ever been through this before. We didn't know how to act. At 4:00 p.m. I walked into a crowded bar filled with laughter and passengers on a Florida-bound aircraft grounded for the next five days, but happy to be alive. They laughed to hide their sobs. It could have been them. No one showed up at the book signing, including the author.

Seven years later America is still at war. And during those years I have grown increasingly aware of every war Pennsylvania has fought alongside—and sometimes against—America, from its prenation infancy until today. You have no idea how many Pennsylvania battlefields have saved this country. At least, I had no idea until I started working on this third edition of *Pennsylvania Curiosities.* All the quirky characters, roadside oddities, and offbeat stuff are here better than ever. But what has impressed me in my research—and astonished me as a lifelong Pennsylvanian—is how Pennsylvania has been in the thick of the fight of every war that mattered on or off this continent, and how these places are around us all the time and we hardly ever notice. In Pennsylvania, Gettysburg and Valley Forge and Shanksville are real towns, not symbols.

I wish to acknowledge every brave man and woman who served to defend this magnificent, fertile, mine-ravaged, oil-sucked, crooked

acknowledgments

★ ★

rectangle of American inland, not quite on the Atlantic Ocean, but certainly blessed by God for the people it produced, from the fictional Captain Miller who taught high school English and coached baseball in the fictional town of Addley, Pennsylvania, the one who with his dying words told Private Ryan on the bridge to "earn this," to my father, Philadelphia-born army sergeant Harry Benjamin DeLeon, who never talked about how scared he was on that ship off the coast of Japan awaiting the invasion in August 1945. He was thirty-six years old with a wife and two kids at home. He survived, and because of that, you're reading this. Thanks, Dad.

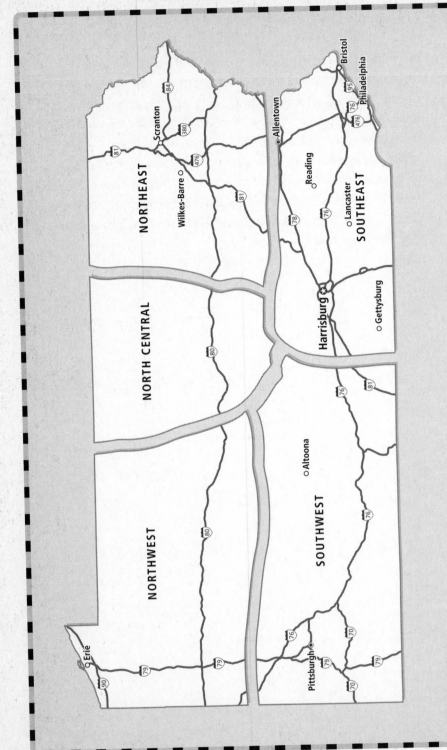

contents

* *

★ ★

Why? Oh, Why? Oh, Why O?

Why is Wyoming, a Louisiana Purchase territory that became the 44th state admitted to the Union in 1890, renamed for a Pennsylvania valley more than 2000 miles away? Why did Connecticut go to war with Pennsylvania and send an army to gain control of the same valley? Why did the British Redcoats allow their native American Indian allies to slaughter men, women, and children in northeast Pennsylvania during a Revolutionary War battle that, thanks to a famous Scottish poet, became known around the world as the Wyoming Massacre?

Why? And why haven't you ever heard about any of this before? That's the way I felt when I started doing research on the first edition of *Pennsylvania Curiosities* in the summer of 2000. My plan was to find "quirky characters, roadside oddities, and other offbeat stuff," which I found in abundance (or as we in Pennsylvania might say, "out the kazoo"). But what blew me away were the stories about places and faces I thought I knew well, only to realize I knew hardly anything. And this was after three decades as a newspaper columnist writing about Pennsylvania, in general, and Philadelphia, in particular.

What the experience has taught me, especially while working on *this* edition of *Pennsylvania Curiosities,* is that what I don't know—make that *didn't* know—about Pennsylvania could fill a book, especially this book, the third and most up to date in the *Pennsylvania Curiosities* series. My traveling companion, as she was during the research for the first and second editions, was my daughter Molly, our youngest, who was in fifth grade during our first foray across the state and was about to enter her senior year in high school during the "Oh, Dad!" summer of teenage embarrassment in 2007.

Pennsylvania: A place full of history

Do Pennsylvanians Tawk Funny?

Pennsylvania is a lot like England and America, which Winston Churchill once described as "a great people divided by a common language." Yes, all or at least most Pennsylvanians speak English. But Pittsburgh speaks English its way, Scranton its way, Philadelphia its way, and, well, there's a reason that the Pennsylvania Dutch aren't called Pennsylvania English. *New York Times* "language" columnist William Safire noted the differences between spoken Pennsylvanian and spoken English when in 1983 he wrote about a friend who "roots for a football team he calls the Iggles [and] talks in a patois so incomprehensible" that he asked for help in understanding "words and pronunciations peculiar to people from Philadelphia." Because I grew up in Philadelphia, I am more familiar with the "patois" Mr. Safire spoke of, although real Philadelphians don't use words like *patois*.

To speak proper Philadelphian, it helps to understand the following terms:

FLUFFYA: Ciddy of Brotherly Love

SENDA CIDDY: downtown Fluffya

KWAWFEE: what you buy at Dunkin' Donuts

WOODER: clear liquid that turns brown in kwawfee

WINDA: glass rectangle on the side of a house

WINDIZ: more than one winda

SHTREET: asphalt path used by cars

PAYMENT: concrete path used by people

CROWNS: those little wax sticks you get in Crayola boxes

KELLER: crowns come in different kellers

ACKAMEE: big supermarket

INKWIRE: Fluffya's morning newspaper

PIXTURE: painting or photo hanging on the wall

PURDY: good looking, as in "purdy as a pixture"

CHIMBLY: hole in the roof that lets the smoke out

YOUSE: second person singular, "Youse lookin' at me?"

YIZZ: plural of youse

YIZZLE: contraction of youse will, as in "Yizzle be comin' over tonight, won'tchizz?"

VETCH-T-BLS: t'maydahs and p'taydahs

BUDDER: something to put on p'taydahs or a samitch

WUNST: half of twiced

STRAWBIDJEZ: a department store

FIFF: shtreet between Forf and Sixt, also called Fiss Shtreet

AKKROST: something you have to do to Fiff to get from Forf to Sixt Shtreet

AWN: opposite of awf

DINT: a denial, as in "I dint do it"; sometimes pronounced "ditt'n"

WOOTNA: would not have, "Hey, even if I cooda, I wootna done it."

SUMP'N: not nothin'

POCK A BOOK: what a man wouldn't be caught dead carrying

TAL: cloth used to dry off after a shower

AST: to inquire in the past tense, as in "I ast Gloria for a date, and she tole me to go take a wawk."

WIDGES: in your company, as in "Hey, I'll go widges!"

HON: variation on Sir, Ma'am, or Miss as practiced in Philadelphia eating establishments, as in, "Yo, Hon, watches want with that hamburger?"

DOUNNASHORE: anywhere but here, a summer destination, the Lannick Ocean, you have to drive across Jersey to get to it.

GAWNA: to depart or proceed to, as in, "And to think I was gawna taker dounnashore."

(con't.)

SKOOK'L: name of a river that nobody can spell—S-C-H-U-Y-L-K-I-L-L—, means "hidden river" in Dutch.

ADDYTOOD: cajones, huevos, what Fluffyans are proud to have, you got a problem widdat?

GAZ: expensive fuel that makes cars go, what you get from eating a bad hoagie, sometimes causes newborns to appear to smile

SPIGOT: where wooder comes out in the zink when you're making kwaffee, same thing as a faucet but people notice which word you choose, faucets think they're smarter than spigots.

Philadelphia and Pittsburgh share a heritage of nobody knowing what the heck people who come from either place are talking about. Is it the words we choose to speak, or how we say them, like what the people in Pittsburgh call their own city:

PIXBURG: Pennsylvania's second largest ciddy, where the Mon meets the Ohio.

YUNZ: same as youse, only more nasal

WE UNZ: first person plural, "We unz were here first."

YINZER: native of Pixburg, a person who can speak perfect yunz.

DAHNTAHN: sedda ciddy Pixburg, great view from the top of Coal Hill, also pronounced "dawn tawn."

DA BUCOS: once great National League baseball team, sometimes called "da Parrots."

DA STILLERS: two or more moonshiners, the greatest NFL team ever from Pennsylvania

GIANT IGGLE: Pixburg area supermarket chain, what Fluffya's NFL team would be called if it could win one stinkin' Superbowl.

STEEGLES: name of the NFL team representing Pittsburgh and Philadelphia during World War II

DA PENS: name of NHL team that defeated the cross state Flyers in order to meet Detroit in the 2008 Stanley Cup finals, what Redwings forwards would have worn underneath if they had to play the Flyers.

DA IGLOO: where da Pens play

FARCE FAR: what Smokey da Bear says only yunz can prevent

IT'S A BURG THANG: Pixburg expression Fluffyans wouldn't understand

SLIPPY: what roads get when wet

AHT: opposite of in

SLIBERTY: slippy suburb section called East Liberty

SAHSIDE: Pixburg Dixie, south side of the Monongahela Rivers, working class and hipster neighborhoods with South Philly addytood.

STILL MILLS: what Pixburg used to have a lot of, why it was called "The Still Ciddy"

JUMBO: a big baloney sangwich, a Pixburg hoagie

QUIT JAGGIN DAT JUMBO: stop playing with your food

POND: what 16 ounces equals, "Same as that beer in your hand, gimme one of those cold ponders."

DAWN: a masculine name, short for Dawnald

BAW KNEE: muy bonita, a feminine name, Scottish for "pretty," as in "baw knee lass," male name of 1970's hit comedy cop show, "Baw-Knee Miller"

EYE SEE LITE: a cold bottle of beer, and not one of them boutique beers neither; what a broke customer tells his bartender at last call.

POP: Coke, Pepsi, any carbonated beverage; quaint midwestern term for what anyone east of Altoona calls "soda"

(con't.)

SPUTZIE: a noisy little bird

RADIO TOWER: steel-belted rubber around a wheel, cars use four at a time

IMP n ARN: a shot and a beer, Imperial and Iron Ciddy

GUM BANDS: what rubber bands are called in Pixburg

MOUNT WARSHINGTON: Coal Hill, best view of dahntahn, great place to watch da Stillers or da Parrrots play if you have a pair of binoculars.

With a working knowledge of the dialects in Pennsylvania's largest cities on the state's southeastern and southwestern extremities, understanding Northeast and Central Pennsylvania—an area known as Coal Country—should be a piece of cake. But not necessarily. "Hayna," for instance, is an expression everyone up and down the line from Wilkes-Barre to Scranton uses or understands, but I have yet to meet someone who can explain it. "Hayna, you know, it means 'you know what I mean?'" an Old Forge resident told me. "Hayna or no." Make sense? OK, then you should have no problems with understanding north central Pennsylvania speak:

HAYNA VALLEY: where people who say "hayna" live

WIXBERRY: what Scrantonyans call Wilkes-Barre, also Wuxe Bare

GIMME A STEG: I'll have a cold beer, please

MELK: white liquid kids drink before they're old enough for a Steg

PIGGIES: cabbage rolls that can be eaten with melk or beer

HALUSHKI: cabbage again, sautéed with pasta

DA YOU: the University of Scranton

DEE ACKAMEE: same as in Fluffya, "Meet me at dee Ackamee."

MAYAN: ancient Mexican civilization, also "that belongs to me"

LECKTRIC: Scranton is called the Lecktric City

BREFISS: first meal of the day

BAFF ROOM: where you go after eating brefiss

DRAFF: beer served cold from the tap

LIE BERRY: classy place with books

DINKYBANK: large pile of mine waste, usually slag; very pretty when covered with snow

SHENDO: Shenandoah, town surrounded by dinkybanks

ON TICK: running a tab, credit, the tick or checkmark entered in the record book of the store giving credit

CARLOAD OF ROCK: a bounced check, failure to pay the tick. Miners were paid by the carload—of coal. A carload of rock was worthless.

SCRA'UN: big city up the line from Wixberry

PROLLY: in all probability; quite likely

LEFT HANDERS: non-Catholics

PUBLICS: left handers attending non-Catholic school

PANKED DOWN: hair flattened on the head; hat hair

MEER: what people look in to make sure their hair isn't panked down

OVER TOWN: in the direction of downtown, as in "I'm going over town" when town is on the other side of the ridge, hill, or mountain

JAHAFTA: "Was that really necessary?"

BUGGY: cart to carry groceries at the Ackamee

BADEN SUIT: what you wear to go swimming

AFTERLATER: later than now, when I'm done here. "I'll go widges afterlater."

COUPLA: as few as two, as many as twelve, especially beers, as in "I stopped for a coupla." All depends on whether you go home afterlater.

AIN'T LEFT: not allowed, permission denied. "Left" is past tense of "let," as in "I'd like to come out tonight, but I ain't left." Usually applies in the wake of arriving home afterlater from a coupla.

(con't.)

FIGHTIN' AMISH: oxymoronic nickname for Kutztown University's championship rugby team. Like the Fightin' Quakers of Penn.

The Pennsylvania Dutch have added their own flavor to the Pennsylvania language stew. How else do you think Kutztown High School could come up with a cheer that goes, "Ring baloney once! Ring baloney twice! Hey, yah, Kutztown sure is nice!"

GETT'N TO WET'N: looks like rain

LEP'NEN: county adjoining Lancaster; a type of baloney

STOP BEING SO SHUSSLY: can't you walk without tripping over your own feet?

OUTEN THE LIGHTS: don't waste electricity

THE BABY'S GREXY: my, what a cranky baby

WOOTZ: a person who makes a pig of himself at dinner

RAISON STROP: Amish buggies don't have them painted on the sides, but hot rods do

FRESSING: indulging a sweet tooth, a wootz with candy

HURRIEDER: what you can't do in traffic stuck behind an Amish buggy

MISHTY: nickname for an Amish person

DIPPY X: flip those eggs over easy

CROTCH: enclosed place to park the car

THROW MAMMA FROM THE CAR A KISS: kiss me from the window

QUIT YER BRUTZIN: you're acting like a grexy

COME THE HOUSE IN: come on in, but wipe your feet first

TASTES LIKE MORE: are you serving seconds?

ROOCHY: restless sleeper, tossing and turning

SKOOTCHY: what the person lying next to a roochy usually does

1

Southeast

When you think of Pennsylvania, what do you see? Amish carriages? The Liberty Bell? Hershey chocolate? The bronze statue atop Philadelphia City Hall of William Penn (not Benjamin Franklin, as many visitors assume)? Rich rolling farmland? Three Mile Island nuclear power plant, the site of the worst nuclear accident in American history? The battlefields of Gettysburg? The silent steel mill in Bethlehem? Billy Joel singing "Allentown"? Just about everything that immediately leaps to mind about Pennsylvania can be found in the Southeastern part of the state.

The Southeast stretches from the Delaware River (the same one Washington crossed to get to Jersey) on the east to just beyond the state capital of Harrisburg in the west (where in 2006 incumbent elected officials from all over the state were voted out of office by the dumpster load following an unannounced vote at two in the morning to raise their own pay). The Southeast's southern boundary with Maryland is the most famous border line in America, bearing the hyphenated name of its surveyors, Charles Mason and Jeremiah Dixon.

But the Southeast is also home to lesser known Pennsylvania curiosities: the smallest church in the world, for instance, and the home of Pennsylvania's only president, James Buchanan, who was the only bachelor president and possibly gay. America's only canonized saints lived in the Southeast and you can see the mummified remains of one in a glass coffin in the basement of a Philadelphia church. The Southeast is a great place to start because, after all, didn't America start here?

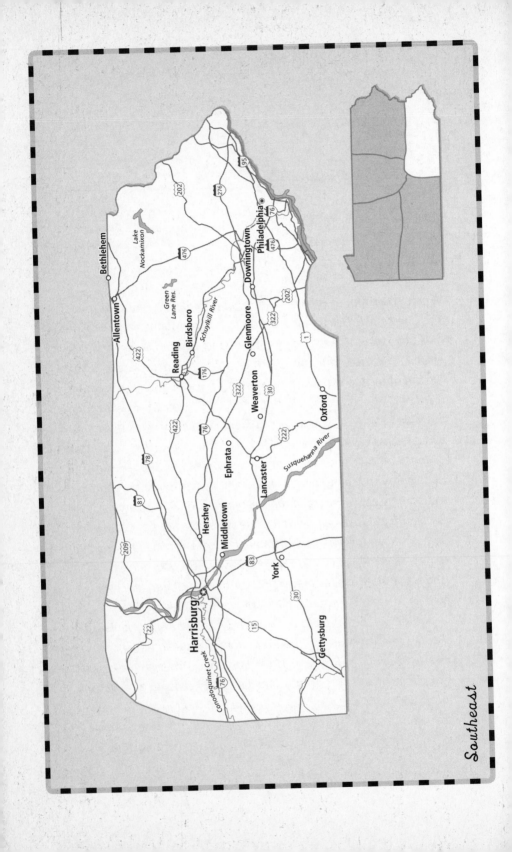

Southeast

Daniel Boone Was a Pennsylvania Kind of Guy
Birdsboro

Daniel Boone was a man. Yes, a real man." So goes the theme song to the old Daniel Boone TV show starring Davy Crockett (or was it Fess Parker?). *Daniel Boone* was also a Quaker, or at least he started life that way. Boone was born in 1734 in a log cabin in Berks County in what is now called Birdsboro. There is a stone farmhouse where his log birthplace once stood, but the original earth-floored cellar and spring remain from the structure that Boone called home for the first sixteen years of his life. That was about as long as the frontiersman ever stayed in one place, because from the time he turned twenty-one until his death at the age of eighty-five in Missouri in 1820, Daniel Boone was a man on the move.

The Daniel Boone Homestead off Route 422 is a collection of eighteenth-century buildings maintained and operated by the Pennsylvania Historical and Museum Commission. You can learn about Boone's travels in a twelve-minute video in the visitor center. ("Them Boones was always lookin' for more elbow room, if you know what I mean," says the colonially dressed narrator of the documentary.) Daniel was the sixth of eleven children born to Squire Boone and his wife, Sarah. The Boones were Quakers from Devonshire, England, who had come to Pennsylvania seeking the religious freedom and opportunities promised by the commonwealth's proprietor, William Penn.

Young Daniel was a gun-toting Quaker. He became a proficient shot with a long gun that would become famous as the Pennsylvania rifle when he moved to Kentucky in later life. After Squire Boone had a falling out with his fellow Quakers over the issue of one of his children marrying a non-Quaker, the family began a trek southward and westward that would take them through Maryland and Virginia and finally to North Carolina, where they settled when Daniel was sixteen. At the age of twenty-one, Daniel married Rebecca Byrne, a woman who would spend most of her life wondering where that

★ ★

husband of hers had gotten himself this time—either being captured by Indians or leading a raiding party or exploring new territory and settling communities named in his honor, such as Boonesborough, Kentucky. Daniel was home enough to leave Rebecca with ten children, however.

Daniel Boone's Pennsylvania years were the stuff of storybooks, which means you could make up stories about them because so little is known about his youth. He did return to his birthplace twice, in 1781 and 1788, to visit relatives who had purchased the homestead from his father. Today the homestead is as much about the settlers who carved out a life in the sparsely populated wilderness of central Pennsylvania. There is a flintlock rifle range where specialty competitions are held on the 579-acre property that the state took over in 1938. There is a total of seven structures on the site, including a restoration of the original eighteenth-century smokehouse, blacksmith shop, and sawmill.

The Daniel Boone Homestead, on Daniel Boone Road in Birdsboro, is open year-round. Call (610) 582-4900 or visit their Web site at www.danielboonehomestead.org.

Where the Blob First Oozed
Chester County

POLICE LIEUTENANT DAVE: "Just because some kid smashes into your wife on the turnpike doesn't make it a crime to be seventeen."

That line from the 1958 movie *The Blob* should have been enough to alert viewers that this wasn't just another B horror movie; it was a teenage angst B horror movie. Why won't grown-ups listen when we tell them there's a flesh-absorbing ball of goo rolling around the Pennsylvania countryside?!

The Blob was Steve McQueen's first starring movie role and he played—what else?—a teenager who is on a lovers' lane with his girl-friend when a meteor crashes nearby. They go to investigate, but a hobo finds the crash site first. He pokes the meteor with a stick and it breaks open to reveal a clear gooey center, which quickly leaps onto the hobo's hand. That's when Steve McQueen and his girlfriend find him screaming on the side of the road. They rush him to the local doc, and soon the hobo, the doctor, and Nurse Kate have all been blobsorbed.

The rest of the movie consists of McQueen and his teenage buddies trying to wake up authorities to the otherworldly menace. By the time of the movie's climax, the rolling ball of bloodred silicone is as big as a house, or at least the Downingtown Diner, which the Blob is oozing over when McQueen discovers it can be stopped by cold. (In the end they parachute a crate holding the Blob onto an Arctic ice floe. The credits read "The End" with a big question mark.)

The Blob was one of the great horror classics of the late '50s. It was filmed entirely in Montgomery and Chester Counties by Valley Forge Films in Yellow Springs. Something of a Blob cult has formed and there are pilgrimages to famous Blob sites, such as the Downingtown Diner and the Colonial movie theater in Phoenixville, where the Blob oozed through the projectionist's viewing holes and gummed up the audience during the "Midnight Spook Show."

A few years ago, thirty members of the Horror and Fantasy Film Society of Baltimore took a Blob tour led by Wes Shank, a Montgomery County resident who purchased the actual Blob—a five-gallon container of red silicone used as an animated prop in the movie—from Valley Forge Films in 1965. In addition to the Colonial Theatre and the Downingtown Diner (the original has been torn down, but another was built on the same site), the Blob tourists visited what is now a Meineke Discount Mufflers shop in Phoenixville where the Blob ate a mechanic working under a car. Also on the tour was Jerry's Supermarket (now the "I Got It at Gary's" drugstore) on Lewis Road in Royersford, where Steve McQueen and his girlfriend hid in the walk-in refrigerator to escape the Blob. "The average person probably thinks we're a bunch of crazed fanatics, which we probably are," said Wes Shank during the Blob tour. "But it's all in good fun."

★ ★

The German Connection

Ephrata

When William Penn declared his province of Pennsylvania to be a "free-religion zone," in the lingo of today, no group of people took him up on his offer more than members of various German Christian sects with names like Amish, Mennonite, Moravian, Schwenkfelder, and others who fall under the larger group name *Brethren*. There are more than twenty Brethren groups, each an offshoot of another, the result of disagreements over various issues of faith.

The repression of their faith at home brought these German immigrants to Pennsylvania.The followers of Menno Simons, a Dutch Roman Catholic priest who broke away from the church in 1536 over the issue of infant baptism, settled in Germantown, now part of the city of Philadelphia, in 1683. These Mennonites were called Pennsylvania Dutch because of the birthplace of their founder, but they were German speaking, as were members of the Amish Church, a more conservative group within the Mennonite Church, founded in the 1690s.

Germantown was just what it sounded like—a town full of Germans—and in 1729 the German Christians in northwest Philadelphia were joined by one hundred immigrants of a new religious order called Schwarzenau Brethren (Church of the Brethren or Dunkers), led by Alexander Mack. In 1732 a conservative and charismatic member of Mack's Brethren order broke away to form a cloister of celibate members (German Seventh Day Baptists) in Ephrata, Lancaster County. In 1740 a group of German missionaries, followers of the Bohemian priest John Hus, who was burned at the stake as a heretic in 1415, settled first in Nazareth and later Bethlehem. They called their church Unitas Fratrum (Latin for Unity of the Brethren) and intended to convert Native Americans and black slaves to Christianity. They were all Germans but were called Moravians because they took refuge in Moravia during a period of persecution.

★ ★

Another group, the Schwenkfelders, arrived in Philadelphia in 1734 and settled in Montgomery County along the Perkiomen Creek. The group takes its name from a pious German nobleman, Caspar Schwenckfeld von Ossig, a contemporary and early supporter of Martin Luther and the Reformation. But Schwenckfeld found the direction of Luther's Protestantism to be as extreme and exclusionary in its own way as the Catholic Church. His controversial writings toward a more ecumenical "Middle Way" of Reformation led to his exile. After his death in 1561, followers of his ideas increased in number until religious persecution drove them from Europe to America. The loosely organized Schwenkfelders did not become a society until 1782 and the Schwenkfelder Church did not officially exist until 1909. Today there are five Schwenkfelder Churches—three in Montgomery County and two in Philadelphia—with a total congregation of 2,300. The most famous Schwenkfelder is probably Pennsylvania's former U.S. senator Richard Schweiker, who also served as secretary of health and human services under President Ronald Reagan.

Although their numbers are small today, the influence of these early religious immigrants from Germany can be seen throughout eastern Pennsylvania. Bethlehem, Nazareth, and Lititz were all founded by the Moravians, and until the 1850s only members of that faith could live in those closed communities. Bethlehem continues to be the administrative capital of the Northern Province of the Moravian Church in the United States. There are approximately 18,000 Moravians in Pennsylvania attending services at twenty five churches throughout the state. The Moravians continue their missionary work; in fact, the largest Moravian community is on the African continent. The Amish and Mennonites have spread throughout the country, but the largest numbers are found in Pennsylvania, Ohio, and Indiana. Lancaster County is the center of Amish Country, where their private and separate lifestyles have become a major tourist attraction. Most laymen can't tell the difference between Amish and Mennonite dress, but if you see an Amish-looking guy driving a car, he's a Mennonite.

The cloister formed in 1732 at Ephrata is empty now (you might expect this from a celibate religious order). After the death of founder Conrad Beissel in 1768, the number of white-robed brothers and sisters dwindled from a high of 300 to 135 in 1770. The Seventh Day German Baptist Church, as it was incorporated in 1814, managed to struggle on with a handful of followers until it dissolved in 1934. The grounds and gothic European buildings of the Ephrata Cloister were taken over by the Pennsylvania Historical and Museum Commission in 1941, and today the site is a National Historic Landmark. The cloister is open for tours showing the spartan nature of monastic life. (Ephrata Cloister, open 9:00 a.m. to 5:00 p.m. Monday through Saturday, and Sunday noon to 5:00 p.m.; admission charged; 717-733-6600. The mailing address is 632 W. Main Street, Ephrata, PA 17522. For the most current information go to www .ephratacloister.org.)

The Little Church
Glenmoore

"What is it we're looking for, Dad?" asked my then ten-year-old daughter, Molly. "We're looking for the smallest church in the world," I told her. "What does it look like?" she asked. I hadn't a clue. In fact, I didn't know if it even existed. I had been told by a newspaper-delivery-truck driver about what he described as "the smallest church in the world" off Route 282 in Glenmoore, Chester County. "You can't miss it," the truck driver had told me.

Famous last words if ever I've heard them. The biggest church in the world, now maybe that you can't miss. I drove through Glenmoore the first time without realizing that that little cluster of buildings I passed awhile back was, in fact, a town. Then I went through it a second time (it looks different coming from the other direction).

Downtown Glenmoore consists of an intersection with no traffic light and one antiques shop next to a convenience store, where I stopped to ask for directions.

★ ★

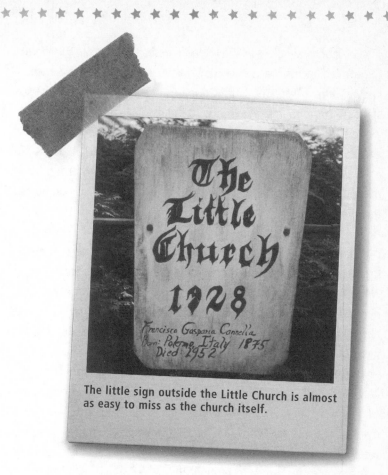

The little sign outside the Little Church is almost as easy to miss as the church itself.

"Excuse me, guys," I said to the two teenagers behind the counter, "there's supposed to be a really, really small church around here.
Have you ever heard of it?" They both shook their heads. I was half
backing out the screen door when one boy said, "You mean really
small?" I nodded. He pointed down Route 282. "It's a couple of
miles that way on your right. But be careful; it's real easy to miss," he
said. "It's about as big as a car."

For the record it's about the size of a one-car garage or a big
toolshed, if toolsheds were made out of flagstone. Also for the
record, the Little Church, as the sign outside describes it, is located in
Cornog Crossing, another one-intersection town about 2 miles south

★ ★

of Glenmoore, where Marshall Road crosses Route 282. The kid at the convenience store was right: You'd pass right by it if you didn't know where it was. The Little Church is nestled under trees just six steps from the roadway. Whether it's the smallest church in the world is an issue best left to Mr. Ripley, but it's the smallest one I've ever seen—about big enough for three people plus an altar. It's big enough for a really intimate wedding, which it has been used for on occasion, according to Dorothy Lambert at the Exxon station across the street.

The sign outside the church reads: THE LITTLE CHURCH, 1928; FRANCISCO GASPARIA CANNELLA; BORN: PALERMO, ITALY, 1875; DIED: 1952. The story behind it is a sweet one. Francisco Cannella came here from Italy to work the nearby quarry in the 1920s. Like many immigrants he left his wife and children behind, determined to work and save until he had raised enough money to bring them all to America. Francisco went one better. He made a promise to God that he would go to church every day if God would allow him to bring his family from Italy. God and Francisco's hard work paid off. The only problem was that in order for Francisco to honor his pledge, he had to travel 9 miles to the nearest Catholic church in Downingtown in all kinds of weather on a dangerously winding road. But the Italian stonemason was a man of his word, so he built the Little Church with his own hands, and each day until the day he died he went there to thank God for bringing his family to America.

Francisco's children still live in the house behind the Little Church. Upon hearing the inspiring story of a father's love and faith, my own darling child commented, "Can we go home *now?!*"

The Keystone China Syndrome
Harrisburg

In March of 1979, *The China Syndrome,* starring Jane Fonda, Michael Douglas, and Jack Lemmon, opened in movie theaters around the country. The movie dealt with a fictional accident at a nuclear power

✶ ✶

station; its title came from the notion that a meltdown in a nuclear reactor would burn a hole through the earth all the way to China. In reality, a character in the movie says, a meltdown of a nuclear reactor would burn a hole through the earth until it hit groundwater, sending plumes of radioactive steam into the air that would "contaminate an area the size of Pennsylvania." Two weeks later the real thing happened at Three Mile Island (TMI) Nuclear Power Station near Harrisburg.

At 4:07 a.m. on March 28, 1979, the alarm sirens began wailing at the TMI facility on an island in the middle of the Susquehanna River. A faulty valve had allowed air to enter the cooling system, causing the nuclear reactor core to overheat. Sixty-nine boron control rods smashed into the reactor core to stop the nuclear fission, but it was too late. The worst commercial nuclear power accident in American history was under way. The temperature reached 4,300 degrees inside the reactor core in Unit One of Three Mile Island's two nuclear reactors. At a temperature of 5,300 degrees, a China Syndrome meltdown would have taken place as the nuclear material burned through the containment vessel into the riverbed. Pennsylvania was spared its own Chernobyl by a matter of degrees.

The images of the accident at Three Mile Island are unforgettable: mass evacuations, headlines about a huge hydrogen bubble, President Jimmy Carter padding around in ridiculous-looking paper decontamination slippers on a visit to the plant. It was all quite scary, but you'd never know it on a visit to Three Mile Island twenty-some years later. Unit One has been shut down ever since that day, but Unit Two is still churning out the nuclear heat that boils the water that turns the turbines that produce electricity for much of central Pennsylvania. Two of the four 372-foot-tall cooling towers still spew ominous-looking but benign clouds of mist. The towers dominate the Dauphin County landscape the way City Hall Tower once dominated Philadelphia. But there's no William Penn statue atop these cooling towers, only the misty memories of what might have been.

★ ★

Like the Knox Mine Disaster, which drove a stake through the heart of Pennsylvania's deep anthracite mining industry, the accident at Three Mile Island not only crippled the commercial nuclear-power-generating movement in Pennsylvania but ended it in the United States. No nuclear generating station has been built in America since the accident.

Today you can have your picture taken with the TMI cooling towers looming like boogeymen overhead. The TMI Visitor Center that operated on the island for more than twenty years is now permanently closed due to increased security surrounding nuclear plants following the 9/11 attacks.

Chocolate City, USA
Hershey

What Philadelphia means to liberty, what Pittsburgh means (meant) to steel, what Heinz means to ketchup, the town of Hershey means to (a) kisses, (b) bars, (c) orphans, (d) chocolate. You have thirty seconds to answer. No, make that fifteen. In fact, time's up.

The answer, of course, is all of the above. Hershey symbolizes many things to many people, not the least of which is the bittersweet subject of orphans. And behind it all is the name Milton S. Hershey, the candy-making visionary who created a factory town and a product famous all over the earth.

The Hershey Bar is an American icon born and raised, like its inventor and namesake, in central Pennsylvania, just a stone's throw from the state capital, Harrisburg. Born in 1857 in the village of Derry Church to a devout Mennonite family, young Milton Snavely Hershey completed a formal education only through fourth grade. He worked first as a printer's apprentice and then as a candy maker's apprentice. At the age of eighteen, he moved to Philadelphia to open a candy shop, which failed after six years. Hershey moved to Denver, then Chicago, then New Orleans, then New York City, trying in each city to establish a successful candy-making business. In 1883 he returned to Lancaster, Pennsylvania, where he incorporated the candy-making techniques he had learned in his travels, key among them the use of fresh milk in the making of caramel. His Lancaster Caramel Co. was a success, and in 1893 he purchased new German-manufactured candy-coating machines, which he later used to manufacture his recipe for a milk chocolate candy bar he would name Hershey.

In 1900 Milton Hershey sold his caramel candy business for a tidy sum of $1 million. He used the money to move back to his birthplace of Derry Church, where he built the largest chocolate factory in the world. So successful was the Hershey Chocolate Co., and so generous and foresighted was Milton Hershey—he built employee housing of a quality-of-life design never seen before, as well as an inexpensive public transportation system to allow employees to live in nearby towns—that Derry Church was renamed Hershey.

In 1909 Milton Hershey and his wife, Catherine, who had no children of their own, established a trade school for orphaned boys. In 1918, three years after the premature death of his wife, Hershey placed his entire fortune of $60 million in a trust fund for the support of his school for orphans. Today the Milton S. Hershey School has a residential enrollment of 1,500 financially needy boys and girls between the ages of four and eighteen, no longer orphans necessarily, who live on a 10,000-acre campus. Milton Hershey, who lived to the ripe old age of eighty-eight, was technically penniless at the time of his death in 1945. Penniless but rich beyond measure, he had given away all his wealth and assured the future education of countless thousands. And it only gets better. In 1963 the Hershey School Trust donated $50 million to establish the Milton S. Hershey Medical Center and the Hershey College of Medicine, which opened in 1967.

Meanwhile, the business Hershey founded thrived, as did the city bearing his name. In the 1930s during the Great Depression, Milton Hershey launched a building program to make sure his employees still had work. They constructed a grand hotel, a sports arena, a community center, and a new corporate headquarters. Later, the gardens and public park and zoo that Hershey built with corporate funds were developed into one of the most popular theme parks in the United States. Hershey, Pennsylvania, is now a destination for families seeking fun and sweets, a Chocolate Disneyland with streetlights that look like Hershey Kisses.

Hershey Bars may be an American icon, but the unlikely yarn of Milton Hershey, the kid with the fourth-grade education who persevered through failure to establish one of the great business and philanthropic empires in the United States, is a true Pennsylvania success story equal to that of Stephen Girard, John Wanamaker, and Andrew Carnegie. A sweet story about a sweet man, a nice guy who finished first.

Pennsylvania's Bachelor President
Lancaster

The only Pennsylvanian to become president of the United States is best remembered for being the chief executive who preceded Abraham Lincoln in the White House. Under James Buchanan, the United States inched inexorably toward civil war, even though he was considered a pro-South president. His one term in office was marked by the Supreme Court's dreadful Dred Scott Decision, which Buchanan considered binding as law. Dred Scott was a slave who escaped to a free state and who sought legal protection in the courts. Ultimately, the Supreme Court ruled that slaves had no rights as citizens, even on free soil. No historian ranks Buchanan among the nation's best presidents, and some would argue that he deserves to be listed among the worst. Perhaps it's only a coincidence, but in Buchanan's hometown of Lancaster, Buchanan Avenue begins where Lemon Street ends.

Buchanan was America's only bachelor president; his niece, Harriet Lane, performed the hostess duties of the First Lady. His failure to marry alone would be enough to start tongues wagging as to Buchanan's sexual preferences, although he has been "outed" in

★ ★

many gay publications in recent years because of his long-term relationship with William R. King, a senator from Alabama who died while serving as vice president of the United States under Buchanan's predecessor, Franklin Pierce. Buchanan and King shared a room at a Washington, D.C., boardinghouse for several years while each served in Congress. One of President James Polk's law partners derisively labeled the two roommates "Mr. and Mrs. Buchanan." Several politicians referred to King as Buchanan's "better half," and President Andrew Jackson was known to call King "Miss Nancy" or "Aunt Fancy."

Buchanan's estate, Wheatland, is open for tours in the city of Lancaster. The grand brick Victorian country home is decorated with souvenirs from Buchanan's days as envoy to Russia and ambassador to Great Britain, including signed portraits of Queen Victoria and Prince

Wheatland, in Lancaster, home of Pennsylvania's only president, James Buchanan.

Albert. Still intact at Wheatland is the back porch where Buchanan was sitting in June 1856 when the news arrived that he had won the Democratic nomination for president. Fanning himself in the summer heat and sitting in shirtsleeves, Buchanan made a brief acceptance speech. Buchanan once wrote that the only reason he went into politics was "as a distraction from a great grief which happened at Lancaster when I was a young man." The grief was the death of his former fiancée, Anne C. Coleman, who died shortly after breaking off the engagement for unknown reasons.

Wheatland's hours vary by season. For the best information go to www.wheatland.org or call (717) 392-8721.

Main Line Rhymes
The Main Line

Philadelphia's Main Line is a string of suburban neighborhoods running west of the city along the Main Line of the Pennsylvania Railroad. What Larchmont is to New York, what Grosse Pointe is to Detroit, what Beverly Hills is to Los Angeles, the Main Line is to Philadelphia. More blue blood than blue collar, the traditional Main Line is the C. K. Dexter Haven and Tracey Lord old-money Philadelphia portrayed in *The Philadelphia Story*. In fact, Katharine Hepburn is an alumna of Bryn Mawr College, one of the Main Line's (and the nation's) most prestigious institutions of higher education. In interviews Hepburn would often mention through her trademark clenched teeth that, after all, "I am a Bryn Mawr girl."

Today the Main Line is indistinguishable from any other wealthy suburb when seen from a car traveling along Route 30 (Lancaster Avenue). But within a few blocks in any direction can be found some of the grandest mansions and gated estates this side of Buckingham Palace. To get a flavor, turn right off of Montgomery Avenue at the Merion Cricket Club and meander among the swells.

Most of the towns along the Main Line were renamed by the president of the Pennsylvania Railroad in the 1890s. Pennsy president

George Roberts named his train stations after towns in his ancestral home of Wales. The train station in Elm was called Narberth, the one in Athensville was called Ardmore, the one in Humphreysville was called Bryn Mawr, and so forth. Technically, the communities voted to change their names to the same names as the train stations, but it was more out of self-defense.

Ironically, the one community without a Welsh name gives its name to the famous commuter train that serves the Main Line—the Paoli Local. Paoli, the western end of the original Main Line about 20 miles from Center City, is named after Corsican patriot Pasquale Paoli (actually, it's named after a tavern named for the Corsican patriot).

There's a way that Philadelphians with too much time on their hands remember the order of the towns along the Main Line. It's a mnemonic, two of them actually. The first goes as follows: Old Maids Never Wed And Have Babies (Overbrook, Merion, Narberth, Wynnewood, Ardmore, Haverford, Bryn Mawr). The second one is a bit more labored: Really Vicious Retrievers Snap Willingly, Snarl Dangerously. Beagles Don't, Period (Rosemont, Villanova, Radnor, St. Davids, Wayne, Strafford, Devon, Berwyn, Daylesford, Paoli).

Barnes to City: Matisse Must Wait
Merion

The Barnes Foundation has been itching for a divorce from the suburbs to marry the city for seven years. But the relocation of one of the world's most valuable privately-owned collections French Impressionist, Post-Impressionist and early Modern paintings—not to mention important American paintings, African sculpture, Old Masters and ancient Roman and Greek artwork—has been delayed by lawsuits and endless legal appeals. The status of the Barnes Foundation's move from a leafy residential street in suburban Merion in Montgomery County to a site on the museum-rich Benjamin Franklin Parkway across the street from the Franklin Institute in Center City Philadelphia is not much changed from the second edition of *Pennsylvania*

★ ★

Curiosities published in 2004. Except that the state of Pennsylvania has earmarked $25 million to the $100 million relocation project and New York architects have been hired to design the new Barnes Foundation with three times the space but in total harmony with the concept of the old Barnes Foundation. As the third edition (*PC3*) goes to press, the court battles continue, this time led by a group of sub-urban residents who want to stop the Barnes moving, as opposed to a group of suburban residents who went to court to stop the Barnes from staying. The whole business has been so thoroughly cantanker-ous—personally, politically, and judicially—you can't help but imagine the foundation's namesake, Dr. Albert Barnes, looking down (or per-haps up) on the proceedings with a smile on his face.

Still a Tough Ticket to Get
Merion

By all reports and documentary evidence, Barnes was a cranky young man who grew into cranky old manhood while amassing a fortune with which he purchased artwork valued, conservatively, at $3 billion. Barnes grew up in Kensington, one of Philadelphia's crankiest working-class neighborhoods. He brought the chip on his shoulder and his col-lection of art to his home in Montgomery County, where it has been giving the art world and the neighborhood fits ever since the Barnes Foundation opened in 1922 at 300 North Latch's Lane in Merion.

Barnes was brilliant as well as ornery. He graduated from the University of Pennsylvania's Medical School in 1892 at the age of twenty. As a young man Dr. Albert Barnes developed a patent medi-cine called Argyrol, an antiseptic, which he manufactured and which made him a millionaire many times over. In 1913 Barnes began collecting art seriously. By 1920 he owned the largest collection of Renoirs outside of France, along with works by Cézanne, Matisse, Seurat, van Gogh, Picasso, Gauguin, Degas, Rousseau, Manet, Miró, Cassatt, Chagall, Pissarro, Titian, El Greco, Goya, Rubens, Delacroix, Daumier, Modigliani, van Goyen, and Toulouse-Lautrec, among oth-

★ ★

ers. Then Barnes hung his thousand paintings on the walls of his house—dozens of them per wall, stacked almost from floor to ceiling—and he placed his hundreds of pieces of sculpture in these same rooms. Then he dared anyone to actually come and see them.

At least that's the way it seemed to the art world that wanted to flock to the Barnes Foundation he created in 1922. Albert Barnes had his own ideas about how his art should be presented and who should see it. He wanted students, not critics or admirers. He had developed a scientific approach to the appreciation of art, and he wanted his art classes to reflect his theories. His classes were open to anyone, but his collection was not. You couldn't "drop by" the Barnes Foundation. And what you would find if you did were countless masterpieces unidentified by artist or period or subject but arranged on the walls to reflect the scientific principles of art—space, line, color, light, and focus—that Barnes wanted to express by his individual choices.

His will forbade any changes in the way his art was displayed, and after his death in a car accident in 1951 at the age of seventy-eight, several lawsuits were filed seeking greater public access to the priceless Barnes collection. In 1961 the lawsuits filed by the *Philadelphia Inquirer* and the State of Pennsylvania were settled out of court, and the Barnes Foundation agreed to open its doors to the public—reservations required months ahead of time—two days a week.

Since then the collection has been made even more available to the public, which resulted in lawsuits brought by neighbors trying to prevent tour buses from parking in the leafy neighborhood. Even the board of the Barnes Foundation has gone to court seeking to overturn Albert Barnes's restrictive rules regarding how the art should be displayed. In 1992 a court ruling allowed a onetime world tour of some of the Barnes masterpieces to raise money for the upkeep of the collection.

The Barnes collection includes 180 works by Renoir, 69 by Cézanne, 60 by Matisse, 44 by Picasso, 18 by Rousseau, and a mere 7 by van Gogh. The Barnes Foundation is open to the public three days a week, varying by season. Advance reservations are still required. As the museum is moving, please check the foundation's Web site for the most current information: www.barnesfoundation.org.

Where Edsels Go to Die
Oxford

When the Ford Motor Company decided to introduce an automobile named for Henry Ford's son, Edsel, in 1957, America was not ready for a car with a horse collar grille that *Time* magazine described as "an Oldsmobile sucking a lemon." The Edsel had a lot of neat technological advances, such as a push-button transmission in the center of the steering wheel, but the doomed model was so ugly that it was discontinued after 1960. Only 150,000 Edsels were manufactured during that time.

Hugh Lesley was a twenty-five-year-old farmer in 1957 when the Edsel was introduced. If it wasn't love at first sight, it was certainly an enduring love. Lesley couldn't afford a new Edsel (they sold for $3,500) but in 1960 he managed to buy a used 1958 Edsel convertible for $750. Then he bought an Edsel station wagon, and then a sedan. By 1962 Lesley owned eight Edsels. It was only the beginning. By the early 1990s Lesley was being hailed as the owner of the world's largest collection of Edsels. Today almost 175 Edsels, many of them rusting hulks, are scattered like the bones of an elephants' graveyard on Lesley's farm, Lemongrove, off Route 472 west of Oxford in Chester County.

"A good running '58 can get about $10,000," Lesley said of the Edsel collector's market. Most of his do not fall into the category of "good running." He's got a few of the Edsels in better condition under a roof in a big barnlike shed, but he estimates only twenty "with a little work" are in running condition. His collection is fairly famous among Edsel restoration circles, and he gets an average of one phone call a week from someone seeking a hard-to-find replacement item. "I try to help out people who need parts," he explains.

★ ★

Lesley's collection includes his first Edsel, which sits under a tarp outside. "I still have it, but it's all worn out," he says. Since 1992 his claim to owning the world's largest collection of Edsels has been surpassed by Leroy Walker of Beulah, North Dakota, who had more than 210 Edsels at last count. "He's got his spread all over the prairie," Lesley said, adding, "He's been here to see mine." You know how Edsel guys have to stick together.

Rocky's Back Where He Belongs
Philadelphia

Is it art? Who cares? The Rocky statue, depicting Sylvester Stallone as the million-to-one shot who made almost as many movie sequels, has found a permanent home in front of the Philadelphia Museum of Art, even if not at the top of the steps. Decried as a "movie prop" by art purists and hailed as a 8-foot, 6-inch tall bronze symbol of Philadelphia by less-critical art and movie lovers, the statue by sculptor A. Thomas Schomberg was finally installed in front of the museum on Benjamin Franklin Boulevard in November of 2006, ending a twenty-four-year-long battle over where the statue belonged.

It all started in 1981 during the shooting of *Rocky III* when the Rocky statue was placed at the top of the art museum's steps, made famous by the original *Rocky* movie in 1976. The statue, like the steps, became a tourist attraction—and not because of the thousands of masterpieces inside the neoclassical building. At some point Stallone let it be known he wanted his gift to the city to remain where it was in perpetuity (remember, this was a few *Rocky* sequels ago). During the ensuing civic discussion, the statue was removed and placed in storage. Public opinion in Philadelphia seemed evenly divided among those who wanted the statue to remain at the top of the iconic steps and those who wanted it displayed in a more appropriate place, such as outside the Spectrum, where Rocky battled Apollo Creed for the heavyweight championship in the first two *Rocky* movies. This being Philadelphia, there was also a sizable minority who wanted the gift

Stand in the bronze footprints of Rocky Balboa at the top of the steps of the Philadelphia Museum of Art.

Rocky (Sylvester Stallone) leaped up and down in triumph here after running up the steps.

statue from a Hollywood star tossed into the Schuylkill River (the *nerve* of this guy!). Cooler heads prevailed. The statue was reinstalled at the top of the museum steps for a two-month period during the opening of *Rocky III* and then installed outside the front entrance to the Spectrum, where it remained until 1990, when it was returned to the top of the art museum's steps during the filming of *Rocky V,* renewing the statue-site controversy once again.

By 2006 the thirtieth anniversary of the original *Rocky* and the year of the release of fifth sequel, *Rocky Balboa,* resistance was futile. By now books had been written about the inspiration and personal impact that running up the Rocky steps had had on people from all over the world. The story of a club fighter from Philadelphia who wanted to prove he "weren't just another bum from the neighborhood" by going the distance with the champ had won the hearts of the world, not to mention the Fairmount Park Commission and the City Art Commission and every other commission whose approval was necessary to relocate the Rocky statute to a shady spot at street level in front of the Philadelphia Museum of Art just to the right of the Rocky steps. A pair of size-nine bronze footprints with the name Rocky beneath them remain embedded at the top of the steps where each year tens of thousands of visitors raise their arms in triumph and do a little victory dance. It's quite an amazing thing to see. And you don't even feel self-conscious if you find yourself doing it.

Stanley Kubrick, Arnold Toynbee, David Mamet, and Me
Philadelphia

If you were to Google my name and type *Clark DeLeon Pennsylvania* into the search field, one of the first things you'd see is an Amazon .com listing for *Pennsylvania Curiosities.* However, if you were to type *Clark DeLeon Toynbee* into the search field, you would find numerous stories of a true mystery, a concrete conundrum—one that grows curiouser and curiouser with each passing year. It/they are commonly called "Toynbee tiles," the UFOs (Unidentified Flat Objects) that

★ ★

A typical "old school" Toynbee tile embedded in Chestnut Street in Center City Philadelphia.

appeared out of nowhere on crosswalks of busy urban intersections in Philadelphia and Pittsburgh—and New York and Baltimore along with Boston, Washington, Chicago, Atlantic City, St. Louis, Detroit, Cleveland, Columbus, and Toledo, not to mention Rio de Janeiro, Brazil, Buenos Aires, Argentina, and Santiago, Chile. These flat, colorful, license-plate-size messages are made of a flexible linoleum-type substance that literally bonds to the asphalt and despite constant foot and car traffic remains legible, in some cases, for close to twenty years. And the repetitive message formed by hand-cut tiled letters is the same in every city with slight variations: TOYNBEE IDEA/KUBRICK MOVIE 2001/RESURRECT DEAD/ON PLANET JUPITER.

Curious yet? The Toynbee mentioned is English historian Arnold Joseph Toynbee (1885–1975) whose work may or may not have influenced film-maker Stanley Kubrick (1928–1999) who did produce a science fiction movie called *2001: A Space Odyssey*, which may or may not have had something to do with resurrecting the dead on the planet Jupiter because, to this day, no one can really explain what that movie is about. At the end of *2001*, there is a big fetus floating in space that looks like the lead character, Keir Dullea—who hasn't been seen since, incidentally—and resurrecting the dead on planet Jupiter probably made as much sense as any other explanation.

But no one has been able to explain the Toynbee tiles. Who is responsible? Is it the work of a cabal or of a lone tiler behind the grassy knoll? In Cincinnati the Toynbee tiles were dubbed "graffiti from Mars" by a Scientologist, and they became an issue in the 2001 mayor's race when the Democratic incumbent refused to comment about them to a reporter, and a Republican city councilman admitted he didn't know much about them other than "I'm happy someone is paving the streets around here." In a 1999 *New York Times* article, the Toynbee tiles were described as "public displays of paranoia" perhaps because of tiles like the one imbedded in Forty-ninth Street and Fifth Avenue, which carried the additional message, MURDER EVERY JOURNALIST I BEG YOU.

In newspaper stories and Web sites (www.toynbee.net, www.resurrectdead.com) devoted to the Toynbee tiles, which made their first appearance on Philadelphia streets sometime in the late 1980s, the trail starts, or ends, with me and playwright David Mamet. In 1983 Mamet wrote a short one-act play called *4 A.M.* about an all-night talk radio host who gets a strange call from a guy who wants to talk about Arnold Toynbee, Stanley Kubrick, and the possibility of resurrecting human life on the planet Jupiter. Mamet, whose works include *American Buffalo* and *Glengarry Glen Ross,* has said he made up the entire story as "an homage to Larry King," who used to have an all-night talk radio show.

But the Rosetta Stone of the Toynbee tiles ends up being my column in the *Philadelphia Inquirer* on March 13, 1983. I wrote a daily column in the *Inquirer* from 1974 to 1994 called "The Scene," and on that day I wrote the following, under the headline, "Theories: Wanna Run That by Me Again?":

> Call me skeptical, but I had a hard time buying James Morasco's concept that the planet Jupiter would be colonized by bringing all the people of Earth who had ever died back to life and then changing Jupiter's atmosphere to allow them to live. Is this just me, or does that strike you as hard to swallow too? Morasco says he is a social worker in Philadelphia and came across this idea while reading a book by historian Arnold Toynbee, whose theory on bringing dead molecules back to life was depicted in the movie *2001: A Space Odyssey.*
>
> "There are no scientific principles I've found that can make this possible," Morasco said, "especially colonizing the planet Jupiter, which has a very poisonous atmosphere. The possibility of giving that planet an oxygen atmosphere is beyond even science fiction writers' imaginations."
>
> Now that quote may sound as if Morasco doesn't believe it can be done, but that's not true. He thinks that between Toynbee and Stanley Kubrick there is a way to pull it off. That's why he's contacting talk shows and newspapers to spread the message. He's even founded a Jupiter colonization organization called the Minority Association, which he says consists of "Me, Eric, Eric's sister who does the typing, Frank . . ."
>
> You may be hearing more from Morasco. And then again, you may not.

I have no idea of the real name of the man I spoke to on the phone in March 1983, but his name probably wasn't James Morasco.

A Tale of Two *P*s

Pennsylvania is among the handful of states (along with New York, California, Texas, and Florida) that can claim to be home to seven major-league sports franchises among the Big Four—NFL, MLB, NBA, and NHL. But Pennsylvania is the only state with two Major League Baseball teams that have used the same letter—*P*—as the club logo for more than a century. In the west there is the spartan yellow or black P of the Pittsburgh Pirates and in the east there is the swirly white or red P of the Philadelphia Phillies. Both teams play in the National League. And that is where the similarities end.

The Phillies P may as well stand for "perpetual." It is the only team in Major League Baseball that takes its name directly from the name of the city it represents. The Philadelphia Phillies joined the National League in 1883 and is the oldest team in the senior circuit that has never changed names or city of origin.

Pittsburgh entered the National League in 1887 as the Pittsburgh Alleghenys, or more correctly, the Allegheny Alleghenys, since the team played on the north side of the Allegheny River in the city of Allegheny, which didn't become part of Pittsburgh proper until 1907. The proud Pirate nickname was first attached to the franchise in 1890 as a term of derision by other teams because of the robber baron mentality of ownership and the team's propensity to steal the best players from other clubs, most famously second baseman Lou Bierbauer of the Philadelphia Athletics. Pittsburgh fans and players embraced the pirate insult the way the 2004 Red Sox adopted the self-description "idiots." The Pirate patch didn't officially appear on the Pittsburgh uniform until 1912, but they were commonly referred to as brigands, pirates, and buccaneers by 1903, when Pittsburgh represented the National League in the first World Series, won by the Boston Red Sox in the eighth game of a best-of-nine.

The last time the Phillies won the World Series was 1980. The time before that was . . . well, there was no time before that. Phillies fans

(con't.)

have come to look at that lone championship ring the same way a groom looks at his wedding band—"forsaking all others, until death do us part." Pittsburgh Pirates fans could wear a different World Series championship ring for every finger on their left hands. The Pirates five World Series titles are the second most in the National League, behind ten wins by the St. Louis Cardinals.

As for memorable World Series moments, the Pirates are remembered for being the first team to win a championship on a ninth-inning home run. It happened in 1960 when second baseman Bill Mazeroski won the seventh game with a walk-off home run against the Yankees, a team that had outscored Pittsburgh thirty-eight to three in the three Yankee victories. The last time a World Series was decided by a ninth-inning home run was 1993. With the Phillies leading the Blue Jays six to five, Philadelphia closer Mitch "Wild Thing" Williams gave up a three-run blast to Joe Carter in Toronto. That was the same series where the Phillies led the Blue Jays fourteen to nine in the seventh inning of game four at Veterans Stadium, only to lose fifteen to fourteen in a record-setting slugfest that Philadelphia fans immediately dubbed the Greatest Game That Ever Sucked.

In fairness it should be noted that the Pirates haven't appeared in a World Series since 1979. Since then the Phillies have had a ticket to the Big Dance three times, winning in 1980 and falling to the Baltimore Orioles in 1983 before giving Canada its second consecutive World Series championship in 1993. In fact, since the Pirates, at the time boasting Barry Bonds, Bobby Bonilla, and Andy Van Slyke, won their third straight National League East division title in 1992, the once-proud Pittsburgh franchise hasn't enjoyed a single winning season. When my daughter, Molly, and I visited Pittsburgh in the last week of June 2007, the last-place Pirates were on a five-game losing streak on the West Coast, and the newspaper sports pages were bristling with stories of a planned fourth-inning mass walkout by

Pittsburgh fans when the Pirates returned home to play the Washington Nationals at PNC Park. "Fifteen years of losing baseball is enough," was the protest slogan of disgruntled fans. The Pirates players responded by winning seven of their next ten. In August Pittsburgh actually won more games (nineteen) than they lost (fifteen). But in September the Pirates walked the gangplank and played like they had eye patches over both eyes, losing thirteen of their final fifteen.

Amazingly, on the other side of the Allegheny Mountains, the Phillies were doing the exact opposite, winning thirteen of their final sixteen, and winning the Eastern Division on the last day of the season, their first division pennant since 1993. The victory was all the sweeter for Pennsylvania baseball fans because, like a hound dog chasing an escapee from a chain gang, the Phillies had run down the season-long first-place team from the city called New York. The Mets' collapse during the last two weeks of the 2007 season was both epic and delightful. The Phillies swept the Mets in New York in mid-September starting the New Yorkers into a five-to-twelve tailspin, bringing joy into the hearts of Pirates and Phillies fans alike. The only major-league team fans in both cities hate more than the Mets are the Yankees. And the Rangers. The Giants, of course.The Knicks. We hate pretty much every New York team except the Jets, who we don't really care about. When was the last time the Jets beat an NFL team from Pennsylvania in an important game? I rest my case.

As I write this on June 10, 2008, the Phillies are in first place by three and a half games over the Marlins, and the Pirates are in last place, again, nine and a half games behind the Chicago Cubs. That's why they play the games. To find out who wins in the end. Because ya never know.

The only James Morasco living in Philadelphia died at the age of eighty-eight in 2003. He was a carpenter by trade, not a social worker, and he would have had to have been an especially spry seventy-something-year-old to have tiled Philadelphia—let alone New York, Baltimore, and Pittsburgh—during the first heyday of the Toynbee-tile era from the late 1980s through the mid-1990s. But a new wave of Toynbee tiles, with subtle but distinctive differences in size and wording, began in (gulp) 2001. In September 2006 National Public Radio aired a five-minute piece about the Toynbee-tile phenomenon featuring www.resurrectdead.com creator Justin Duerr, David Mamet, and me. As recently as November 2007, a new Toynbee tile appeared at the intersection of Thirty-eighth and Walnut Streets in West Philadelphia on the University of Pennsylvania campus. Meanwhile, in Buffalo, New York, a mutant form of the message tiles called House of Hades has appeared on downtown streets featuring specific language (KILL MEDIA and HELLION JEWS) peculiar to the more paranoid versions of the Toynbee tiles.

It's Always Funny in Philadelphia
Philadelphia

One of the darkest hit comedy series on cable TV in the last couple of years has been the FX network's *It's Always Sunny in Philadelphia*, which its creator, Philadelphia-born and St. Joseph's Prep graduate Rob McElhenny described as *"Seinfeld* on crack." The series centers around four friends in their late twenties (McElhenney, Glenn Howerton, Kaitlin Olson, and Charlie Day) and Danny DeVito, who plays the biological father of one of "the gang," born out of wedlock, as well as the divorced father (but not biological) of two others. Think of *Sunny* cast as a *Friends,* in which everyone is stabbing each other in the back, and the Philadelphia bar they run called Paddy's Pub, as in *Cheers,* where everybody knows your name and Social Security number and has cleaned out your savings account.

The show is wickedly funny and totally without redeeming social value. In fact *It's Always Sunny in Philadelphia* is gleefully psychopathic, as if the cast consisted of Hannibal Lecter, John Wilkes Booth, Lucrezia Borgia, Carrot Top, and the Sweathogs from *Welcome Back, Kotter.* When they find a healthy baby in a dumpster, DeVito's character says, "Put it back where you found it." The characters not only sleep with each other but with each other's parents. One character shows up at an AA meeting insisting he's not an alcoholic and carrying a beer. Other characters take drugs—Whatcha got?—crack, ecstasy, steroids. They burn down buildings and set each other on fire, they slip knockout drops to priests and then taken obscene photos of them when they pass out, they run for political office so they can take bribes, they sell drugs for the mob, and they're shallow, criminal, vain, sexist, insincere, racist, and dumb as posts. There is no motive too shallow, no scheme too stupid, no morality untrampled upon. And not only is it hilarious in a way that creeps you out for laughing, but it's a big hit in Ireland and Sweden as well.

The original pilot was shot on a digital camcorder by McElhenney, Day, and Howerton, who claimed the total budget for the original episode in August 2005 was $200, although DeVito told David Letterman on his late-night show on September 6, 2007, that the bottom line was actually $85. The show is shot in California with occasional on-location Philadelphia scenes with cast members. Like its Scranton counterpart, *The Office* on NBC, *It's Always Sunny in Philadelphia* opens with establishing shots of Philadelphia landmarks like South Street, Boathouse Row, the Ben Franklin Bridge, Logan Circle, and Thirtieth Street Station. *Sunny* is the kind of show that would do a city proud, so long as the mayor of that city was Jerry Springer.

Philadelphia has more wall murals than any city in the country. The Mural Arts Program, originally an anti-graffiti outreach, has completed almost 2,000 wall murals in neighborhoods throughout the city, including this homage to homegirl Patti LaBelle at 34th Street and Mantua Avenue on Broad Street in West Philadelphia, across the railroad tracks from the zoo.

A Milestone for the *L* Word

Philadelphia

Ironically, the Philadelphia Phillies almost-championship season in 2007 (they won the National League East Division over the Mets on the last day of the season and proceeded to get swept in three games in the first round of the National League playoffs by the Colorado Rockies) came during the same season as an embarrassing and much-publicized major-league sports milestone. By dint of perseverance, longevity, bad luck, and decades of indifferent and tightfisted management, the oldest continuous franchise in Major League Baseball did what no other team in any professional sport has ever done in recorded history, including the smackdowns between Rome and Carthage during Punic War League seasons.

It happened on April 15. It was a Sunday. The Phillies were hosting the world champion St. Louis Cardinals in the final game of a three-game weekend set at Citizens Bank Park in South Philadelphia. The Phillies were on a three-game winning streak and enjoying the rarified statistic of being two games over .500, something the long-suffering franchise has enjoyed infrequently at any given time during 124 baseball seasons. A sellout crowd of 44,872 enthusiastic fans had gathered to see if their Fightin' Phils would win their fourth in a row or make history. No one had left by the ninth inning when that question had long been answered. The Phillies were down to their last batter, trailing the Cardinals ten to two. The crowd was on their feet and cheering when the reigning major-league MVP, Ryan Howard, struck out and made it official. The Phillies had become the first professional sports team to lose 10,000 games.

Woo-*hoo!* We're Number *ONE!!* Phillies' fans had been anticipating, dreading, or ignoring this day for more than a year. Although it was as as obvious as global warming, many chose to embrace denial. At the start of the 2007 season, the Phillies needed forty-five losses to hit the magic 10,000-loss milestone; some fans mused, "Maybe the Braves (the second-losingest MLB team) will lose 350 in a row while we go undefeated for the next two years." It was not to be. Fans of the only team with two numerals before the comma in the loss column greeted the accomplishment with signs reading, TEN THOUSAND LOSSES FOR OUR PHILLIES AND I WAS HERE! or ZERO TO GO, or a variation on a famous try-try-again quotation by Thomas Edison: I HAVE NOT FAILED. I'VE JUST FOUND 10,000 WAYS THAT WON'T WORK. In a weird way, understandable only by lifelong fans of Philadelphia sports teams, we appreciated the Phillies staving off the ignominious moment until they could do it so spectacularly at home.

Most baseball fans don't know that the stylish Phillies logo worn by current players is a retro throwback to the swooshy-font "Phillies" logo worn by players on the ill-fated 1964 Phillies. That team broke the heart of millions by losing ten out of twelve in the final two weeks of a season during which they seemed destined for a World Series until the last day. What's interesting about the Phillies uniform jersey logo is that it splits down the middle with the zipper. Unzipped it reads "PHIL" on the right panel and "L . . . LIES" on the left. What's the extra *L* stand for? Don't ask. A team doesn't lose 10,000 times without becoming painfully familiar with the *L* word. Consider what it

★ ★

takes to lose that many times: To match that record, a team founded today would have to lose one hundred games a year for one hundred years. That's pretty impressive stuff.

The late James Michener, the best-selling author and lifelong Phillies fan who grew up in suburban Bucks County, lived to see every one of the Phillies five World Series appearances, including the single championship in 1980. But that took him ninety years on earth, eighty-five of which were object lessons in "next year" and usually much worse. Michener described the loony hope of the diehard Phillies faithful in a verse that goes like this: "Garland them with timeless lilies! Although they are a bunch of dillies, Who give honest men the willies. We love them for their sillies. Hail, The Phillies."

Perhaps this was the same sentiment, if not the poetic wording, that lead a fan to sneak into Baker Bowl, the dilapidated North Philadelphia ballpark where the Phillies played for fifty-one and a half seasons, but never so dramatically and dreadfully as between 1918 and 1938. During those twenty years the Phillies enjoyed one winning season (two games over .500) and ten last-place finishes, averaging ninety-nine losses a season. During those two decades the dominant feature of the ballpark was a humongous 60-foot high right field wall along Broad Street (by comparison Boston's "Green Monster" in Fenway Park is only 30 feet high). Covering most of the wall was an advertisement for deodorant soap that declared in huge white block letters against the green backdrop, THE PHILLIES USE LIFEBUOY. The sneaky fan, bearing a bucket of white paint and big brush, added the words, AND THEY STILL STINK! In Philadelphia that's what you call "addytood."

Don't Remember the Name, but I'd Know That Face Anywhere
Philadelphia

One of the most famous bars in Philadelphia has no sign out front. And the people who hang out in Dirty Frank's like it that way. Not that they aren't friendly at Frank's; it's just that the bar and its eclectic clientele prefer to "fly under the radar." In a city burgeoning with

Frankly, my dear, there is no need for a sign outside Dirty Frank's bar in Center City Philadelphia. How many famous Franks can you spot?

hip, trendy singles bars, Dirty Frank's proudly displays the cardboard plaque awarded by *Philadelphia* magazine in its annual "Best and Worst of Philly" issue, designating the bar as the "worst place to meet a Jewish dentist." In a city of neighborhoods, Dirty Frank's is Philadelphia's favorite neighborhood dive. Artists, lawyers, writers, construction workers, homeless people, students, retirees, judges, and strippers—you never know who you'll be sitting next to at Dirty Frank's.

The lore of Dirty Frank's is the stuff of legend. There was the time that a young folk singer named Bob Dylan was chastized for using foul language by Frank's founder, John Segal. Segal had bought the bar in 1958 from the original owner (whose name was Frank and whose reputation for hygiene was suspect). The nickname Dirty hung

★ ★

over Frank's like smog, until eventually it was embraced by all. What made Frank's special was that kindly John Segal, a retired watch repairman with the Reading Railroad, didn't understand the unwritten rules of racial and class prejudice of the late 1950s. By the late 1960s, Frank's was an oasis of outcasts, a human ark containing one of everything Noah had left behind.

I was there one time in the 1980s when, during the confusion of last call, a customer asked the doorman at Frank's to hold something for him while he used the men's room. Only later, when everyone had left the bar, including the customer, did the doorman realize that he had been left holding a human prosthesis. Somewhere in Philadelphia, a man was walking around without his artificial arm. I wrote about the incident in my daily column, "The Scene," for the *Philadelphia Inquirer,* and the following day a woman called me to say that her brother had returned home late the other night missing his arm. She wondered if the prosthesis could be his. I asked her a question only a professional reporter would ask: "Left or right?" Brother and arm were soon reunited.

Today Dirty Frank's is still a no-sign-outside bar. But its status as a neighborhood institution was officially recognized when an artist with the city's Mural Arts Program was hired to render unto Frank's everything but the name. Images of famous Franks, both obvious and subtle, now adorn the south and west walls of the corner bar. The most obvious celebrity Franks flanking the front door are Frank Zappa and Frank Sinatra. Other easily identifiable Franks are Franklin Delano Roosevelt, Boris Karloff (as Frankenstein), Aretha Franklin, tender chicken purveyor Frank Perdue, and, of course, Philadelphia's most famous citizen, Ben Franklin. But only students of architecture and gay congressional politics would recognize Frank Lloyd Wright and Barney Frank. Baseball fans will recognize Phillies pitcher Tug McGraw, but fewer will know that his given name was Frank Edwin McGraw (there was a memorial service at the bar for the Tugger after his death from brain cancer in January 2004). It takes a minute to figure out the "frankness" of the saintly monk feeding a bird (Saint Francis of Assisi), likewise for the large foreign coin pictured (a French franc), and the doorman at the entrance to the Emerald City in the *Wizard of Oz* (actor Frank Morgan). But what about that hot dog with mustard? A frankfurter, of course. Curiously, the image of Philadelphia's biggest Frank and former top cop and mayor, the late Frank Rizzo, is not included despite the fact that he once commanded the police district then located 2 blocks away. . . . Come to think of it, that might be the reason.

Dirty Frank's is located at the corner of Thirteenth and Pine Streets in Center City.

Living History That Doesn't Hurt
Philadelphia

No words cause the eyes of members of the MTV generation to glaze over faster than the *United States Constitution*. Your typical teenager reacts to a discussion about the Constitution with a sort of catatonic despair, like those young guys in the Energizer battery commercial trapped in a car on a cross-country trip with a driver who knows meaningless facts about every state they enter. "Delaware was the first state to ratify the Constitution," the driver says as his passengers turn up the volume on their CD headsets. "Man, am I glad we wrote *that* thing up."

"That thing" is the oldest existing national governing document on earth, a system of laws and agreements in principal created by parties who barely agreed on anything except that this so-called Constitution that they had hammered out would have to do "for now." Like attendees at a doomed marriage on the wedding day, many of the founding fathers gave the new Constitution "six months, tops." Little did they dream that more than 200 years later, this government "conceived in liberty and dedicated to the proposition that all men are created equal" would not have perished from the earth. Nor would they imagine that such a successful document would be

Here's Looking at Chew

The last of a breed of realist painters died in Wheeling, West Virginia, on November 24, 2000, and with him passed a piece of Pennsylvania history. His name was Harley Warrick and you've probably seen his handiwork while driving along backroads or highways, along Route 30 between Gettysburg and Chambersburg, or Route 255 between Dubois and St. Mary's, or several places along the Pennsylvania Turnpike between Lancaster and Somerset Counties. Wherever you've seen a CHEW MAIL POUCH TOBACCO sign on the side of a barn, you've probably seen Warrick's brushstrokes.

Harley Warrick wasn't the only man to paint Mail Pouch ads on barns throughout Pennsylvania and the Midwest, but by his reckoning, at the time of his death at the age of seventy-six, he had painted or repainted 20,000 barns with the famous black, white, and yellow message CHEW MAIL POUCH TOBACCO. TREAT YOURSELF TO THE BEST. In the process he helped create and preserve a piece of vanishing Americana that is going the way of the dodo and Burma-Shave signs. Mail Pouch barns used to be as common as Sheetz convenience stores throughout Pennsylvania, but now you've got to keep your eyes peeled or you could miss the faded lettering on the side of the barn on Route 309 between Hazleton and Tamaqua.

"The first thousand were a little rough, and after that you got the hang of it," Warrick said in a 1997 interview, recounting his fifty-plus years painting Mail Pouch barns. He started working for Mail Pouch as a painter fresh out of the Army in 1946. He and a helper would travel the countryside, painting two barns a day, six days a week for a weekly salary of $32.

Mail Pouch Tobacco company started advertising on the sides of barns and other high-visibility buildings in the late 1800s. The original slogan was "Clean Lasting Chew" rather than "Treat Yourself to the Best." Thousands of barns were painted, from Pennsylvania to Oregon.

Mail Pouch Tobacco barns can still be seen along the Pennsylvania Turnpike and along backroads and highways in various parts of the state.

The beginning of the end for Mail Pouch signs was the 1965 highway beautification act, which prohibited advertising within 660 feet of federal highways. Then came bans on tobacco advertising. In 1969 the company discontinued the barn-painting program, but they kept Warrick working repainting existing barns. By the time Mail Pouch barns achieved historic landmark status, Warrick was something of a historic landmark himself. He worked for Mail Pouch full-time until 1992; in his retirement he built and painted Mail Pouch barn bird-houses, bird feeders, and mailboxes.

Today "Chew Mail Pouch" barns are becoming as rare as brass spittoons or smoking sections in restaurants. There are still perhaps a hundred in Pennsylvania, but fewer each year as time and progress take their toll.

★ ★

so taken for granted, unappreciated, and misunderstood by the very people who enjoy its protections—or, some would say, suffer its inadequacies—generations after it was written.

On July 4, 2003, the long-awaited, and even longer under construction, National Constitution Center at Sixth and Arch Streets on Independence Mall in Philadelphia opened with a bang . . . well, more like a thud, actually. In truth, it was a near disaster. Supreme Court justice Sandra Day O'Connor was at the microphone at the conclusion of the grand-opening remarks. Selected members of the audience stood nearby holding on to long ribbons that were supposed to break and officially open the new facility. The ribbons were attached to a large wooden framework over the stage. Justice O'Connor gave the signal. The audience members pulled the ribbons. But the ribbons didn't break. Instead the large wooden framework that was improperly anchored to the floor fell forward like a 14-foot-tall doorjamb. The top part missed Justice O'Connor's head by inches, and several dignitaries, including Mayor John Street and National Constitution Center president Joseph Torsella, got clobbered. "We all could have been killed!" a stunned Justice O'Connor said into the microphone.

The mayor and new center's president were taken to local hospitals. Mayor Street emerged with his arm in a sling and Torsella was treated for a lump on the noggin. It was an inauspicious, not to mention nearly catastrophic, opening for a national museum dedicated to celebrating and understanding an architecturally brilliant document with serious structural flaws.

Much like the U.S. Constitution itself, the National Constitution Center survived the shaky start and has already become one of the most frequently visited sites in Independence National Historical Park, which includes the new Liberty Bell Center and Independence Hall. Before touring the interactive video and computer exhibits in the Constitution Center, visitors first experience a lively and inspirational pep talk in a twelve-minute multimedia presentation hosted by a live actor and augmented by images projected on the walls of the intimate theater. These performances begin every thirty minutes, fifteen times a day during daily operating hours, and they emotionally prepare visitors for the exhibitions depicting the powerful and often startlingly contradictory meanings people have taken from the same words in the Constitution throughout American history.

Fortunately there are plenty of gizmos, computers, videos, and fun displays to keep kids and adults interested during the tour as the deeper significance of the historic document sinks in painlessly. Kids can see themselves on a video monitor sworn in as president of the United States, and adults can compare their height and paunch with life-size bronze statues of the delegates to the Constitutional Convention in 1787. It is a brilliantly rendered and marvelously designed experience that brings life and modern meaning to words etched on parchment more than two centuries ago.

Visit www.constitutioncenter.org for more information.

Trivia

Over the years the owner and employees at Mid-City Tire in South Philadelphia have adopted so many stray cats that the city erected a cat crossing sign near the shop at Seventh Street and Washington Avenue.

Never Too Late to Join
Philadelphia

Philadelphia has always been a clubby city. Per capita, Philadelphia has more clubs than a deck of cards: sports clubs, veterans' clubs, eating clubs, social clubs, Mummers clubs, ethnic clubs, political clubs, union clubs, military clubs, professional clubs, and my personal favorite, ridiculous clubs. Two of the most ridiculous clubs are the Friday the 13th Club and the Procrastinators Club. We'll get to the Procrastinators Club later.

The Friday the 13th Club was founded in 1936 by an advertising man named Phil Klein who understood that newspapers and wire services love wacky stories with no redeeming social value. So he created a club consisting of himself and clients seeking publicity, who gathered each Friday the 13th to tempt fate by opening umbrellas indoors, breaking mirrors, walking under ladders, spilling salt, and allowing black cats to cross their paths. The Friday the 13th Club held its meetings in various public places over the years—the zoo, the Market Street subway, the Forrest Theatre stage, the Belmont Avenue entrance ramp to the Schuylkill Expressway—always on a Friday, always on the 13th of the month, and always called to order promptly at 12:13 p.m.

The Friday the 13th Club met an average of once a year, although there were multiple Friday the 13ths in 1942, 1974, and 1996. Phil Klein, who died in 1982, had written a sunset provision into the Friday the 13th Club by producing a calendar that listed every Friday the 13th from 1936 through the year 2000, when the club would disband. "To give the world a break, we should all be dead by 2001," wrote Klein in the club bylaws.

And so it was that on Friday, October 13, 2000, the Friday the 13th Club held its final public function in the Swann Fountain in Center City Philadelphia. Leading the festivities was Phil Klein's younger brother, Harry, age eighty-two, and Phil's son Arthur, age sixty-six. "Years of walking under ladders, throwing salt over your shoulder, it's no fun," said Arthur before the last meeting. "Maybe I'll get some luck now." Perhaps the greatest legacy of the Friday the 13th Club was making the word *triskaidekaphobia* (fear of the number 13) a common spelling bee word in Philadelphia schools.

And now on to the Procrastinators Club, which they got around to founding in 1956, and which has been led by acting president Les Waas since then because the club hasn't yet counted the votes from the 1957 club elections. Like Klein, Waas was an advertising man who saw a good idea and ran with it, if procrastinators ever actually run. The first meeting was scheduled for the Bellevue Stratford Hotel and then postponed as a joke. The Philadelphia newspapers loved the idea and Waas contacted a bunch of friends to have an actual luncheon meeting of the Procrastinators Club, which began promptly at dinnertime.

Over the years club membership has grown to more than half a million, 5,000 of whom actually filled out the membership application, which says "Read later" on top. For dues of $12, members receive a License to Procrastinate plus a subscription to *Last Month's Newsletter,* which is published every twelve years. And what exactly is procrastination? "Procrastination is putting off till later those things which are not necessarily done immediately, and also putting off those things preferably we don't like to do, in the interest of those things eventually never needing to be done," explains Waas.

Over the years newspaper and radio stations have looked forward to reporting on the Procrastinators Club predictions for the new year, which are usually reported twelve months late. "We're the only people who have a 100 percent accuracy rate on our prognostications," Waas says. "Also we're the only people who can be called 'the late' so-and-so and still be around to hear it."

The club motto is the urgent message "Procrastinate Now!" and its national holiday is "Be Late for Something Day," held each year on the day after Labor Day. In 1980 when the Phillies won the World Series, the Procrastinators Club issued a proclamation congratulating the team for waiting ninety-seven years to win its first World Champion-ship. In past presidential elections the Procrastinators Club issued an early endorsement for Buchanan—James Buchanan, Pennsylvania's only president, elected in 1856. Why Buchanan, who died in 1868? "Because only live politicians cause deficits, high taxes, wars, etc.," says Waas. "And dead presidents make better currency."

Pennsylvanians in Heaven
Philadelphia

There are only four Americans officially canonized as saints in the Catholic Church, and two of them are from Philadelphia.

Saint John Neumann was the bishop of Philadelphia and the founder of the parochial school system in the United States. You can see him in the flesh, so to speak, in a glass coffin in the lower church of St. Peter's Church at Fifth Street and Girard Avenue in North Philadelphia. His remains were moved there in 1963 after the Pope declared him "Blessed," which is the last step before sainthood. Saint John Neumann was canonized by Pope Paul VI in Rome in 1977, one hundred and seventeen years after his death in 1860. The Shrine of St. John Neumann, which houses his remains, includes a small museum that tells the story of his life. Also on display are various instruments of self-mortification worn by the saint during his life on earth, such as a hair shirt of coarse fibers that made every movement uncomfortable, and a "discipline" collar with sharp edges that made every turn of his head excruciating.

Mother Katherine Drexel, who was canonized on October 1, 2000, is entombed in Bensalem, Bucks County, inside the convent of the Sisters of the Blessed Sacrament, the religious order she founded in 1891. She died in 1955 at the age of ninety-six. Her path to sainthood was much faster than Saint John Neumann's primarily because of the miracles attributed to her intercession in the relatively few years after her death. In 1974 Robert Gutherman, an altar boy who assisted in serving Mass at the convent, was diagnosed with a debili-

★ ★

tating disease that doctors said would leave him deaf for life. Two bones in his right ear had literally dissolved. The Sisters of the Blessed Sacrament told his parents to pray to Mother Katherine Drexel. That night in the hospital, fourteen-year-old Robert heard a voice calling his name, heard it in his deaf ear. The next day the amazed doctor found that his ear bones were regenerating spontaneously. There was no medical explanation, although the family knew the reason.

The second miracle attributed to Mother Katherine Drexel also involved the deafness of a Bensalem child. Amy Wall was one year old when she was diagnosed as incurably deaf. Her parents, who had seen a TV show about the Gutherman miracle, obtained a piece of cloth from the habit worn by Mother Katherine, placed it on the child's ear, and prayed. Four months later, Amy Wall began hearing

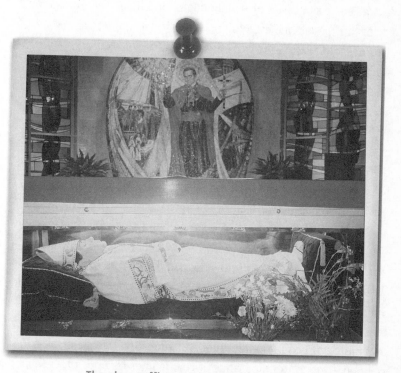

The glass coffin containing the remains of Philadelphia's Bishop John Neumann, America's first saint.

for the first time in her life. When asked before the canonization of
Saint Katherine Drexel why she had been chosen for the miracle, Amy
(then age seven) said, "Because God loves me and I love God."

The lives of Philadelphia's two saints could not have been more
different in origin or more similar in purpose. The "Little Bishop,"
as Neumann was affectionately known (he stood 5 feet, 3 inches),
was born in Bohemia in 1811. He immigrated to America seeking
to serve immigrant Catholics and, after being ordained a Redemptor-
ist priest, was assigned a parish on the frontier of Niagara, New York,
where there were many German immigrants. Later he served
as rector at St. Philomena's Church in Pittsburgh and St. Alphonsus
in Baltimore before being consecrated Bishop of Philadelphia in 1852.
As bishop he ministered to the Irish immigrants in Coal Country (he
spoke Gaelic and seven other languages) and the Italian immigrants
of South Philadelphia, establishing the first Italian parish, St. Mary
Magdalene de Pazzi, after he purchased a former Methodist church.
Neumann became an American citizen in 1848, and he established
the first system of diocesan schools in his new country after he
arrived in Philadelphia in 1852. On January 5, 1860, Bishop Neumann
suffered a stroke while walking on the street not far from Philadelphia's new Cathedral of SS Peter and Paul on Logan Square. He died
before last rites could be administered, but there is no doubt where
his soul dwells.

Katherine Drexel was a socialite from one of the richest families
in Philadelphia in the late 1800s. Her father, Francis Drexel, was a
banker and business partner with J. P. Morgan. The Drexels were
wealthy but charitable, and they opened their home three days a
week to distribute food, clothing, and money to needy people. After
entering the convent at the age of thirty, Katherine used her inheritance of $20 million to establish twelve schools for American Indians
and more than one hundred rural and inner-city schools for black
children. Among the thousands of children her religious order helped
over the years was basketball legend Kareem Abdul-Jabbar, then a

fourth-grader known as Lew Alcindor. He attended Holy Providence School in Bensalem in 1956 when it was called a mission school for "Indians and Colored People." The experience may have influenced Jabbar's later life, because in 2000 he wrote a book about his experiences as a volunteer high school basketball coach on the White Mountain Apache reservation in Arizona. You could say that Mother Drexel works in mysterious ways.

The Shrine is open every day from the beginning of the first daily mass at 7:30 a.m. until the end of the last daily mass at 5:30 p.m.

One Hundred Years of Mummery
Philadelphia

The Mummers Parade on New Year's Day is Philadelphia and Pennsylvania's gift to the world. The gift comes wrapped in spangles and feathers and banjoes and saxophones, and it takes the better part of ten hours to unwrap.

A cold-weather Mardi Gras—that's the best description I can come up with to describe the indescribable, a parade of 10,000 performers stretching for miles from South Philadelphia to Center City, strutting, marching, and cakewalking from dawn to dusk and into the night. It is a Philadelphia institution, a parade that comes but once a year and is the focus of thousands of families in neighborhoods around the city and suburbs for the entire year leading up to it.

So what's a Mummer? Fair question with a long answer, the end of which still doesn't answer the question adequately. *Mummer* is a word of German origin that means "disguise." The original Philadelphia Mummers didn't even call themselves mummers. They called themselves shooters, because it was their tradition from colonial days to celebrate the new year by dressing up in costume and firing guns in the air. To this day the official name of the organization is the Philadelphia Mummers and Shooters Association, although guns have long since been holstered.

★ ★

Mardi Gras in Philadelphia

The ancient tradition of dressing up in elaborate costumes to celebrate the new year, or the return of the sun after the winter solstice, dates back to the Roman Saturnalia, when kings would dress as beggars and beggars would dress as kings. The whole concept of role reversal was key to the all-male (until the late 1970s) Mummer tradition: men dressed as women, called "wenches" in Mummerspeak. And until 1964, when the use of blackface was banned in the parade because of offensive minstrel racial stereotypes, white men would dress as black men in fancy top hats and canes, calling themselves "dudes."

Dudes and wenches were the heart of the Comic Clubs, one of the four divisions in the Mummers Parade (comics, fancies, string bands, and fancy brigades). The parade today is far different from that first city-sponsored march "up the street" in 1901 to dedicate the new City Hall. For years the Mummers clubs would march informally up and down streets in "the Neck," the South Philadelphia neighborhoods situated on the neck of land between the Delaware and Schuylkill Rivers. The clubs would perform to the delight of spectators and homeowners who would voluntarily—and sometimes not so voluntarily—invite the well-armed Mummers into their houses for hot pepper pot soup or, better yet, hot cider or whiskey. Occasionally, well-lubricated Mummers clubs would confront each other while marching down the same street from opposite directions; these chance meetings frequently turned cranky rather than collegial. Alcohol and firearms have a way of mixing poorly.

In fact, it was the city's desire to control the violence on New Year's Day in South Philadelphia that led to the organized parade with the line of march uniformly north toward City Hall, where judging would be done and prizes awarded. To this day the intense rivalry between Mummers clubs is the competitive fuel that drives individual clubs to outdo each other each year, especially the string bands and fancy brigades, whose elaborate choreography, costumes, and musicianship rise to utterly more improbable levels of ingenuity and excellence every New Year's Day. In fact, that is the source of continuing friction among the Mummers. The comics contend that they are the heart of the parade, and they will march in any and all weather. The string bands and fancy brigades have hundreds of thousands of dollars invested in their elaborate satin and feathered "suits" and props, which will be ruined by rain or high winds. Thus, a number of parades have been postponed in the last twenty years, which has caused ill will among the already fractious Mummers clubs and the loyal fans who line Broad Street sidewalks six deep to watch the parade.

The Mummers Parade returned to its South Philly roots and its historic Broad Street route north to City Hall on January 1, 2004, during

what Mummers and tens of thousands of spectators universally hailed
as the best parade in twenty years. The weather was more than
cooperative; it was perfect—brilliant sunshine, temperatures in the
high forties, and the merest hint of a breeze, which caused sequins
to shimmer, banners to wave, and plumes to fan. The sidewalks on
the parade route through Center City were eight and ten people
deep with spectators, and sidewalks were gridlocked by a new generation of Mummers fans in strollers. On this, the first New Year's
parade up Broad Street in the new millennium, a century-old Philadelphia Mummers tradition was restored.

For all things Mummer, visit www.mummers.com.

The Frogs of Two Street
Philadelphia

James "Froggy" Carr was a tough little kid with an improbably deep
voice (hence the nickname) from Second Street in South Philadelphia.
The area is known affectionately as Two Street and is home to the
majority of Mummers clubs, including the James "Froggy" Carr NYB
(New Year's Brigade). The Frogs, as they are known, is an old-school
comic club—all wenches all the time—that was formed by Froggy
Carr's buddies after he died from a freak injury while playing a pickup
game of tackle football in 1970. He was twenty years old at the time.

Froggy would have been fifty-three on New Year's Day 2004,
when the Mummers Parade returned to Broad Street after a four-year
experiment of marching on Market Street. Outside the Froggy Carr
Clubhouse on Second Street in South Philadelphia, men, boys, and
even a few women dressed as wenches began gathering about 8:00
a.m. under brilliant sunshine. In an ancient rite of mummery, men
helped men with their makeup or helped zip up a friend's dress from
behind. There was nothing metrosexual about it. This is as tough
a group of working-class guys dressed up as women as you'll ever
see. And there are a lot of them—more than 600, the largest wench
brigade in the Mummers Parade. One Frog flew in from Baghdad for

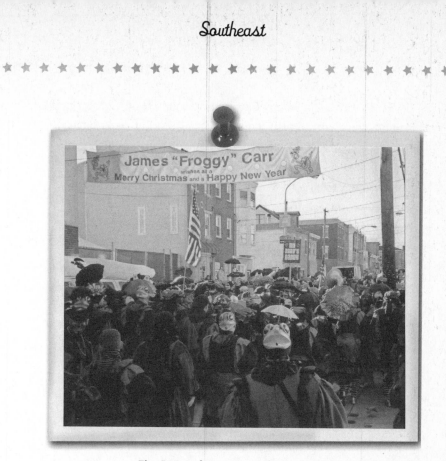

The Frogs of Two Street frolic: Philadelphia Mummers strut in the new year wearing "wench" costumes in the comic division.

the occasion. Marine Lieutenant Colonel Paul Schreiber, who had spent much of the previous year serving with American forces in Iraq, marched with Froggy Carr during his two-week holiday leave. Another unlikely Frog, Sally Daly, a seventy-year-old grandmother from South Philly, was marching in her fifth Mummers Parade.

The 2004 theme was "Jamaican Me Froggy," with the wenches wearing dreadlocks instead of the traditional pigtails. The marchers each wore frog masks backwards on their heads. A plastic tube led from each marcher's mouth to an inflatable noisemaker that would unroll from the frog's mouth like a tongue. The pièce de résistance, a controversial one at that, was a 20-foot-long prop that resembled a hand-rolled cigarette that would have made Bob Marley smile.

"Irie, Frog mon!" The Froggy Carr house band, a church group called the Spiritual Rockets, played reggae on brass instruments—"Let's get together and feel all right . . ."— as the massive comic brigade wound its way through the streets of South Philadelphia to serenade friends and pay tribute to the families of friends who had died the previous year. In fact, the Frogs dedicated this parade to a fellow wench from a rival club who had died in a car crash while sitting at a stoplight the previous September.

The Frogs' trademark chant "Who dat? Who dat? Who dat Froggy Carr?!" could be heard from blocks away as they marched up Broad Street, creating a buzz of recognition and appreciation among veteran Mummers Parade spectators. Despite their numbers and enthusiasm, the Frogs generally finish out of the money, if not actually in jail. One year Frogs Captain Mike Renzi ended up in police custody when Renzi protested the police confiscating dozens of cases of beer from the Frogs' support truck. This happened the first year the parade route was switched to Market Street. The leaderless Frogs responded with a spontaneous sit-down strike on Market Street, which prevented the parade from moving past them. Forty-five minutes later the police arrived with flashing lights and sirens to return the Frogs captain so the parade could continue. Even tough Philadelphia cops don't want to tangle with 600 guys in dresses having a bad-hair day.

Unlike past years, in 2004 the Frogs were not disqualified from the judging for the usual laundry list of Froggy behavior "unbecoming a Mummer." They finished third in the comic-brigade category despite arriving at the starting line of the march an hour late (all that marching around South Philly to greet friends before heading to Broad Street) and despite displaying a prop joint the size of the *Titanic*. During the live TV broadcast of the parade at the City Hall judging stands, TV directors well acquainted with the many surprises of Froggy Carr cut to a commercial when the "Jamaican Me Froggy" prop steamed into view under Billy Penn's hat.

The Pennsylvania X Files
Philadelphia

What Roswell, New Mexico, is to UFOs and what Bermuda is to mysterious triangles, Philadelphia is to disappearing warships. The so-called Philadelphia Experiment would definitely qualify as one of the X Files if Agents Mulder and Scully had decided to look into it. But it happened well before their time, during World War II, even though the story has yet to go away. As recently as November 28, 2000, the U.S. Navy's Office of Naval Research issued an updated statement on its "Frequently Asked Questions" page on the Internet addressing the Philadelphia Experiment. "Allegedly, in the fall of 1943, a U.S. Navy destroyer was made invisible and teleported from Philadelphia, Pennsylvania, to Norfolk, Virginia, in an incident known as the Philadelphia Experiment," began the navy's earlier statement on September 2, 1996. "Records in the Operational Archives Branch of the Naval Historical Center have been repeatedly searched, but no documents have been located which confirm the event, or any interest by the Navy in attempting such an achievement."

I don't know about Agents Mulder and Scully, but such a denial makes a lot of people suspicious. When I logged on to the Philadelphia Experiment from A to Z home page on the Internet, I was visitor 581,305, indicating a continuing interest in the story, which first surfaced in the 1950s and was brought to prominence by a popular movie of the same name in the 1980s. The story, if not the facts, behind the Philadelphia Experiment follows.

In June of 1943 the USS *Eldridge*, a destroyer escort, was fitted with an experimental electromagnetic generation system at the now Philadelphia Naval Shipyard. The goal of the experiment was to make the ship invisible to radar. At 0900 hours on July 22, 1943, the *Eldridge* radar invisibility system was tested in front of naval observers. A greenish fog was said to have enveloped the ship, making it invisible to radar. Then the fog vanished along with the ship, which was no longer visible to the human eye either. After fifteen minutes

Size Matters

The population of the city of Philadelphia has been shrinking almost since the day I was born. In 1950 Philadelphia was the third-largest city in America and home to more than two million people. Since then the city has lost one quarter of its population—more than 500,000 people—most of whom moved to its suburbs in Pennsylvania and New Jersey. Today Philadelphia is America's fifth largest city, with a population of just under 1.5 million. If you add the population of the three adjoining Pennsylvania counties (Bucks, Montgomery, and Delaware), the southeast Pennsylvania metropolis is well over three million people.

Including the suburbs in the city population may seem like fudging the statistics. However, in this case it is more than fair because Philadelphia is America's "smallest big city," literally. Of America's ten largest cities, Philadelphia is the smallest in area. Philadelphia has 135 square miles, compared to New York's 303, Los Angeles's 469, Chicago's 227, and Houston's awesome 579. Philadelphia's last growth spurt took place in 1854, when the city and county consolidated to its present size. Before that the city limits were within the boundaries of what is now called Center City, a 12-block-by-20-block rectangle from Vine Street to South Street, from the Delaware River to the Schuylkill.

As a Philadelphian it bugs me to see cities with three times the area taking our top-city ranking, census after census. In 1960 Los Angeles surpassed Philadelphia, knocking us to fourth place. In the 2000 census Houston hopped over Philly, sending us to fifth place. By 2010 Philadelphia could drop as many as five slots to tenth because four Wal-Mart–size cities with populations of over one million are chomping at the bit. Sixth-place Phoenix (1.3 million people) has an area of 474 square miles; seventh place San Diego (1.2 million people) has 324 square miles; Dallas, which is named after a former Philadelphia mayor, George Dallas, is eighth (1.18 million people) with 342 square miles; and running neck and neck is ninth-place San Antonio (1.14 million people) with 407 square miles. It's gonna happen sooner or later. Philadelphia is like a mom-and-pop-size hardware store with four Home Depots competing for its sales.

Meanwhile, Philadelphia gives Pennsylvania what only one other state on the East Coast has—a city of more than one million people. Shrinking Baltimore, number seventeen on the list, has a population of 651,000. Tiny Boston, number twenty, has 589,000 people packed into its 48 square miles. Booming Atlanta, number thirty-nine, has about the same area as Philadelphia and a population of 416,000. Only enormous Jacksonville, Florida, number fourteen, with 757 square miles and 735,000 people, seems likely to pass a million in the next ten or twenty years.

New York, New York—let's give the devil his due—is in a league of its own. "There are eight million stories in the Naked City" began the epilogue of a famous TV crime show in the '60s. There are still eight million, despite a temporary dip to 7.3 million in 1990. There is a telling difference between New York State and Pennsylvania, though. New York State has a population of nineteen million, and almost half of those people live in New York City. Pennsylvania has a population of twelve million, and approximately 12 percent of those folks live in Philadelphia.

Still, Philadelphia dominates Pennsylvania's population like the Big Pretzel. You'd have to take the combined populations of thirty-six of the state's next largest cities and towns—in order of ranking: Pittsburgh, Allentown, Erie, Reading, Scranton, Bethlehem, Lancaster, Harrisburg, Altoona, Wilkes-Barre, York, State College, Chester, Bethel Park, Norristown, Williamsport, Monroeville, Plum, Easton, New Castle, Lebanon, McKeesport, Johnstown, Hazleton, West Mifflin, Pottstown, Baldwin, Murrysville, Wilkinsburg, Carlisle, Chambersburg, West Chester, Hermitage, Lansdale, Sharon, and Greensburg—to surpass the population of Pennsylvania's largest city. However, excluding Philadelphia, if you added up the populations of the seventy-one Pennsylvania municipalities with populations of 10,000 or more, you'd get a little over two million people. Add Philadelphia to that, and you get 3.5 million. That means the vast majority—more than 70 percent—of Pennsylvania's twelve million people live in small towns.

Curious, no?

the order was given to shut down the electromagnetic field, and the *Eldridge* returned to view at anchor where it had been all along. Upon boarding the ship after the experiment, the naval observers found the crew members to be nauseated and disoriented.

The crew was replaced with a new crew, alterations were made to the electromagnetic equipment, and another test was conducted on the *Eldridge* at 1715 hours on October 28, 1943. This time the ship vanished in a burst of intense blue light and reappeared hundreds of miles away at what is now the Norfolk Naval Shipyard, where it was observed by the crew of a civilian merchant ship, the SS *Andrew Furuseth*. Minutes later, the ship vanished from Norfolk and reappeared in Philadelphia. This time, when the observers boarded the *Eldridge*, they not only found that some crew members were violently ill and out of their minds, but some sailors were missing altogether and five of the crew had been horribly fused to the metal of the ship's structure.

Or so the story goes. The truth is out there, as the *X Files* TV show likes to remind us. The Navy's latest statement on the Philadelphia Experiment offers transcripts of deck logs from both the *Eldridge* and the *Andrew Furuseth*, showing that the *Eldridge* was never in Philadelphia during the summer or fall of 1943 and that the *Andrew Furuseth* was not in Norfolk on October 28, 1943.

Not Your Average Cabbage Garden
Philadelphia

Philadelphia's Fairmount Park has long held the title of "world's largest urban park." In fact, when you look at a map of Philadelphia, one of the most notable features is the amount of green parkland in the heart of the city. This was no accident, although the original motivation behind preserving green space was to protect the city's water supply from industrial pollution. Today Fairmount Park is a system of landscaped and natural parkland totaling 8,000 acres, with fingers of green touching dozens of neighborhoods. In fact, it is possible to walk from Philadelphia's City Hall in Center City to the Montgomery County line 12 miles away without ever stepping outside of Fairmount Park.

Trivia

The Hidden Indian

In the heart of the Wissahickon Valley in Philadelphia's Fairmount Park, in the middle of a gorge where it's hard to imagine that you are surrounded by a city of a million and a half people, there is an outcropping of rock. And on that outcropping of rock crouches a 12-foot-tall Indian in full headdress. It is a limestone statue of the last of the chiefs of the Lenni Lenape, who inhabited the area in the 1700s. The actual chief, Teedyuscung, may or may not have resembled the noble warrior who peers out over the valley with his hand shading his eyes. But "finding the Indian" in Fairmount Park has become one of the traditions of parents and children since the statue was installed in its out-of-the-way location, accessible only by a dirt trail up steep terrain.

The statue of Teedyuscung originally stood in front of a tavern on Henry Avenue during the 1800s. It was moved to its current difficult-to-find location in 1910. It is one of the best-kept secrets of Fairmount Park, and it can be found by intrepid explorers off Forbidden Drive (great name, huh?) near the stone bridge over the Wissahickon Creek at Rex Street. The fate of the original Teedyuscung is a sadder story. After taking his people to the Wyoming Valley in what is Luzerne County today, Teedyuscung died in a fire set by rival Iroquois tribe members in 1763.

★ ★

"Is it possible you have never seen Fairmount Park?" wrote the well-traveled writer Lafcadio Hearn to a friend in New York after a visit to the Centennial Exhibition in Philadelphia in 1876. "Believe me then it is the most beautiful place in the whole civilized world. Your Central Park is a cabbage garden by comparison." Such rave reviews for Fairmount Park were exactly what the city leaders were counting on when they created the park in 1865. In fact, one of the assemblymen in the two city councils governing the city in the mid-1800s urged his fellow legislators to vote in favor of creating the park, using the kind of language usually associated with ending poverty or guaranteeing world peace. Said Assemblyman James Miller in 1865, "We have it in our power, by saying aye to this bill, to give Philadelphia as fair a landscape and as charming a scene as ever gladened the eye of mortal man since the gates of Eden were closed to human eyes—a place where children may play, the young may ramble and the aged rest—a place where philosophy may linger, art may revel, and beauty may find a perpetual home. Seldom in your lives will you have the opportunity of doing so much good by a single vote. . . . The blessings of childhood will follow you, the benediction of age will be upon you, and the generations to come will hold your name in grateful remembrance."

Most Philadelphians couldn't tell you who James Miller was, but certainly they are grateful for the park he and his fellow legislators gave the city. Visit at www.fairmountpark.org.

City of the Dead
Philadelphia

Philadelphia has its share of prominent and architecturally significant cemeteries, none more prominent and architecturally significant than Laurel Hill Cemetery on the edge of North Philadelphia. Overlooking the Schuylkill River, Laurel Hill's seventy-eight acres are laid out like a promenade for the living rather than a resting place for the dead. Designed by Scottish architect John Notman, upon opening in 1836 Laurel Hill immediately became a destination for city-bound Philadel-

Armless woman raises the coffin lid to allow the soul of the departed to rise to heaven at a grave site at Laurel Hill Cemetery in Philadelphia.

phians seeking a rural retreat, a place to picnic and stroll among the marble monuments.

Located 3½ miles from Center City, Laurel Hill's landscaping set the tone for later development of Fairmount Park, which eventually spread to its very gates. Within the cemetery, which was declared a National Historic Landmark in 1998, are hundreds of exquisitely sculpted monuments, such as the tomb of William Warner, young son of William and Anna Catherine Warner, who died on January 20, 1889. The tomb shows a woman pulling aside the top of a stone sarcophagus, allowing a spirit, a face shrouded by wings, to soar to

★ ★

heaven. Over the years this striking work has been vandalized (both of the woman's arms are missing), but like a Venus de Milo of the departed, her serenity is enhanced by the loss of her extremities.

On the back of the tomb is the monument maker's signature, "A. Calder, Philadelphia." That would be Alexander Milne Calder, the artist responsible for the huge bronze statue of William Penn and the other 250 pieces of statuary adorning City Hall. The date of young Warner's death reveals that Calder was in the middle of the forty-year-long project that was the design and construction of City Hall when he accepted the commission to sculpt this grave monument. As you can see, the artist did not treat this stunning work with any less attention than he devoted to the statues on City Hall.

Among the better-known Philadelphians buried in Laurel Hill Cemetery are Anna Jarvis, the founder of Mother's Day; George Meade, the victorious Union general at the Battle of Gettysburg; and Owen Wister, the author who wrote the first "western" novel, called *The Virginian*. Laurel Hill is open daily for tours.

To learn more, visit www.thelaurelhillcemetery.org.

Old Baldy and the Invisible Hero
Philadelphia

Even in his hometown George Meade doesn't get the credit his role in history deserves. Ask the average Philadelphian who commanded the Union troops at the Battle of Gettysburg, and chances are he or she will draw a blank. But even the most Civil War–history-impaired high school graduate north of the Mason-Dixon Line can tell you that the Confederate troops at Gettysburg were led by General Robert E. Lee. Nevertheless, it was Union general George Gordon Meade who won the biggest battle ever fought on the North American continent—and the turning point of the Civil War. Yet despite his victory defending native soil, among most Pennsylvanians, George Meade has about the same name recognition as the correct answer in the Final Jeopardy category "Sixteenth-Century Prussian Monarchs."

The Schuylkill: A Spelling Bee of a River

Most rivers in Pennsylvania have names of Indian origin: Susquehanna, Allegheny, Monongahela, Lehigh, Lackawanna. Even the Delaware, which is not an Indian name (it takes its name from the English Lord De La Warr), became the name commonly used to identify the Indian tribe known as Lenni Lenape.

The Schuylkill, however, is of Dutch origin (the word, not the river). There are many regular commuters on the expressway that bears the river's name who will swear that the word *Schuylkill* in any language means "this lane ends suddenly." But in Dutch it means "hidden river," which, in fact, makes the term Schuylkill River as redundant as Rio Grande River.

The Schuylkill was named by Henry Hudson, the English explorer under Dutch hire who gave his name to a river in New York. During one of his explorations in the early 1600s, Hudson sailed up the Delaware River and passed without noticing the mouth of the Schuylkill, which was covered with reeds. On his way back down the Delaware, Hudson saw the mouth of the Schuylkill for what it was. He explored its navigable sections and gave it the name "hidden river."

As difficult as the Schuylkill was for Hudson to find, the name he gave the river has proved difficult for first-time visitors to pronounce and a continuing challenge for even lifelong Pennsylvanians to spell. There is a hard "C" sound at the beginning, not a soft "Sh": skoo-kill (although Philadelphians tend to pronounce it skook'll). *Schuylkill* is always a spelling bee champion breaker. Someone—certainly not Henry Hudson—came up with a mnemonic to help kids remember how to spell it: Seven Cooties Hurry Up Your Leg—Kick It Lots, Lee!

★ ★

There are reasons for Meade's comparative obscurity in relation to his Confederate equivalent. The Virginian, Lee, was majestic, soft spoken, regal, and handsome. The Pennsylvanian, Meade, was none of the above. Even at his best, George Meade was hard to take and plug-ugly to boot. He was notoriously short tempered and harsh with subordinates. With his bulging eyes and pinched mouth, Meade was nicknamed "old snapping turtle" by Union enlisted men. In some circles the name of Lee's iron gray warhorse, Traveller, is better known than the name of the general who defeated Lee at Gettysburg. Considerably fewer people know the given name of General George Meade's horse—a name befitting the mount of such a Civil War antihero—Old Baldy. Unlike his master Old Baldy was in the news as recently as the year 2003 because two Philadelphia museums went to court over who owned the horse's head.

In his youth Old Baldy was named Baldy, a deprecating honorific bestowed not for lack of hair, but for the patches of white on his chestnut head. Unlike Traveller, Baldy wasn't built for comfort (there were whispers that Lee's mount was an "ambler" or Tennessee walking horse). Baldy was a warrior, steadfast and imperturbable in battle, wounded fourteen times, left for dead at Antietam, and found grazing in a field the next day. At Gettysburg Baldy took a bullet in the lung meant for his irascible master. Baldy not only survived the war, but outlived Meade by ten years. He became "Old" Baldy after he served as the riderless horse at Meade's funeral in 1872. The heroic horse died at the age of thirty in December 1882 in rural retirement outside Philadelphia. After Old Baldy's death, two Civil War veterans formerly under Meade's command, fueled by sentiment and, perhaps, holiday grog, dug up the horse's remains, removed the head, and had it stuffed by a taxidermist. Old Baldy's noggin was the guest of honor at many a reunion of veterans of the Grand Army of the Republic (GAR). Eventually, the stuffed head joined the collection of the GAR Museum and Library in Philadelphia. In the late 1970s the GAR Museum loaned Old Baldy to Philadelphia's Civil War Library Museum,

★ ★

where it has proudly hung in its own display case ever since. In fact, a monthly gathering of Civil War enthusiasts has been meeting at the museum for the past twenty-five years under the name Old Baldy's Round Table. Check out www.netreach.net/~cwlm/obcwrt.htm.

Perhaps it was the stories in Philadelphia newspapers that the impressive collection of the financially troubled Civil War Library Museum might be sent south to a new Civil War museum under construction in Richmond, Virginia, the capital of the Confederacy. Whatever the cause, in April 2003 the GAR Museum went to court to seek the return of Old Baldy's head. The matter seemed to be resolved by the announcement in October 2003 that a brand-new Civil War/Underground Railroad museum would be built in Philadelphia with city, state, and federal funds, ensuring that Old Baldy will remain in his hometown.

But let's return to the issue of why George Meade remains a relative footnote in American history in comparison to dozens of lesser Union and Confederate officers. It's almost as if there were a conspiracy of silence against him. In truth, there was a conspiracy of silence against him. It was joined by just about every Civil War newspaper correspondent covering the Army of the Potomac, which Meade commanded until the end of the war. Meade's snapping turtle personality turned what should have been a memorable rags-to-riches story into historic obscurity. After a succession of bungling Union commanders from McClellan to Pope to Burnside to Hooker, a telegram delivered at 3:00 a.m. on June 28, 1863, informed General Meade, then commander of the Pennsylvania volunteers, that he had been given command of the entire Army of the Potomac. Lee and 80,000 Confederate troops had invaded Pennsylvania, and they were advancing on Philadelphia. Meade was ordered to use his own judgment to stop the enemy advance. Four days later Meade met Lee at Gettysburg.

But instead of being hailed as a savior, Meade was criticized in the press for failing to crush the retreating Confederate army. Thin-skinned and indignant, Meade openly despised the press corps. This

Dixie Starts Here

Throughout American history there have been pairings of names that have become instantly recognized—Lewis and Clark, Woodward and Bernstein, Sears and Roebuck, Barnum and Bailey—but no two Pennsylvania names have had a greater impact on the way America sees itself than Mason and Dixon.

The story of what brought Charles Mason and Jeremiah Dixon to Pennsylvania in 1763 begins with a dispute almost a century earlier between William Penn and Lord Baltimore. In 1682, when Pennsylvania's "proprietor" William Penn arrived in his newly granted colony, the Calverts, the founding family of Maryland, had been settled for exactly fifty years. Both the Calverts and the Penns had been granted land by kings of England (both kings, as luck would have it, were named Charles). Charles I granted Lord Baltimore the province of Maryland in 1632. Charles I was separated from his crown, and subsequently his head, by Oliver Cromwell, and Charles II eventually assumed his father's throne in 1661. Maybe the records were lost along with the first Charles's head, but no sooner had the second Charles granted a charter to William Penn than the Calverts and Penns were yelping at each other over who owned what and where.

What would become the state of Delaware, for instance, was in dispute. Pennsylvania claimed "the lower three counties" as hers. Maryland said otherwise, and the people living in the three counties that compose the state of Delaware were already acting like an independent colony by the time two Englishmen, an astronomer and a surveyor by the names of Mason and Dixon, were sent over to clear up the mess.

The British courts had ruled that the east-west boundary line between Pennsylvania and Maryland should begin exactly 15 miles due south of Philadelphia, which Mr. Mason and Mr. Dixon soon discovered placed them in New Jersey, of all places. But they persevered and four years later had completed the Mason-Dixon Line, which included an arc representing the Pennsylvania-Delaware border, as well as a north-south line representing the Delaware-Maryland border. But the Mason-Dixon Line that became famous through American history as the demarcation line between North and South, free and slave, Union and Confederate, was the east-west line separating Pennsylvania and Maryland.

The literal Mason-Dixon Line runs for 233 miles along 39° 43' north latitude. It ends where Maryland meets West Virginia at the Pennsylvania border in Fayette County about 5 miles west of the Youghiogheny River Lake. The more symbolic Mason-Dixon Line between North and South was created by the Missouri Compromise in 1820. The line extended from Pennsylvania's southern boundary west to where the Ohio River empties into the Mississippi and farther west along 36° 30' north latitude.

The Missouri Compromise separated America into free and slave states until the Civil War. By that time the South was known to all, friend and foe, as Dixie. In fact, Dixie takes its name not from Jeremiah Dixon but from the nickname for French currency used in the big river port in New Orleans. "Dix" was French for "ten-spot." Dixie was also the name of a popular black character in a minstrel show from 1850; Dixieland was where he lived.

made him no different than many Union generals, most notably
William Tecumseh Sherman. But Sherman is a household name compared to Meade. The reason for Meade's obscurity can be traced
to an incident during the Battle of the Wilderness in May of 1864.
Meade was enraged by a story written by *Philadelphia Inquirer*
reporter Edward Crapsey, who suggested that if it weren't for General Grant's aggressiveness, Meade's caution would have caused a
Union defeat. By twenty-first-century reporting standards, Crapsey's
criticism was almost apologetic. "Not that General Meade was at the
point of committing a blunder unwittingly," Crapsey wrote, "but his
devotion to his country made him loathe to risk her last great army
on what he deemed as chance."

Meade went nuclear. He had Crapsey brought to him in irons
and ordered the reporter expelled from camp. But first Crapsey was
placed backward on a mule and led for hours around the Union
camp with a sign hanging from his back that read LIBELER OF THE PRESS.
The drum corps followed this one-mule parade, playing "The Rogue's
March." Crapsey's humiliating treatment by the military became a
cause celebre among the press corps. His fellow journalists informally agreed to keep Meade's name out of the newspapers in future
articles, unless it was absolutely necessary and, if so, only the merest of mentions. It didn't take long for Meade to notice his new lack
of public recognition. In a letter to his wife, Meade wrote, "I find
the paper barely mentions the Pennsylvania reserves, and my name
never appears." Despite the fact that Meade served with distinction
through many battles until Lee's surrender at Appomattox, the war
correspondents' conspiracy of silence made him all but invisible by
war's end. Meade was the last major general of the Civil War to have
a serious biography written about him. It was published in 1897,
more than thirty years after his death. Today, more than a century
later, Meade continues to be largely ignored even in his hometown,
where a horse's stuffed head gets more press than the man who
once rode him.

★ ★

The GAR Museum (215–289–6484) is located in the Frankford section of Philadelphia. The Civil War Library Museum (215-735-8196) is at 1805 Pine Street.

It's Not Weird, It's Mütter
Philadelphia

Whenever I told friends and acquaintances from Philadelphia that I was working on a book called *Pennsylvania Curiosities,* almost immediately would come the comment, "You gotta have the Mütter Museum in there." Of course, the Mütter Museum is in here. If there were an encyclopedia listing for "Curiosities, Pennsylvania," it would include a little illustration of the Mütter Museum of the College of Physicians at 19 South Twenty-second Street, Philadelphia.

Where else could you see the cancerous tumor removed from the jaw of President Grover Cleveland during a secret operation aboard a private yacht in 1893? Where else could you find a body cast of the original Siamese twins, Chang and Eng Bunker, who underwent an autopsy at the College of Physicians after their death in 1874? Where else could you find the "soap lady," a victim of yellow fever in the 1800s whose corpse turned into a soaplike substance after being buried in alkaline soil?

What would become the Mütter Museum started with a collection of anatomical pathologies donated by Dr. Isaac Parrish in 1849. It was expanded by the larger collection donated by Dr. Thomas Dent Mütter in 1856, including bladder stones removed from Chief Justice John Marshall and the skeleton of a woman whose rib cage had been compressed by the habitual wearing of a tight corset. The collection now includes a mind-boggling number of medical abnormalities and antique medical instruments, including the first wooden stethoscope invented in 1816, Florence Nightingale's sewing kit, and a full-scale model of the first successful heart-lung machine designed by Philadelphia physician Dr. John H. Gibbon in 1953.

Although by laymen's standards, the Mütter Museum ranks high on the "Ewwwww!" meter, it is a serious museum of medical history. There is a display of 139 skulls from eastern and central Europe as well as the skeleton of a man whose bones appear to have razor-sharp edges, causing him to live and die in almost unimaginably excruciating pain. And then there is the exhibit of the Mega Colon, a piece of large intestine that more closely resembles a giant caterpillar 27 feet long and 8 feet in circumference. It was removed from inside a man who failed to survive the operation.

The Mutter Museum's public-friendly profile was raised in recent decades through the tireless efforts and irreverent personality of museum director Gretchen Worden, who joined the museum staff as a curatorial assistant in 1975, and who rose through the ranks to become the public face (and saucy voice) of the formerly stodgy medical institution until her death in 2004. Gretchen would share with visiting journalists and prurient pals such off-exhibit items of interest as astounding abnormalities of male genitalia. Since her sudden death at the age of fifty-six after a long battle with Hodgkins Disease, the museum has created a Gretchen Worden Room filled with some of her favorite anatomical grotesqueries floating in formaldehyde-filled jars. But not, you know, that one.

Now That's a City Hall!
Philadelphia

There is a famous tower in Copenhagen, Denmark, built in the early 1900s and decorated with a mosaic depicting "The Eight Wonders of the Modern World." Included among them is Philadelphia's City Hall, a modern wonder that celebrated its one-hundredth birthday in 2001. City Hall stands at Philadelphia's ground zero, geographically, politically, and architecturally. It is literally the center of Center City, occupying four and a half acres where Broad Street would intersect Market Street. Like the middle of a compass, all Philadelphia directions—north, south, east, and west—use City Hall as their starting point.

Why He's Called the Founding "Father"

One of Philadelphia's best-known "inside" jokes has to do with the statue of William Penn atop City Hall. The 37-foot-tall bronze statue shows the Quaker-hatted Penn standing with his left hand resting on a copy of Pennsylvania's Charter of Privileges spread out on top of a tree trunk. His right hand is turned downward and bent at the wrist slightly below his waist with his 2½-foot-long fingers pointing outward in the direction of Shackamaxon, the location on the Delaware River where Penn signed his famous treaty with the Indians under a spreading elm tree.

As luck or circumstance would have it, Shackamaxon is northeast of City Hall, which is the direction Penn is facing, which means that Penn's face is never in direct sunlight, which further means his outstretched hand is seen only in silhouette shaded from the sun by his body. When seen from the northwest, which happens to be the straight line down the Benjamin Franklin Parkway from the Philadelphia Museum of Art, the outstretched fingers of William Penn's hand seen in silhouette below his waist look more like his, well, let's put it this way—no wonder he's called Pennsylvania's Founding "Father."

The "dirty" angle of viewing William Penn has been the subject of both civic embarrassment and mirth, not to mention the topic of irreverent Philly T-shirt humor. It is the kind of detail proper Philadelphians pretend not to notice, although the desire to ignore the obvious can lead to ridiculous attempts to disguise it. For instance, in the fall of 1972, the *Philadelphia Inquirer* published a business magazine supplement featuring a prominent photo of William Penn atop City Hall on its cover. What was not prominent, in fact, what was missing altogether, was any sign of William Penn's offending hand, which had been airbrushed out of the photo.

★ ★

Everything about City Hall is big. The 37-foot-tall bronze statue of William Penn on top of City Hall tower is the largest statue on a building in the world. The 548-foot-tall tower itself is the tallest masonry structure in the world. At the time of its construction, it was the largest municipal building in the country, literally twice the size of the U.S. Capitol. And the "time of its construction" was a period of almost forty

After taking forty years to complete. City Hall has overlooked Central City for more than a century.

years. Ground was broken in 1871 and the interior of the building wasn't finished until 1909, although the building was officially "presented" to the city in 1901 by the special Commission of the Erection of Public Buildings appointed by the state legislature.

You'll note that the name of the commission refers to Public "Buildings" not "Building." One of the first surprises citizens of Philadelphia experienced regarding City Hall was that it was one massive structure rather than four separate buildings occupying the intersection of Broad and Market. This led to City Hall being dubbed the "world's largest traffic obstruction" by countless millions of drivers, whether behind the wheel of a car or the reins of a horse and carriage in 1871.

Everything about City Hall is too much: 88 million bricks; enough marble, granite, and limestone to pave eighteen football fields; 250 individual pieces of statuary—the building simply overwhelms. When conceived, it was to be Philadelphia's statement about itself to the world, as overinflated as the building itself. Its architectural style, French Second Empire, had fallen out of style before the building was even completed. What was supposed to be a point of civic pride was seen as a civic embarrassment by many. In a nation falling in love with skyscrapers, City Hall was about as lean and mean looking as a wedding cake. Whereas New York's skyline reached for the stars, Philadelphia's squatted on its haunches. For eighty-five years no building in Philadelphia surpassed the top of City Hall tower (thirty-four stories) due to a charming "gentleman's agreement" known as the Billy Penn's Hat Rule.

Today there are several buildings in Center City taller than City Hall, its once dominant tower now a minor player in the city's skyline. Residual resentment toward City Hall as a symbol of Philadelphia stodginess has turned to affection. No one would dream of tearing down City Hall, as they proposed in the early 1950s. (It was discovered that it would cost more to demolish the structure than it did to construct it.) They just don't *build* buildings like City Hall anymore. In 1957 the American Institute of Architecture declared City Hall to be "perhaps the greatest single effort of late nineteenth-century architecture." During the new millennium, City Hall is getting a face-lift that will take an estimated eight years and cost $125 million, which is about $100 million more than the cost of building it.

Free walking tours of City Hall are offered Monday through Friday at 12:30 p.m. Tours of the City Hall tower start every fifteen minutes from 9:30 a.m. to 4:30 p.m. Monday through Friday. The tour office is located in Room 121 of City Hall. Call (215) 686-2840.

The Liberty Bell: Cracks, Typos, Missing Chunks, and All
Philadelphia

I love the story of the Liberty Bell because, well, it's so totally American. It is a story of flaws overcome and scars worn proudly. It is a story of false starts and ingenious solutions. It is a story of misunderstandings and myths that make the simple truth all the more powerful.

★ ★

For instance, the Liberty Bell never rang on July 4, 1776. And it was the Civil War, not the Revolutionary War, that brought the Liberty Bell to the attention of the world. And the famous "crack" most people recognize is actually a repair. And only a Pennsylvanian would probably notice or be chagrined by that fact that the word *Pennsylvania* is spelled unlike we spell it on the bell that countless millions have seen and touched.

First things first. The bell began life in 1751 when the Pennsylvania Assembly ordered a bell for the State House (now Independence Hall) in Philadelphia. The chairman of the assembly, Isaac Norris, ordered the bell from Whitechapel Foundry in London, specifying in his instructions: "Let the Bell be cast by the best Workmen & examined carefully before it is Shipped with the following words well shaped in large letters . . . By order of the Assembly of the Province of Pensylvania for the State House in the city of Phila 1752." (Note the spelling of Pennsylvania in Norris's instructions.)

The bell arrived in Philadelphia in September 1752. The first time it was tested, Norris wrote, "I had the Mortification to hear that it was cracked by a stroke of the clapper without any other violence as it was hung up to try the sound." To the rescue came John Pass and John Stow, two Philadelphia foundry craftsmen, who agreed to recast the 2,081-pound bell for a price of 36 British pounds, not to mention the immortality of having the names Pass and Stow forever emblazoned in large letters on the Liberty Bell.

Nobody had heard the sound of the original bell sent from England, so they had nothing to compare it to, but the community verdict on the Pass and Stow bell was a resounding "HATED it!" The assembly voted funds to purchase a new bell from London, but when it arrived in 1754, everyone but Pass and Stow was disappointed to discover that it sounded no better than the Philadelphia recast. The new bell from England was placed in the State House cupola to ring the hours, and the Pass and Stow bell remained in the State House steeple to ring on special occasions. (In 1772 neighbors passed around a petition complaining that they were "incommoded and distressed" by the constant "ringing of the great Bell in the steeple" of the State House.)

The bell never rang on July 4, 1776, because the Declaration of Independence was at the printer's being reproduced. It summoned Philadelphians to the first public reading of the Declaration in the State House Court-yard on July 8, 1776. A year later the bell was removed from Philadelphia along with all the other bells in town to prevent the invading British troops from melting them down into cannonballs or Wilkinson sword blades.

Anyone notice which word is misspelled on the Liberty Bell?

After the Revolutionary War the bell returned to the State House, where it rang on special occasions such as the deaths of Presidents Washington, Adams, and Jefferson, and Supreme Court justice John Marshall. No one agrees on when the new crack first appeared, except that it was discovered before 1846 and that a repair job was attempted by drilling out the existing hairline crack so that the sides of the bell wouldn't rub together and cause a buzzing sound when rung. On February 14, 1846, while tolling for Washington's birthday, the buzz returned, along with the discovery of a new hairline crack. That was the end of the bell's ringing days, but only the beginning of its story.

Even before the crack became famous, the bell was adopted by the antislavery movement because of the Biblical inscription from

★ ★

Leviticus around the top of the bell: PROCLAIM LIBERTY THROUGHOUT ALL THE LAND AND UNTO ALL THE INHABITANTS THEREOF. To the abolitionists, the operative word in that passage was *all* as much as *Liberty*. The first use of the term Liberty Bell is dated 1839 in a poem about the bell in the antislavery publication *Liberator*.

The Civil War cemented the reputation of the Liberty Bell as a symbol for a fractured nation seeking to heal itself. After being put on display during the 1876 Centennial Celebration in Philadelphia, the Liberty Bell toured the country several times. New Orleans, Chicago, Charleston, Boston, St. Louis, and San Francisco all hosted the bell during celebrations between 1885 and 1915. In those thirty years souvenir hunters had managed to chisel and chip away thirty pounds of metal from the bell's mouth (you can see for yourself). After that, the city of Philadelphia, which owns the bell, passed legislation forbidding the bell from ever leaving the city again. And it never has. (The Liberty Bell, enclosed in glass, can be seen daily from 9:00 a.m. to 5:00 p.m. at the new Liberty Bell Pavilion constructed in 2003 and located between Fifth and Sixth on Market Street. Admission is free. www.nps.gov/archive/inde/liberty-bell.html.)

Thinking about the Rodin Museum
Philadelphia

The Gates of Hell hangs in Philadelphia and *The Thinker* sits before it, pondering, perhaps, the choices one faces in life. These sculptures by the great French artist Auguste Rodin reside in a tiny but impressive museum on the Benjamin Franklin Parkway, Philadelphia's gateway boulevard modeled after the Champs-Élysées. The gardened gateway to the Rodin Museum itself is modeled after the facade of the Chateau d'Issy, which Rodin had moved to his studio in Meudon, France. Inside the museum are 125 sculptures completed by Rodin, the largest collection of his work outside Paris.

For this jewel box of a museum we have a movie-palace magnate to thank. Jules E. Mastbaum was a Philadelphia movie theater mogul back in the days when red carpets and velvet curtains and white-gloved ticket takers greeted arriving moviegoers, back in the days when movies were an event rather than a couple of hours to kill at the mall multiplex. You could fit a half dozen Rodin museums into one of Mastbaum's movie theaters back in the 1920s when Jules Mastbaum began collecting the works of the artist, who died at the age of seventy-seven in 1917. Among those works is *The Thinker,* perhaps the most famous statue in the world. Philadelphia's 800-pound bronze is one of seventeen casts made of the original. Mastbaum commissioned the museum housing Rodin's works to complement the massive Philadelphia Museum of Art a few blocks away. Among the masterpieces in the Rodin Museum are *The Burghers of Calais, Eternal Springtime,* and Rodin's epic bronze doors, *The Gates of Hell,* which the artist worked on for thirty-seven years. Get more information at www.rodinmuseum.org.

Mario Lanza and the Corner Boy Cult
Philadelphia

Back in the mid-1970s, actor Tony Randall starred in a TV sitcom called *The Tony Randall Show* in which he played a Philadelphia common pleas court judge. In the first episode he meets his new administrative assistant named Mario Lanza. "Are you related?' asks Randall. "To who?" asks the assistant. "Mario Lanza," says the judge. "I am Mario Lanza," comes the reply, without a trace of self-consciousness. Mario is, after all, as common a name in South Philadelphia as Todd and Ashley are in the suburbs. Ironically, the most famous Philadelphia Mario wasn't a Mario at all. Alfredo Cocozza was Mario Lanza's given name. His friends called him Freddy.

Freddy Cocozza was a barrel-chested South Philly corner boy who was as good with his fists as he was with his voice. He was encouraged to leave South Philadelphia High School because of fighting, and his only class picture from that period was during his days at Vare Junior High School in South Philadelphia. He is seen standing in

★ ★

the back row just a few students away from another famous Philadelphian also good with his fists, future mayor Frank Rizzo. You can
see that class picture and other artifacts from the career of Freddy
Cocozza at the Mario Lanza Museum located in the Settlement Music
School in South Philadelphia. Mario Lanza (his mother's maiden name
was Maria Lanza), one of the greatest American tenors ever to sing on
records and film, became a James Dean–type cult figure among opera
buffs after his death at the age of thirty-eight. By then Lanza's career
in Hollywood as a movie matinee idol was already in a downward spi-
ral. Lanza had an operatic temperament, and he made enemies.

But in Philadelphia where he grew up, he is remembered as one of
the guys. Friends started the Mario Lanza Institute in his honor over
forty years ago. A museum featuring his clothes and recordings and

At the Mario Lanza Museum in Philadelphia, framed
newspaper headlines report his death in 1959.

gold records started in the back of a record store on Snyder Avenue and then moved to the Settlement Music School, not far from where Lanza grew up on the 600 block of Christian Street. The handsome young corner boy with the voice of an angel was discovered by Hollywood after World War II. His first movie, *That Midnight Kiss,* with Kathryn Grayson and Ethel Barrymore, made its world premiere in Philadelphia in 1949. Lanza played a truck driver from Philadelphia who dreamed of being an opera star. In his next movie he played a fisherman who dreamed of being an opera star. In his next movie he was an opera star who dreamed of making a comeback. His last movie was *The Student Prince;* the white military uniform he wore in that role is on display in the museum. Lanza died in Rome in 1959 in the midst of a European comeback attempt.

The Mario Lanza Museum moved in 2002, and the current location is at 712 Montrose Street. It's housed in a parish house next to his former church St. Mary Magdalen dePazzi, and it is literally around the corner from the house on Christian Street where Lanza was born and raised. It's still a mom-and-pop museum run by volunteers from among the Lanza faithful, but this time it is on the ground floor, rather than the fourth floor of its last home at the Settlement Music School a few blocks away. Stop in at www.mario-lanza-institute.org/museum.htm.

They're Called Hoagies, Aren't They?
Philadelphia

Everyone knows that hoagies come from Philadelphia, right? But why? Why *hoagie?* And why have Philadelphia hoagies taken on a mystique of sorts that is absent from similar sandwiches in other cities? Elsewhere, these sandwiches are called heroes, subs, torpedoes, blimps, and—only in and around Norristown, Pennsylvania, for some reason—zeps. Certainly those names are more descriptive of the general shape of hoagies, long Italian rolls cut lengthwise and filled to overflowing with meats, cheeses, and veggies. They *do* resemble

submarines, torpedoes, blimps, and zeppelins, not to mention that
they require a heroic appetite to finish.

But for some reason the mythology of hoagies has spread
throughout the land, especially in the last fifteen years or so. You
began to see and hear the word *hoagie* in places you never saw or
heard it before—in *New Yorker* magazine cartoons and David Letter-
man monologues—key indications that hoagies have become hip.
Now hoagies are mainstream American junk food, like buffalo wings
and Philadelphia cheesesteaks.

But the word hoagie—where did it come from? What follows is
the more-or-less official version: During the First World War, Philadelphia's already booming shipbuilding industry went into overdrive.
The shipyards provided ample work for skilled and unskilled Italian
immigrants who arrived in Philadelphia in great numbers around the
turn of the century. In 1890 there were 6,799 Italian-born citizens in
Philadelphia; by 1920 there were 63,223, the vast majority of whom
settled in South Philadelphia, not far from the city's largest private
shipyard on Hog Island in the Delaware River.

The workmen at Hog Island were called Hoggies. An Italian Hoggie would typically carry his lunch in an oil-stained paper bag that
contained an Italian roll sliced in half, slathered with olive oil on each
side, and filled with cheese, tomatoes, lettuce, onions, peppers, and,
if he was lucky, slices of salami. Imagine the aroma wafting around
the workplace or a crowded streetcar from one of those sandwiches.
Imagine someone saying, "I gotta get one of those sandwiches those
Hoggies eat." So it doesn't take much imagination to see how the
new sandwich sensation became known as a hoggie. How one of
the *g*s became an *a* is anyone's guess. And how the "hah" sound
morphed into the "ho" sound is a question for linguists to argue
(although if it were up to marketing analysts the answer would be,
"Don't you think *hoagie* sounds entirely too *piggy?*").

So Philadelphia, exclusively, enjoyed its hoagies by that name for
the better part the century, always certain of the hoagie's superior-

ity over the less enigmatically named subs, blimps, torpedoes, and heroes enjoyed by other cities. But sometime around 1990, the same way people in other cities started saying "Yo!" after all the *Rocky* movies, the word hoagie was embraced by people who wouldn't know Hog Island from Hoagy Carmichael.

One problem Philadelphians have with the success of hoagies as an export is with the rampant corruption of the "meaning" of the word hoagie. A hoagie can contain any number of meats, except chicken. A hoagie can be doctored to taste with any condiment, except mustard (for a long time, mayonnaise was the line, but that battle is long past). And a hoagie can be served cold from a refrigerator or, better, at room temperature. But never from an oven. A hoagie baked in an oven is called a grinder.

And a hoagie can never be what I found on an Internet Web site from Bedford, Indiana, under the heading "Hoagie Recipe": "In a large bowl mix together Velveeta, chipped ham, sliced eggs, diced onion, diced pickles, and chopped olives. In small bowl mix together mayonnaise and chili sauce. Add small bowl mixture to large bowl mixture and mix. Put mixture on buns of your choice and wrap each one in foil. Refrigerate until almost ready to serve. Heat in 450-degree oven for 15–20 minutes. Makes approximately 16 hoagies if you use hot dog buns."

Whatever that is, it's not a hoagie. And whatever a hoagie is, it had to be invented in Philadelphia. Or Norristown—after all, zep is a great name for a hoagie.

The "Invention" of the Philly Cheesesteak
Philadelphia

Unlike the hoagie, the origin of Philadelphia's other five-star contribution to the American junk food pantheon, the cheesesteak (or for the lactose intolerant, the steak sandwich), is pretty much accepted as gospel. Like the fried baloney sandwich, the steak sandwich just sort of happened. But unlike fried baloney, the Philadelphia steak

★ ★

sandwich became a national gastronomic, not to mention marketing, phenomenon.

It was during the dark days of the Great Depression (don't all inspirational American success stories start out that way?) when Pasquale "Pat" Olivieri, the son of Italian immigrants who was born in South Philadelphia in 1907, was having a particularly bad day behind the counter of his hot dog stand at Ninth and Wharton Streets. No business, no prospects, and worst of all, Pat Olivieri was sick of eating hot dogs. So he splurged. "Get me some beefsteak," he said to his cousin, flipping him a dime to buy a chunk-a chunk-a burnin' love from the local butcher. Pat sliced the beefsteak into thin slices, tossed it into a skillet on top of some siz- zling oil, and cooked himself a nice sandwich, which he was about to eat when— behold—a cus- tomer poked his head over the counter and asked, "What's that GREAT SMELL? I want what- ever that is."

Pat Olivieri, hungry no doubt, was not a dope. He sold the sandwich out of his hand, the proverbial shirt off his back. And so a

It's four a.m. in South Philadelphia, time for a cheesesteak.

Steak Wars: May the Cheese Be with You

In 1966 something unbelievable happened to Pat's cheese steak kingdom. A rival steak sandwich shop opened on the southeast corner of Ninth and Passyunk, catty-corner to Pat's Steaks, calling itself Geno's. In the forty-some years since, the Great Steak Wars of Philadelphia have continued 24/7. The only days Geno's and Pat's are closed are Christmas and Easter. The war reached a peak in the mid-1980s when Geno's owner Joe Vento hung a banner across Ninth Street that said, "Geno's. The freshest meats, cheeses, and breads. Also clean!" You didn't have to read too deeply between the lines to understand who that last part was aimed at.

Throughout the Great Steak Wars, local politicians have wooed customers of each steak shop without declaring their personal preference. In one of the most brilliant diplomatic moves of his career, then-President Bill Clinton held a reelection rally in the middle of the intersection between the two steak shops in 1996. After the rally Clinton and then-mayor, now-governor Ed Rendell walked to Pat's and ate a cheesesteak. When they finished they marched over to Geno's and ate a cheesesteak there. Then the ex-president of the most powerful nation on earth told the assembled thousands that he couldn't choose which steak was better because they were both so good. That Clinton could charm the stripes off a zebra.

Such cheesesteak political correctness was abandoned in 2008 when during the Pennsylvania Democratic presidential primary, Barack Obama and Hillary Clinton bypassed Geno's during their mandatory Philadelphia cheesesteak photo opportunity. Geno's owner Joe Vento had placed a sign in the window asking customers to order in English. Many took this as an anti-immigrant announcement. It even ended up under arbitration before the Pennsylvania Human Relation Commisssion. All the candidates abandoned Geno's after that. And to think all Joe Vento was trying to do was get people to pronounce "cheese wit" the proper way in Philadelphia: "Cheese wid."

unique food industry was born. "Pat's King of Steaks" became a family dynasty that continues today. The original Pat's is still on the southwest corner of the triangle formed by Ninth Street, Wharton Street, and Passyunk Avenue, the "fertile crescent" if you will, of the cheesesteak culture. You can see a bronze plaque in the sidewalk outside the counter at Pat's, where Rocky Balboa stood dripping sauce on his shoes in the original *Rocky* movie.

Pat's became a twenty-four-hour-a-day operation, an all-night diner open to the elements, but customers didn't care. There was something about freezing one's buns off while waiting for a sizzling cheesesteak at three in the morning. People stood in line (still do, in fact) meekly waiting for the counterman to shout, "Next," at which time a customer had 2.7 seconds to give an order or be ordered to the end of the line. (And you thought the soup Nazi on *Seinfeld* was bad!) "Gimme a cheese with" means a cheesesteak with fried onions. "Two cheese without" means two cheesesteaks without fried onions. And woe be the person who asks the question, "What's with?" At that the counterman says, "Hey, fellas, we got one." All the kitchen crew put down their spatulas, crowd their faces into the 2-by-2½-foot window, and shout, "With onions! STOOPID!" You don't want to be standing at the front of the line when that happens.

Philadelphia Sky Walkers
Philadelphia

There is no written record of the first time children in Philadelphia tied the shoelaces on a pair of sneakers together and then flung them over telephone wires, but chances are the first sneakers hanging from telephone wires were sighted within days of the telephone conversation that started with the words, "Mr. Watson, come here. I want you."

I threw sneakers up on the wire as a kid, and so did my friends. It was a way of retiring a well-worn pair of Keds or Converse All-Stars, sort of like a Viking funeral in the sky. All who looked upward would know that these shoes served someone well.

Sneakers hanging from the wires. A Philadelphia tradition continues at Eighth and Lehigh in North Philly.

The custom of tossing sneakers over telephone wires almost disappeared in Philadelphia during the 1980s, a period that coincided with the rising popularity of footwear that required a second mortgage to purchase. The price tag on a pair of "sneaks" increased in direct proportion to multimillion-dollar endorsement contracts offered to athletes by Nike, Puma, and Adidas. No one was tossing a pair of hundred-dollar energy-transfer cross-trainers over any stupid telephone wires. But with the prosperity of the 1990s, the sneakers returned overhead, along with hiking boots and any other footwear equipped with laces.

Nowhere in Philadelphia is the concentration of dangling sky walkers more plentiful than the intersection of Eighth Street and Lehigh Avenue in North Philadelphia. Hundreds of pairs of all shapes and sizes and brand names hang from these utility wires less

★ ★

than a block away from a public middle school. The sneakers usually remain until the laces rot from exposure or until the city Streets Department crews remove them because the accumulated weight poses a hazard.

The Cowboy in the Rearview Mirror
Philadelphia

Frederic Remington was one of the most famous sculptors and illustrators in the late nineteenth and early twentieth centuries. It was Remington, on assignment to Cuba to illustrate Spanish atrocities and Cuban rebels before the outbreak of the Spanish-American War, who cabled the complaint to newspaper magnate William Randolph Hearst that there were no atrocities, and there was no war. "You provide the pictures," Hearst cabled back. "I'll provide the war." Which he dutifully did.

The Cowboy, overlooking Kelly Drive in Philadelphia, is Frederic Remington's only life-size sculpture.

Remington was most famous for his artwork depicting the American West. His illustrations and sculptures of the drama of western landscapes and native inhabitants, and his sculptures of ranch hands and sodbusters, are classic American art icons. But the only life-size statue Remington ever completed stands on an outcropping of rock along Kelly Drive in Fairmount Park. The bronze, called simply *The Cowboy,* shows a rider pulling hard on the reins of his horse on the edge of a precipice. The horse's tail stands straight out from behind as an indication of fast motion or, perhaps, a stiff head-wind.

Remington himself chose the exact site for the sculpture to stand, overlooking a slight bend in the road immediately below. When Remington chose the site, however, the river drives were cinder-covered horse-and-buggy thoroughfares where the fastest traffic traveled at 10 miles an hour. Now the speed limit is 40 miles per hour and Kelly Drive is a busy and heavily traveled commuter route. Because there is no place to pull over on Kelly Drive to admire the statue, most motorists only see it as a blur flashing past on their way to and from work.

The "Legendary" Blue Horizon
Philadelphia

Walk to the top of the stairs of a certain 140-year-old Victorian brownstone building on Broad Street in North Philadelphia and then turn right. As countless thousands before you have said upon seeing the boxing ring set up in the middle of the Blue Horizon auditorium, with its dark wooden balconies hanging almost over the ring ropes, you may mutter in awe, "This is like something out of a movie."

Yes, it is. That's why fight fans everywhere, without self-inflated bravado, call it the "legendary Blue Horizon." This is the boxing venue hometown fighters dream of: a bout at the Blue, with friends, neighbors, and family cheering their lungs out. This is the inspiration for the Rocky Balboa type of club fighter from Philadelphia, the hometown boy who makes it big. When Philly boxer and USBA heavyweight champion Tim Witherspoon defended his title at the Blue in 1991, the description on the fight card began, "'Terrible Tim' Witherspoon, who has boxed in London's Wembley Stadium, the Omni in Atlanta, the Dunes Hotel in Las Vegas, the Sky Dome in Seattle, and Madison Square Garden, finally hits the big time tonight with his first-ever Blue Horizon appearance in a scheduled twelve-round fight with Art Tucker." If that description was tongue in cheek, you couldn't see it for the mouthpiece.

The Blue Horizon is one of the most intimate and atmospheric fight venues in America, seating 1,200 people in an auditorium that has seen twenty-seven world champions box there at some point during their careers. The USA Network cemented the reputation of the "legendary Blue Horizon" by telecasting live *Tuesday Night Fights* from the Blue starting in 1987. ESPN2 added the Blue to its *Friday Night Fight* venues in 1998. The ancient facility has been struggling to meet modern zoning and fire-code demands in recent years, and its future was uncertain until new ownership invested in much-needed refurbishment. But it is a must-see for serious fight fans, even if they are only serious about watching the showgirls march around the ring with the round cards. See more information at www.legendarybluehorizon.com.

Rock and Roll Ringing Rocks

Upper Black Eddy

Pennsylvania has a number of fields where boulders were deposited by retreating glaciers during the last ice age. Perhaps the most famous is Boulder Field in Hickory Run State Park in Carbon County, where boulders as round as cantaloupes and as big as Volkswagens are piled on top of one another in an eerie landscape surrounded by trees. But there's only one field where you can play rock and roll on the rolling rocks.

Ringing Rocks Park near Upper Black Eddy in Bucks County has been a place of mystery since the original inhabitants noticed that the boulders strewn about the field rang like bells when struck with a tomahawk. The same effect can be produced with a ball-peen hammer these days, and more than one musical group has traveled to the Ringing Rocks in an attempt to create the ultimate rock music. The first rock concert in the field was conducted by Dr. J. J. Ott, who led a group of musicians playing more traditional instruments in a performance for the Buckwampum Society of Bucks County in 1890.

Dr. Ott played lead boulder in the concert. A witness at the time reported, "The clear bell-like tone he was playing could be heard above the horns."

Over the years the theories as to why the Ringing Rocks ring have ranged from Native American spirits to UFOs to glaciers. One thing we know is that the Ringing Rocks are not a glacial deposit. They were the result of erosion, perhaps from an ancient riverbed. Within the past thirty-five years, the mystery of what makes these boulders ring has been explained by geologists as the result of molten magma cooling, placing the unique deposits of hard dark diabase minerals within under enormous stress. The effect of this stress was like tightening a guitar string. The rocks in the center of the field away from trees and under direct sunlight ring better than the rocks along the perimeter. Some people believe that the Ringing Rocks are the result of some bizarre magnetic energy field, which causes compasses to spin wildly and camera film negatives to be cloudy when developed. Scientific tests have revealed no unusual energy emissions from the area, which of course hasn't stopped anyone from claiming that weird things keep happening there. Back in 1987, during the so-called Harmonic Convergence, a group of new age believers gathered around the Ringing Rocks to chant "Om." The rocks did not chant back. (Call 215-757-0571. The park is located 2 miles west of Upper Black Eddy.)

When the Rebels Took York
York

York, Pennsylvania, holds the distinction of being the only capital of the United States ever to fall to Confederate troops during the Civil War. Of course, York wasn't the capital of the United States at the time, nor had it been for almost one hundred years. But York was technically the capital of the United States in 1777, after Congress had fled Philadelphia when British troops occupied the city during the Revolutionary War. It was in York that the Articles of Confederation, America's first constitution, were adopted by Congress.

On June 26, 1863, Confederate general Jubal Early and 9,000 troops marched into York and occupied the town without a battle. The Stars and Stripes were hauled down from the flagpole in the town square and replaced with the Confederate battle flag. York was the largest northern city ever to fall to Robert E. Lee's invading Army of the Potomac. The Confederate occupation of York lasted four days. As the historical display in the York tourist center notes, on June 30, 1863, "Like many future visitors, Jubal Early and men traveled on to Gettysburg."

The House That Hoffman Built
York

Bob Hoffman was a man's man and proud of it. Only a man's man would have the confidence to have a nearly nude larger-than-life-size bronze statue of himself cast and placed along a busy highway outside his place of business. You can see Bob Hoffman in bronze, next to Interstate 83 outside York. The statue stands in front of the Weightlifting Hall of Fame next to the York Barbell Company, which Hoffman founded. Hoffman was already an old man when he posed for the statue, but he still looked strong enough to lift an Oldsmobile.

Inside the Weightlifting Hall of Fame are artifacts from the era known as a "Strongmanism," when weight lifting was the stuff of carnivals and vaudeville acts. There's the 220-pound dumbbell used by nineteenth-century strongman Louis Cyr, who lifted it easily over his head with one hand. Then there's the gaudy belt presented by the *National Police Gazette* to Warren Lincoln Travis for being the World's Strongest Man in 1906. There are photos showing feats (and feets) of strength, such as a strong man on his back supporting a bench holding sixteen men on the bottom of his feet.

The Bob Hoffman Story (1898–1985) is told in another room, showing young Hoffman after he returned to York following World War I. He founded the York Oil Burner Company, the precursor to York Barbell Company. Hoffman organized a weight lifting club among his employees that soon developed into a national weight lifting organization. The first weight lifting championships in America were held in York, which soon became known as Muscletown, USA. Hoffman turned his attention to full-time physical fitness in 1932 when he purchased *Strength and Health* magazine (there's a photo of four men lifting Hoffman and another man in an automobile in front of the publishing company offices). By the time he died at the age of eighty-seven, Hoffman was recognized as the Father of World Weight Lifting and the company he founded as "the strongest name in fitness."

Alongside the Weightlifting Hall of Fame is the Bodybuilding Hall of Fame, which is not about how much you can lift as much as how

Mural of Bob Hoffman, muscleman extraordinaire and York, Pennsylvania, entrepreneur.

★ ★

muscular you can become. Big difference. The heroes, of course, in the Bodybuilding Hall of Fame are the original Mr. America, Steve Reeves, star of many badly dubbed Hercules movies in the 1950s and 1960s, and Mr. Universe, Arnold Schwarzenegger, who, as the caption next to his photo noted, "has had several movie roles since his retirement from competition." There's a photo of Schwarzenegger on the cover of a 1970 bodybuilding magazine where he is identified as "Arnold Strong, movie and TV star." Who knew he'd become governor of California?

The Harley Factory Tour: No Ties Required
York

You're not allowed to bring a camera with you when you take the guided tour of the Harley-Davidson Final Assembly Plant off Route 30 in York. It may have something to do with industrial secrets, but most likely it's a safety measure. The last thing they need at the Harley assembly plant is some wide-eyed biker enthusiast with a camera stepping in front of a forklift speeding around the one-million-square-foot plant. And let me tell you, this tour is for real.

The first thing you have to do is turn over your camera to the tour guide, who locks it up for safekeeping. In exchange you'll receive a pair of plastic safety glasses and a radio receiver with an earpiece. The need for this soon becomes apparent because this is a working factory and working factories are loud. (I said, WORKING FACTORIES ARE LOUD!) Carl was the tour guide for my group of about twenty people, some of whom had come from as far away as Germany to see the inside of an American motorcycle factory. Carl is a retired schoolteacher, and as he led us onto the factory floor from the visitor center, we could hear his heavy breathing in our earpieces. Just when members of the tour were beginning to make amused eye contact about what we were hearing, Carl announced into his headset, "If you hear me breathing it's because I have asthma. If you don't hear me breathing, call 911."

★ ★

As I said, this is a working factory, and the first thing Carl tells us is to stay inside the yellow lines painted on the floor so that we don't wander into the path of forklifts and carts moving heavy equipment from one end of the factory to the other. "That motorcycle you see there," says Carl, pointing to a finished product coming off the end of the assembly line, "was ordered by a customer more than a year ago." Harley's success in recent years has been a combination of a first-rate product meeting incredible customer loyalty and patience. Harley owners are a breed unto themselves. Not only are they willing to wait more than a year for the Harley of their choice, but they seem to rejoice in the process. And so do the Harley employees, a remarkably stable workforce with a turnover of only 1 percent a year in a factory employing 3,000 men and women. "And that 1 percent is people retiring," says Carl.

"You see anyone wearing a tie here?" Carl asks, as the tour group pauses in front of the testing area, where the finished product is taken off the assembly line and run through the gears up to 70 miles per hour on a stationary treadmill. "You can't tell the bosses from the workers because everyone's a worker and everyone's a boss." The uniform of the day is T-shirts and blue jeans, with an impressive number of employees preferring well-worn Harley-Davidson T-shirts. Clearly this is a factory that works on the principle of mutual respect, from management to workforce and back.

The York final assembly plant turns out a new Harley-Davidson motorcycle from start to finish in two hours and twenty-four minutes. One motorcycle comes off the assembly line every two-and-a-half minutes. Each day the plant working on three shifts turns out 570 motorcycles made to customer order. The new Harley plant in Kansas City turns out 250 motorcycles a day, and still demand exceeds supply. The tour itself takes the better part of an hour, and by the end, of it you are bound to be a new member of the Harley cult, even if you ride a rice burner. Tours are free and begin hourly. Afterward you return to the visitor center where you're invited to sit on a new Harley model and dream.

Harley-Davidson Corporate headquarters are in Milwaukee, Wisconsin, but Pennsylvania has been producing the majority of Harley-Davidson motorcycles since 1968. The York final assembly plant actually started life as a World War II munitions factory. In fact, there's still a sixty-year-old military-looking watchtower overlooking the visitor parking lot. Harley-Davidson factory tours are Monday through Friday. For more information, tour hours, and highly suggested reservations, visit www.harley-davidson.com.

2

Southwest

While the hip *East coast girls of Philadelphia were wearing velvet and lace in 1776, Pittsburgh girls, what few there were, dressed in buckskin or whatever was the female fashion on the frontier. Southwestern Pennsylvania was where East met West, civilization met wilderness, European met Iroquois, transportation technology met unpassable mountains. And it has the battle scars to show it. The Pittsburgh skyline surrounds the original site of Ft. Pitt, Altoona has a railroad curve named after it where the battle to cross the Allegheny Mountains was won by the steam engine and Irish laborers, the city of Johnstown shows evidence of its three losing battles against flood water, and the tiny village of Shanksville bears witness to the current war on terrorism.*

The Southwest is defined by the Mason-Dixon line along its lower counties. Its weirdest border feature is to the west with what was originally a pinky finger of Virginia (now West Virginia) that extends as far north as New York City. This means that the high-water mark of the Confederacy was once 50 miles north of Gettysburg. That finger, or panhandle, is defined by the southern shore of the Ohio River, which starts in Pittsburgh and flows north to Monaca. There it turns to the southwest to the border of Ohio and West Virginia and then dramatically southeast, creating this narrow peninsula of West Virginia, which a famously wordy legislator from neighboring Greene County once indelicately described as being "thrust toward Pennsylvania like a pig's genitalia."

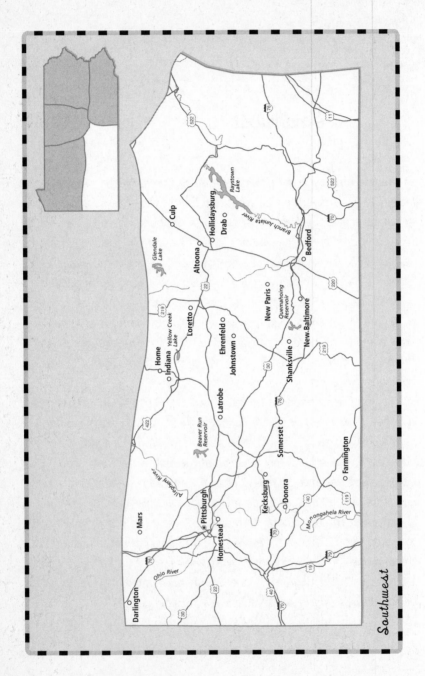

Southwest

✦ ✦

The Curve That Made a City
Altoona

Altoona has been famous for more than 150 years for one thing, a
bend in the railroad tracks called the Horseshoe Curve. In fact, the
only reason there is a city called Altoona (Cherokee for "highlands
of great worth") is that the Pennsylvania Railroad decided to cross
the Allegheny Mountains in 1850. Up until that time, a trip from
Philadelphia to Pittsburgh took three days, in an ingenious but almost
comically complicated series of transfers from train to boat to train to
boat. You'd start out by train in Philadelphia and travel to Columbia
in Lancaster County, where you'd board a mule-pulled canal boat
up the Susquehanna River. After negotiating a series of eighteen
locks, you'd arrive in Hollidaysburg in Blair County, where you would
board the Allegheny Portage Railroad, which carried the entire canal
boat over the mountains to Johnstown in Cambria County. There, an
inclined railroad deposited the canal boats and passengers into the
Conemaugh River for the final leg of the journey through sixty-six
canal locks to Pittsburgh.

There had to be a better way. The problem was that the mountains were too steep for a train to climb and too wide to tunnel
through. It took a Pennsylvania Railroad engineer by the name of J.
Edgar Thomson to come up with the idea of building a curve into
a V-shaped wedge carved out of the mountain in the middle of the
nowhere that was to become Altoona.

Construction started in 1851 and was accomplished by several
hundred Irish immigrants using gunpowder, pickaxes, and pack animals. The massive earth-moving project was literally done by hand.
The 220-degree curve is 2,374 feet long. The distance between the
tracks on either side of the U shape of the curve is 1,800 feet. The
tracks rise 91 feet per mile, and the west side of the curve is 122
feet higher than the east side. Without the curve the grade over the
mountains would have been six to eight degrees, which would have
worn out engines and brakes. With the curve the grade over the

★ ★

A curve so famous they named a beer after it (the Horseshoe Curve in Altoona).

mountains is a manageable 1.8 percent. When it opened in 1854, the Horseshoe Curve was considered an engineering marvel. Virtually all train traffic, both passenger and freight, heading to Philadelphia from the west still uses the two remaining tracks through the curve.

The Horseshoe Curve National Historical Landmark is located 5 miles west of Altoona up a winding stretch of road past the Kittanning Reservoir. On the ride up the mountain, Molly and I saw a black bear standing in the middle of the road—it was exciting. The irony of the curve built for trains and named after a horse's footwear is that it is best seen from an airplane. There is no grand vista available from the opposite slope of the mountain. You can't see the curve from street level, and when you do take the short incline ride from the Horseshoe Curve Visitors Center to the track bed 90 feet above, you can't see the curve from there either. Standing there at the bottom of the U in the curve, all you can see are railroad tracks that bend in the distance in either direction until they are obscured by trees. If you're lucky, a train might pass, but the sight looks remarkably like a train passing. The only difference is the screech of the train wheel flanges holding on to the curve as the train rounds the bend and disappears into the trees. Maybe the dead of winter is the best time to visit the Horseshoe Curve. All that pesky Pennsylvania foliage doesn't spoil the view.

Why Altoona?
Altoona

If one picture speaks a thousand words, then the expression on my daughter Molly's face speaks two: Not again! It was hard for a ten-year-old to travel for hours across the state, rarely taking her eyes off her Game Boy to look at the mountains, and finally arrive at our destination only to discover that it's not an amusement park but a *museum*. A museum about *trains,* no less. (A little-boy museum, if ever there was one.)

The Altoona Railroaders Memorial Museum is much more than a collection of antique locomotives. It is a stirring tribute to a way of life. Altoona started as a working village carved out of a wilderness by necessity and the accident of geography. It became a city, one of the largest in the state, and was one of Pennsylvania's proud industrial workshops until its inevitable decline after World War II. *Railroaders* is the key word in the name of this museum. It's about the people who worked for the Pennsylvania Railroad; it's about life in a railroad town when locomotives ruled the rails.

"A dirty city was a good city because it meant people were working," says Sally Price, a railroad employee featured in one of the exhibits. "We always considered it gold dust, not coal dust. That's what made Altoona run." What made Altoona run was what made Altoona filthy in its heyday, when hundreds of smoke-belching locomotives passed through town on the sixty-four eastbound tracks and seventy-two westbound tracks that dominated the middle of town where the 218 acres of the Pennsylvania Railroad repair shops were located.

Today the museum stands where the great locomotives were once serviced. On the second floor you'll see a life-size figure of a woman crossing the Twelfth Street bridge as the trains pass underneath, causing the kind of updraft made famous by Marilyn Monroe standing over a subway vent in *The Seven Year Itch*. The figure must have

Like most people in the 1920s, Babe Ruth traveled to Altoona by train.

been that of a city girl, because the caption information noted that country girls held down their skirts in the updraft, while city girls held on to their hats. Another item of interest is a classy-looking metal device about the size of an eyeglasses screwdriver. It has a wire loop at the end that was used to remove burning cinders from a person's eyes. (Railroaders Memorial Museum, 1300 Ninth Avenue, Altoona; 817-946-0834. Open 9:00 a.m. to 5:00 p.m. Monday through Sunday April through October; closed Monday November through March. Admission charged. www.railroadcity.com. *Note:* This site has listings of all the Altoona sites mentioned in this book.)

Grand View, No Ship
Bedford County

In its heyday during the 1930s, the Ship Hotel near the summit of the Allegheny Mountains on the Lincoln Highway in Bedford County was a tourist attraction capable of attracting star-caliber guests. Over the hotel's lifespan Henry Ford, Thomas Edison, Calvin Coolidge, Will Rogers, J. P. Morgan, John Barrymore, and Joan Crawford all stayed there. They came for the view, as did other tourists, and they came for the novelty of wining and dining and sleeping in a guest cabin in a wooden ship more than 2,000 feet above sea level. The SS Grandview Hotel started life as a private castle but was modified to look like a ship perched on a mountainside, and after its dedication in May 1932, it did a thriving business even during the Depression. Even though you couldn't find a more dramatic view anywhere else in the state of Pennsylvania, the tourist business for the "Ship Hotel" was scuttled by the opening of the Pennsylvania Turnpike. (The turnpike siphoned off most of the east-west traffic.)

Located on a south-facing bend in the road on Route 30 near the 2,464-foot summit of Pennsylvania's largest mountain range, the SS Grandview Hotel offered a grand view of "three states and seven counties," as the hotel signs advertised. The view is indeed stunning, but you can't see the counties for the trees. The heavily

An artist's rendering of the Ship Hotel was
on display at an antiques store not far from
where the hotel actually stood.

forested panorama spread out below is punctuated by an occasional
farm and lake, but the view does not include those helpful black lines
and dashes to indicate where one state or county ends and another
begins. The SS Grandview was once the most prominent landmark on
the Pennsylvania section of the Lincoln Highway. Today, all that's left
worth seeing of the SS Grandview is the view itself, since an early-
morning fire destroyed the wooden structure on October 28, 2001.
As of this writing, all that remains on the site are the blackened
trees and the concrete foundation rubble of the former hotel, which
had been closed to the public for more than two decades before
the fire. But you can see photos at http://brianbutko.wordpress
.com/2007/12/02/film-of-ss-grand-view-ship-hotel-1972/.

Ironically, without the ship in the way, the Grand View is more accessible to travelers. You can still pull over into the modest parking area that served the hotel and take a gander at a vista that the hotel advertised as encompassing up to 63 miles on a clear day. The three states visible within that view are Pennsylvania (well, DUH-uh!), Maryland, and West Virginia. The seven counties are Bedford and Somerset, Pennsylvania; Allegheny and Washington, Maryland; and Mineral, Hampshire, and Morgan Counties in West Virginia. But believe me, they all look like trees.

Freshly Brewed

Molly checks out the newly renovated but still kitschy Coffee Pot diner, now the visitors information center on the grounds of the Bedford County Fairgrounds. The Coffee Pot has been a landmark on Route 30, the Lincoln Highway, since it was built in 1927 just a few hundred yards west of where it now stands. The last time we saw it during research for the second edition of *Pennsylvania Curiosities*, the Coffee Pot looked like it was down to dregs.

THE COFFEE POT

The Mother of All Highways

Most baby boomers, and even more of their children, have never heard of the Lincoln Highway," concludes a history of America's first transcontinental automobile roadway, published by the Lincoln Highway Association. Being a baby boomer, I took this personally. Whaddaya mean "never heard of the Lincoln Highway"?! Everyone knows about the Lincoln Highway, right? Certainly every Pennsylvanian should have heard of it, considering that eighty-four communities, from Oxford Valley in Bucks County on the east to Smith's Ferry in Beaver County to the west, are part of the Pennsylvania route of the original Lincoln Highway that linked New York with San Francisco.

Then I realized that I'm a little biased, considering that I grew up less than a mile away from the Lincoln Highway, which is called Lancaster Avenue from the Philadelphia area westward to the Lancaster area, where it becomes Philadelphia Pike. By whatever name it is known locally (in Greensburg, Westmoreland County, it's called Pittsburgh Street), the Route 30 portion of the Lincoln Highway meanders for 320 miles across the southern tier of Pennsylvania through some of the most spectacular scenery in the state.

The plan for a transcontinental automobile route was adopted in 1912. It was scheduled for completion in 1915, in time for the Panama-Pacific Exposition hosted in San Francisco. The chief advocate for what he called the Coast-to-Coast Highway was Carl Fisher, owner of the Indianapolis Motor Speedway, who proposed that the roadway be built with private funds. It wasn't until Henry Joy, president of the Packard Motor Car Company, came up with the idea of naming the highway for Abraham Lincoln that funds began pouring in. Pennsylvania is pivotal in the cross-country route that starts at Times Square in New York City and heads south through New Jersey

FILL 'ER UP

During the early years of the Lincoln Highway, gas and snacks were not nearly as easy to find as they are today. Individual gas pumps were located in front of stores on the sidewalks.

Dunkle's Gulf station in Bedford, along the Lincoln Highway, hasn't changed much from the art deco terra-cotta landmark it was upon its construction in 1933. Typical of the ornate roadside establishments built during the heyday of the Lincoln Highway, it looks like a movie prop, but it is indeed a working gas station that has been in the Dunkle family for more than seventy years. A Lincoln Highway Heritage Corridor display stands in front of Dunkle's Gulf with a photo of how the station looked in the 1930. It's hard to tell the difference.

and into Pennsylvania along Route 1. In Philadelphia, the Lincoln Highway makes its big west turn toward the Pacific coast on Route 30, and the route number doesn't change until it becomes Interstate 80 in Granger, Wyoming.

"We're thirteen years older and 1,000 miles longer than Route 66, but for some reason fewer people seem to know about the Lincoln Highway," says Olga Herbert. "I guess we needed a popular TV show named after it." Herbert is the executive director of the

(con't.)

Lincoln Highway Heritage Corridor, a state-sponsored organization that is part of the Pennsylvania Heritage Parks Program. The corridor embraces 200 miles of the Lincoln Highway, through mostly rural and mountainous sections of Pennsylvania, from the York County line on the east to the Allegheny County line on the west. In coming years the Lincoln Highway Heritage Corridor, which was created in 1995, will try to promote more public awareness of the highway's history and its attractions.

Already the corridor is marked by 152 distinctive signs that resemble the 3,000 concrete markers that were placed virtually every mile along the original coast-to-coast Lincoln Highway. The new signs have a big blue *L* with a Lincoln penny above it.

Finding Fort Roberdeau

Culp

My daughter, Molly, and I were driving from Altoona to Lock Haven along Interstate 99 when I spotted a sign that said FORT ROBERDEAU HISTORIC LANDMARK 8 MILES. Pennsylvania had almost as many forts as Carter had liver pills—Fort Pitt, Fort Necessity, Fort LeBoeuf, Fort Mifflin—most dating from colonial times. But I had never heard of Fort Roberdeau. Was it French? What was it defending?

"Wanna go look for Fort Roberdeau?" I asked my then ten-year-old. "Aurgh!" Molly groaned, not at my question but at the treacherous turn of events on the Game Boy she'd been hunched over for the last 40 miles. I took that as a yes.

Now, something odd happens when you turn off the main road in search of something you've never seen or heard of. What does a "Historic Landmark" look like? We exited I-99 at Bellwood and then wound our way up Brush Mountain on State Route 1008. Near the top of the mountain, the view of Sinking Spring Valley opens up below, and I fig-

★ ★

ured Fort Roberdeau must have defended the heights or something. But down the other side of the mountain we went, Molly emitting an occasional "aurgh," through the village of Skelp, where we turned right on State Route 1015 heading toward the village of Culp. (What? No expressway between Skelp and Culp?!) I was beginning to fear that the next village would be Gulp, when I saw another FORT ROBERDEAU HISTORIC LANDMARK sign pointing right on Kettle Road. About a half mile farther was another much-bigger sign pointing to Fort Roberdeau. I turned right, and there, about a hundred yards up the road, was one of those blue-and-yellow Pennsylvania historical markers in the middle of a cornfield. "Fort Roberdeau," it said. "Site of the Revolutionary fort built by Gen. Daniel Roberdeau in 1778 to protect Sinking Valley lead mines. . . ."

Well, that was a long way to go for a short sign. At least that's what I thought at the time. It turns out that there is an actual wooden fort, a restoration of the original Fort Roberdeau, built dur- ing the 1976 Bicentennial, a few hundred yards farther up the road. But I didn't discover that until after we got home. The original Fort Roberdeau was a forti- fied stockade designed to protect the lead-mining operation crucial to the Continental Army's need for ammunition. Miners were threatened by Indi-

After our long search Molly discovers that the sign on the actual site of Fort Roberdeau is as high as an elephant's eye.

★ ★

ans and British sympathizers, but there is no record of any attacks on Fort Roberdeau, which was known as the Lead Mines Fort by the locals. Historically, Fort Roberdeau was what you might call a "one-year wonder." Not only wasn't there any real pressing need for such a garrison due to enemy activity, but the lead-mining operations of the limestone strata of Sinking Springs Valley were more trouble than they were worth. Once the French signed on as American allies in 1778, the need for locally manufactured ammunition was lessened. By the summer of 1779, Fort Roberdeau was abandoned by its garrison, which was needed for duty elsewhere.

Fort Roberdeau is open from mid-May to mid-October. I suggest first calling the fort at (814) 946–0048 to check its hours, although you can see that sign in the cornfield anytime.

Nudist Volleyball Superbowl
Darlington

They've been playing nudist volleyball in Beaver County since the White Thorn Lodge opened in rural Darlington in 1962. Since 1971 the fame of White Thorn's annual week-after-Labor-Day-weekend buck-nekkid volleyball competition had spread throughout nudist circles so that it achieved the status of the official nudist Volleyball Superbowl. The thirty-seventh annual competition will be held in 2008, but this naked Superbowl XXXVII isn't X-rated. It's a family affair that attracts up to 1,500 nude volleyball enthusiasts each year.

Teams play in a round-robin tournament that lasts the better part of two days on the lodge's eleven volleyball courts. Not all the competitors are practicing nudists. "You can tell the ones who aren't," said White Thorn president Lawrence Hettinger. "We call them 'cotton-tails'," a reference to the tan lines so conspicuous among nonnudists.

Still, there are some seeming incongruities at a nudist Volleyball Superbowl. Souvenir T-shirts, for instance. And if you're looking to identify your favorite team by their uniforms, forget it. It's all skins all the time. One nice touch is the nude barbecue grills over at Walt's

Wonderful World of Burgers, where Walt Lippert serves up hamburgers while wearing nothing but an apron to protect himself from grease splatter. "We may be nudists," said Walt, "but we're not stupid."

The nudist Volleyball Superbowl attracts competitors from as far away as Florida, California, and Canada, and the competition is broken down by skill levels. There are men's, women's, and coed divisions. Up to ninety teams participate. Admission is $25 per person and, although clothing is optional, it is frowned upon.

How Donora, Pennsylvania, Changed the World
Donora

I was just a kid the first time I heard the name Donora, Pennsylvania. It was mentioned on a popular network TV cop drama—some 1960s equivalent to all the CSI forensic investigative shows these days—and it involved a life-threatening air-pollution emergency in Los Angeles that no one was taking seriously until this one guy in a lab coat raises his finger and says, "Donora!" like he was shouting, "Eureka!"

"Come again?" says one of the investigators.

"Donora, Pennsylvania, a small steel town near Pittsburgh on a river between two mountains. One day about twenty years ago, there was an air-temperature inversion [this was the first time I had ever heard that term either, which thankfully the guy in the lab coat explained]. That's when cool air clamps down on top of warm air like a lid on a pot. The smoke from the steel mills couldn't escape, trapped between the mountains. Twenty people died in a single day. It was the deadliest air-pollution catastrophe in United States history."

And it remains so to this day. What happened in Donora, Pennsylvania, on Halloween weekend in 1948 scared the bejabbers out of environmental scientists who recognized it for what it was, as a film would document, "an inconvenient truth" that many in post–World War II industrial America would first ignore and then deny. In July 1950 the scholarly journal *California Medicine* reported the findings (note the "allegedly") of a five-month investigation by the U.S.

Health Service into the Donora massacre. "Twenty persons allegedly died as a result of pollutants in the atmosphere and some several hundred more were affected," the journal reported, noting that the Public Health Bulletin No. 306 was an "exceedingly attractive publication about the size of *Fortune* (magazine)." Fortunes, of course, were at stake if U.S. Steel and the Donora Zinc Works had been found liable for the deaths caused by countless millions of cubic feet of untreated sulfur dioxide, fluoride, and other pollutants pumped into the air around Donora year-round—let alone continuously during the emergency of October 30–31, 1948. Well, America wasn't ready to deal with that. Not quite yet.

What you have to understand is that smoke meant life to the Mon Valley mill towns of Western Pennsylvania, to Monessen and Monongahela and Clairton and McKeesport and Braddock and Homestead. When the furnaces shut down, the home hearths suffered. "That's not coal dust; that's gold dust," mill workers would say of the grime that built up so thick each day they could write their names on the hoods of their cars—cars they couldn't have afforded without it. But even by the stoic standards of Mon Valley life, Halloween weekend that year was different. In her 2002 book about the "killer smog" of 1948, *When Smoke Ran like Water,* Donora native and Carnegie Mellon University professor and epidemiologist Dr. Devra Lee Davis described the scene that day through interviews. Like a Stephen King horror movie, an eerie yellow fog rolled into town. At three in the afternoon, car headlights could barely penetrate the curtain of moist smoke. The annual Halloween parade took place on Main Street that Friday afternoon and costumed children disappeared from their parents' sight within a matter of yards. At football practice the day before the big game against Monongahela High School, Donora High coach Jimmy Russell had to yell "Kick!" to let his players know the ball was in the air.

On Saturday fans could hardly see the action. It was like the famous "Fog Bowl" NFL playoff game between the Philadelphia

Eagles and the Chicago Bears when an impenetrable fog rolled into Soldier Field off Lake Michigan obscuring that game to a national TV audience. With Monongahela leading in midgame, from the public-address loudspeakers came a call to Donora's star tight end, Stanley Sawa, telling him to "Go home! Go home now!" With helmet in hand, he ran down Fifth Street to his house to find his father dead. By ten o'clock that morning, nine Donorans had died. By ten o'clock the next morning, eighteen were dead. The local funeral home had run out of caskets by the time the Donora Zinc Works agreed to "dead fire" the furnaces Sunday morning. By that time one-third of the population in a town of 13,000 was seriously ill. Had not heavy rains fallen Sunday afternoon November I and wiped most of the poison from the air, the death toll would have been much higher.

It was Walter Winchell who broke the news of the Donora disaster to "Mr. and Mrs. America and all the ships at sea." The syndicated radio newsman reported on Halloween night, "The small, hardworking steel town of Donora, Pennsylvania, is in mourning tonight as they recover from a catastrophe. People dropped dead from a killer fog that sickened much of the town. Folks are investigating what has hit the area." Today we know that what hit the area was the proverbial piper seeking his pay. The bill on decades of heedless pollution pumped into the atmosphere came due in a deadly and personal way for the citizens of Donora. Their unknowing sacrifice was like a fire bell in the night for the forces of clean air, clean water, and responsible industry. It took years but the movement took hold. In 1965 Pennsylvania passed its first clean-water legislation and, a year later, clean-air legislation. In 1970 an "Environmental Bill of Rights" was adopted. It ain't perfect, but it's so much better than many who suffered can imagine.

★ ★

Great Names Etched in Granite
Donora

One afternoon in June when my daughter, Molly, and I drove across
the Monongahela River bridge that connects Westmoreland County
with Washington County, the first thing we noticed was a big sign
announcing our destination: DONORA. THE HOME OF CHAMPIONS. HUB OF THE
INDUSTRIAL MID MON VALLEY. That's quite a mouthful. A couple of hundred
yards away, I saw something else that made my jaw drop. It was
the Donora War Memorial honoring the men and women who had
fought, and many who had died, for their country in the uniform of
the U.S. military from this western Pennsylvania town with a population of about 5,500. There are nearly 4,000 names etched in the
black granite panels, a breathtaking number from such a small town.
There are forty-one names from the Civil War and sixty names from
Desert Storm, which was the most recent war when the memorial
was planned, but by the time it was dedicated in November 2003,
America was at war again. There are panels ready to add the names
of Donorans who have served in Afghanistan and Iraq.

Stan Musial is one of the names on the Donora War Memorial.
Yes, that Stan Musial. Stan the Man was born Stanislaw Franciszek
Musial on November 21, 1920, the son of Polish and Czech immigrants who lived in a house on Sixth Street in Donora. He won the
National League MVP award in 1943 after batting .357 in a pennant-
winning season for the St. Louis Cardinals. After being drafted
into the navy, Musial served on a repair ship at Pearl Harbor before
returning to the Cardinals in 1946 and winning the MVP again with
a .365 average while leading St. Louis to a World Series victory over
Ted Williams's Boston Red Sox. Musial, whose other nickname was
the Donora Greyhound, was a pitcher in high school. One of his
teammates was Ken Griffey Sr.'s father. Both of the famous baseball
Ken Griffeys were born in Donora—the senior on April 10, 1950,
and the junior on November 21, 1969 (Stan the Man's birthday).
Both became all-stars for the Cincinnati Reds, and at the end of his

★ ★

The Donora War Memorial includes the names of local residents who fought in every U.S. conflict from the Civil War until Desert Storm.

career, Ken Griffey Sr. signed with the Seattle Mariners, which had just signed his rookie son. On August 29, 1990, Ken Griffey Sr. and Ken Griffey Jr. became the first father and son to play together on the same team in Major League Baseball when the Mariners took on the Kansas City Royals. Two weeks later the Griffeys became the first father and son to hit back-to-back home runs in the same game. It only gets better: In St Louis on Sunday, June 20, 2004, Father's Day, with his father in Busch Stadium watching, Ken Griffey Jr. hit his 500th home run, a hit that tied him with Ken Griffey Sr.'s career total of 2,143 hits.

★ ★

First in War: George Washington and Fort Necessity
Farmington

We all know the story, perhaps apocryphal, about young George Washington cutting down a cherry tree and, then when questioned about it, beginning his confession with the words, "Father I cannot tell a lie . . ." Fewer of us know about another youthful indiscretion by the Father of Our Country, who if confronted with the evidence would have to fess up: "I cannot tell a lie . . . I started a world war."

The facts are these: In May of 1754, George Washington, twenty-two and newly commissioned as a lieutenant colonel in the Virginia militia, led a party of forty frontiersmen into the heavily forested wilderness of what is now Fayette County, Pennsylvania, to meet an advancing group of French soldiers moving southeast from Fort Duquesne at the Forks of the Ohio River, what is now downtown Pittsburgh. Earlier Washington had been sent by the governor of Virginia to tell the French forces to leave the land then claimed by Virginia. The French told young George to take a hike. He returned that spring with armed men and Native American allies led by Seneca chief Tanacharison, also known as Half King. Washington's men came upon the French encampment at dawn. The French, not expecting an attack, had not posted sentries, and Washington's men quickly surrounded them.

Then came that ever-popular anonymous trigger finger and historical description "a shot was fired." Could have been a French finger, could have been a Virginia finger, could have been an Indian finger, but the French still rising from sleep caught the worst of it. Thirteen were killed and twenty-one captured. The first shots had been fired in what would become the French and Indian War in North America and the larger global conflict between England and France called the Seven Years' War that did not end until 1763. But the domino effect doesn't end there. The huge cost of the Seven Years' War led England to levy higher taxes on her American colonies, leading inexorably to the Revolutionary War and the Declaration of Independence. And all because of an itchy trigger finger.

The controversy surrounding the skirmish near Uniontown in what became Jumonville Glen was the eighteenth-century equivalent of the Gulf of Tonkin incident, which led to the massive American military buildup in Vietnam. Besides the issue of who shot first and why, there was the question of how the French commander, Ensign Joseph Coulon de Jumonville, died—whether he was killed in battle or executed by a blow from Seneca chief Half King's war club after the surrender. The few French soldiers who escaped returned to Fort Duquesne, and Washington knew a French retaliation "by considerable forces" would be swift. And he was right. No sooner had word of the sneak attack reached the French garrison than a force of 600 French soldiers and 100 Indian allies were on the march under the command of Ensign Jumonville's brother, Captain Louis Coulon de Villiers.

Washington withdrew his men to a position in the Great Meadows 8 miles away where he built a circular wooden stockade and low defensive earthworks at a site he dubbed Fort Necessity. Whatever the French word for "payback" is, it happened on a miserable rainy day five weeks later. Superior French forces taking shelter behind trees surrounded the vulnerable fort on marshy ground in the middle of the meadow. Washington's 300 Virginians bolstered by 100 regular British army troops from South Carolina were running out of dry powder, and more than one hundred were dead or wounded. It could have been a massacre. Instead at 8:00 p.m. the French commander called a truce and offered generous terms for the surrender of Washington's command. His troops would not be taken as prisoners of war. They would be allowed to withdraw to Virginia with their weapons. A little after midnight, Washington signed the document in which he took responsibility for the "assassination" (Washington later said he thought the words meant "death of") of Ensign Jumonville, a document that the French used for considerable propaganda value. And on July 4, 1754, George Washington surrendered his command to hostile forces for the first and only time in his long military career. The French burned Fort Necessity to the ground and returned to Fort

★ ★

Today the site resembles a wooden Stonehenge
in a Western Pennsylvania meadow.

Duquesne to await the return of George Washington under the ill-
fated expedition by British general Edward Braddock the following
year.

Today Fort Necessity National Battlefield is only one of two battle-
grounds from the French and Indian War to be operated by the
National Park Service. It is open sunrise to sunset year round, and visitors can see the Great Meadows and the circular wooden stockade,
which resembles a colonial Stonehenge in this setting. The battlefield
is located 11 miles east of Uniontown on Route 40, the Old National
Road. The Visitors Center (Fort Necessity/National Road Interpretive

and Education Center, (724-329-5811) is open from 9:00 a.m. to 5:00 p.m. year-round except for national holidays. An entrance fee of $5 is charged for individuals fifteen and older. Visit www.nps.gov/fone for the most complete information.

Everyone Knows It's Slinky
Hollidaysburg

Who knew? Certainly not Richard James, who invented it. And not his wife, Betty, who named it. And not even the first customers, who bought out the entire inventory during a Christmas shopper demonstration at Gimbel's Department Store in Philadelphia in 1945. Who knew that a simple spring in a box would become one of the most recognizable toys in the world, an American icon made in Pennsylvania called the Slinky? Who knew that the Slinky would become part of the Smithsonian Institution's permanent Americana exhibit? Who knew that the U.S. Postal Service would honor the Slinky with its own postage stamp in 1999? Who knew it would take a world war to inspire an invention that has lasted longer than the Third Reich?

"It's Slinky! It's Slinky! For fun it's a wonderful toy.

It's Slinky! It's Slinky! It's fun for a girl and a boy.

Everyone knows it's Slinky!"

Everyone knows the Slinky jingle. At least 90 percent of the American adults polled in 1995 knew the jingle, probably because they owned a Slinky as a child or because they had bought one for their own children. Today the sales of Slinky Toys by James Industries in Hollidaysburg in Blair County have equaled the population of the United States—surpassing 300 million. That's a lot of shhhhiiINGG shhhiiIINGGing down the stairs.

It all started during World War II at the Philadelphia Naval Shipyard. In 1943 a young Penn State graduate named Richard James was working as a naval engineer, trying to develop a system to stabilize sensitive monitoring equipment aboard ships in pitching seas. James was experimenting with springs of various sizes when, as the story goes, he noticed one spring fall off a stack of books, uncoiling itself and then righting itself on the book below, before continuing its journey to the next level. "Radar-shmadar," James may or may not have muttered to himself, but in any language it was "Eureka."

For the next couple of years, when he wasn't working to bring the Axis powers to their knees, James worked on his postwar plans to bring millions of kids to their knees to play with his toy without a name. Betty James scoured the dictionary looking for a word that fit the toy. She chose "slinky" because it meant "stealthy, sleek, and sinuous"—not to mention it started with a sibilant.

Slinky it was, a name as simple and delightful as the toy. In 1946 Richard James borrowed $500 to pay a local machine shop to press wire into a coil, 80 feet of wire per coil. He badgered Gimbel's buyers into allowing him to demonstrate his toy to Christmas shoppers, using a portable set of stairs. In ninety minutes, his entire stock of 400 Slinkies was sold at $1 a Slinky. And so it began.

The Slinky story isn't entirely a happy one, although it has remained a family one. In 1960 Richard James abandoned his wife and six children to pursue what his children describe as a "missionary cult" in Bolivia. He nearly bankrupted James Industries in the process with his contributions to the cult. Betty James packed up her children and moved back to her family and hometown roots in Hollidaysburg, where Slinkies have been manufactured ever since, using the same equipment designed by Richard James. Betty, now in her eighties, is still the CEO of James Industries, which is managed by son Thomas James. In 2001 Betty James was inducted into the Toy Manufacturers of America Hall of Fame.

I had to ask about something that has bothered me ever since I followed my first Slinky down the stairs. "What do you call it when the coils of a Slinky get tangled together?" I asked. "Is there a technical name for that?"

"Yes," replied Thomas James. "It's called broken."

The Terrible Truth about Home, Pennsylvania
Home

Unless you live in Indiana County, you've probably never heard of
Home, Pennsylvania, except as the title and location of what is almost
universally considered to be the most grisly, brutal, and disturbing
episode of the *X Files* ever aired on network TV. It was the second
program to air in the fourth season of the *X Files* in 1996. The episode begins with the word *Home,* which dissolves and is replaced by
the word *Pennsylvania.* Agents Mulder and Scully are dispatched to
investigate the discovery of a corpse of a terribly malformed infant.
They discover a Mayberry-type town complete with a sheriff named
Andy and a deputy named Barney, both of whom are horribly mur-
dered by a pair of mutant brothers who live in a farmhouse without
electricity, with a third brother who is actually their father. As Mulder
and Scully close in on the family's terrible secret, they discover the
limbless torso of the mother still alive under a bed on a rolling dolly.
She was still breeding children from this incestuous trio of sons. The
mother tells Scully, "I can tell you don't have no children. Maybe one
day you'll learn the pride . . . the love . . . when you know that your
boy would do *anything* for his mother." The show ends with two of
the sons shot dead by the FBI agents while the other brother/father
carries his mother to the trunk of his car, places her tenderly inside,
and then drives off presumably to find a place to continue breeding
their own children.

Creepy doesn't begin to describe the episode called "Home." Fox
refused to air it again on regular TV, but it still appears on cable TV
reruns and on DVD, where it has gained a cultlike status among *X
Files* aficionados. Although it was shot in rural British Columbia in
Canada, residents of Indiana County are not exactly thrilled by the
notoriety surrounding Home, Pennsylvania, an unincorporated town
with a population of about 180. Whenever he's asked about the *X
Files* episode, Home resident Mike Miller, a blues musician, says, "I
don't know. I was playing a gig the night they shot that" and walks

Why Home? Why Not? Why Ask? Because Who Else Will?

Molly and I were still more than 200 miles from where we live when we arrived at Home. Actually, we passed through Home doing 40 miles an hour on the Buffalo-Pittsburgh Highway, also known as Route 119, one of the lovelier north-south Pennsylvania roadways to take if you want to see what the state really looks like. We were in a hurry to get from Indiana to Punxsutawney before Jimmy Stewart could text message the groundhog and tell Phil to make like a shadow. We were cruising with the wipers on intermittent in a slight drizzle when, on a green bend in the road that revealed wider green fields beyond, out of the corner of my eye, I saw one of those blue Pennsylvania town markers with yellow letters that said VILLAGE OF HOME with more writing underneath. There wasn't much of a town to see: no traffic light or business district, just a fork in the road where Route 85 splits off Route 119 and a little past that a roadside restaurant called, what else, Home Made.

Should I turn around to investigate? This is the problem with traveling with teenagers. They barely tolerate the cool stuff on the itinerary, let alone a "change of plans." Before I could even say, "Let's go back and check out that neat sign," I could hear my own inner father saying, "Ix-nay on the U-urn-tay if you want to avoid an ulk-say by Olly-may." The newspaper comic strip *Zits* described the attitude I was facing in a three-panel-strip in November 2007. Two fifteen-year-olds, a boy and a girl, are talking over lunch. "My new philosophy is to live in the moment," the boy says. "Unless the moment, you know, sucks." In the last panel the boy says, "Then I live in some other moment." And the girl says, "Works for me." And so we motored on toward Punxsutawney, where every day is exactly the same and where there is never a sucky moment. A father can dream, can't he?

But what about Home? When I was researching the second edition of *Pennsylvania Curiosities,* I discovered the Schuylkill County community of Hometown, Pennsylvania, another Home town I had never heard of. Hometown had a story, so why wouldn't Home? But both places offer that precious Abbott and Costello "Who's on First?" possibility. Here's a Pennsylvania state trooper questioning a guy: "Where do you live?" Home. "I know that, but what's the name your neighbors call the place where you live?" Home. "Does your town have a name?" Sure it does. "And that name would be . . . ?" A second guy walks up and tells the first guy not to answer the question. The trooper says, "And why is that?" Because he's from Home and that answer will drive you crazy. "Really, and where might you be from?" Hometown.

If that's stretching a joke, then tell me why people still think a third baseman named "I don't know" is funny.

★ ★

away. Not only is Miller from Home, he is an albino—which is not a bad thing for a bluesman. In college he says he looked like "the illegitimate spawn of Johnny Winter" with shoulder length white blonde hair. Miller described his first day in English class at nearby Indiana State University in 1991 when the instructor asked the class to introduce themselves and where they live. "My name is Mike Miller, I'm from Home, and I play in a blues band." Classmates rolled their eyes in disbelief, and the guy behind him said, "Yeah, right (obscenity). I'm from Home too." Miller had to show his driver's license to satisfy the doubters. "This happens to everyone from Home," Miller said. "The exact same thing happened to my dad during his first day in college right down to the "Yeah, right (obscenity). I'm from Home too."

All this confusion could have been avoided if the new post office for the area hadn't been established inside Hugh Cannon's house in 1834. It was called the "Home" post office because Cannon sorted the mail on a table inside his home. In 1838 a surveyor named Meek Kelly (great-great-grandfather of movie star Jimmy Stewart) was asked to lay out a village by one of Indiana County's first lawyers, Daniel Stannard. Early maps show the village name as Stannardsville or Kellyburg, but the name Home stuck. Besides, how scary could an *X Files* episode called Kellyburg be?

"It's a Wonderful Life" Town
Indiana

Indiana, Pennsylvania, is the perfect name for a mythical all-American hometown. In a town called Indiana, Pennsylvania, you can almost imagine a young Jimmy Stewart walking streets with names like Elm, Maple, and Church, past the library and the courthouse, on his way to his father's hardware store where he'd sweep up after school. You can imagine a photo of Jimmy posing with his proud parents as he leaves home for the first time to attend Princeton University, and later a photo of Jimmy in uniform during World War II, in which he flew twenty-five missions as a bomber pilot. What happens next you don't need to imagine because you've probably seen it on television at least a dozen times, especially around Christmas. You see Jimmy Stewart just back from the war and in despair, standing on a bridge about to hurl himself into the rushing water below. His family would be better off if he was dead, he mutters to himself, if he had never lived at all. And the rest, as they say, is *It's a Wonderful Life.*

In 1946, despite his medals for valor overseas, despite his Academy Award for Best Actor in 1940, Jimmy Stewart was just another out-of-work actor in Hollywood. "Frankly," he wrote about that time, "I was just a little bit scared." Like his Oscar-winning character in *The Philadelphia Story,* the returning GI from western Pennsylvania had seen "hearthfires and holocausts." When director Frank Capra approached him that year to play a role Capra had a hard time explaining, Stewart said, "Frank, if you want to do a picture about a guy who jumps off a bridge and an angel named Clarence who hasn't won his wings yet coming down to save him, well, I'm your man!"

More than fifty years later, *It's a Wonderful Life* is still a classic and Jimmy Stewart (1908–1997) is still an American icon, especially in his hometown, which resembles the fictional Bedford Falls of the movie. Shortly before his death, Stewart wrote a magazine article describing *It's a Wonderful Life* as his favorite movie role. "From the beginning there was something special about the film," he wrote of the elaborate stage set depicting Bedford Falls' main street, with seventy-five buildings and twenty full-grown oak trees. "As I walked down that shady street the morning we started work, it reminded me of my hometown, Indiana, Pennsylvania. I almost expected to hear the bells of the Presbyterian church, where Mother played the organ and Dad sang in the choir."

On May 20, 2008, Indiana celebrated their son's 100th birthday with a week of events entitled, "100 Years of America's Hometown Hero." These included a community church service, a historic

Tough Guy, Tough Town

As devoted as Jimmy Stewart was to his hometown throughout his life, another Hollywood movie star, born and raised in a little town 20 miles away in the next county, walked away as a young man and never looked back. And when he died in Los Angeles in August 2003, his hometown returned the favor. Typical of such obituaries was the wire service report that began, "Charles Bronson, the Pennsylvania coal miner who drifted into films as a villain and became a hard-faced action star, notably in the popular *Death Wish* vengeance movies, has died. He was 81."

He was born Charles Buchinsky, the eleventh of fifteen children born to a Lithuanian immigrant couple. The family moved to the coal fields of Cambria County and lived in a dilapidated shack in the slag heap neighborhood called Scooptown in the town of Ehrenfeld. His family was so poor that young Charles had to wear his older sister's dress to school in first grade, and you can only wonder how hard a boy in a dress had to become to survive in Coal Country. His father died when Charles was ten, and the boy followed his brothers into the mines at a young age, volunteering for the most dangerous jobs because of the higher pay. Unlike middle-class Stewart from a shop-owning family, there was no Princeton in young Buchinsky's future. There was only the hard life of a miner both above- and below ground. He got into fights, spent some time in jail, and, generally speaking, fit right into life in Scooptown, where, as he once described it, "you had nothing to lose because you lost it already."

Being drafted during World War II saved Buchinsky from a life in the mines. After serving in the South Pacific during the war, he moved to Philadelphia, hooked up with the Plays and Players theatrical company, and got married. He was drawn to acting because the pay was relatively good and the lifting was easy. He moved to Hollywood and appeared in some tough-guy character parts in the early 1950s under his real name. In 1954, during the height of the McCarthy anticommunist hearings and Hollywood blacklisting, he changed his last name from the Russian-sounding Buchinsky to Bronson. His Pennsylvania mine experience served him well in such movies as *The Great Escape*, where he played a tunnel rat with claustrophobia digging out of a Nazi prisoner-of-war camp. After Bronson moved to Europe to star in French and Italian films, his jagged, carved-from-a-rock-quarry face launched him to superstardom. In 1971 he was the recipient of the "most popular actor in the world" award at the Golden Globes. In France he was known as *le sacre monstre* (the sacred monster), in Italy, *Il bruto* (the ugly one), but back in Ehrenfeld among old-timers the former Charles Buchinsky was known simply as "Mr. Too-Good-to-Throw-His-Hometown-a-Bone."

Since Bronson's death proposals have been brought before the borough council to erect a sign at the town limits identifying Ehrenfeld (population 250) as the "Birthplace of Charles Bronson" or to rename a street in his honor. Both ideas were voted down. "Why should we do anything for him?" said council president Albert Keller, describing the sentiment of council members. "Charlie didn't do a damn thing for this town." Keller, who knew Bronson's mother—"a fine woman, used to cook for the church picnic"—said the movie star let his former neighbors down the only time they asked for a favor. In 1992 Our Lady of Mount Carmel Church, where the Buchinskys and other Ehrenfeld Catholics worshipped, celebrated its one-hundredth anniversary. The parish sent Bronson a request for a personal message of congratulations to the church of his youth, which could be published in a hundredth-anniversary booklet. "He didn't even write a letter," said Keller. In the end the people from Charlie Buchinsky's hometown felt he'd forgotten his roots, gone Hollywood, literally. "He never gave us any credit," said Keller. "That's what upset people."

★ ★

walking tour, a picnic, live music, an Air Force flyover, and a formal dinner.

At the Jimmy Stewart Museum, visitors can see movie posters, photos, and other Stewart memorabilia. There are film clips of famous Jimmy Stewart movies, and every Saturday afternoon a full-length movie starring Stewart is screened in the intimate museum theater. A bronze statue of Indiana's favorite son, which Jimmy Stewart unveiled during his seventy-fifth birthday celebration in 1983, stands on the lawn of the Indiana County Courthouse at Eighth and Philadelphia Streets. Across the street a sundial marks the former location of J. M. Stewart and Sons Hardware, where his father, Alex, displayed his son's Academy Award statuette in the front window. One block west is a plaque on a stone placed on top of steps leading to a house that no longer stands. The plaque reads: ON THIS SITE WAS THE BIRTHPLACE OF JAMES M. STEWART. It could just as easily have read, ON THIS SITE WAS THE BIRTHPLACE OF A WONDERFUL LIFE.

Jimmy Stewart as classy as ever.

The Jimmy Stewart Museum is located on Indiana's main street, at 845 Philadelphia Street, on the third floor of the Indiana Free Library. It is open 10:00 a.m. to 5:00 p.m. Monday through Saturday, and noon to 5:00 p.m. Sunday.

Floodtown, USA
Johnstown

The last survivor of the original Johnstown Flood died in 1997 at the age of 108. His name was Frank Shomo and he died in his sleep, just as certainly as he would have died as a sleeping infant more than a century earlier when the wall of water arrived at his house 20 miles downstream and a county away from Johnstown, Pennsylvania. His father saved him, and Frank Shomo never tired of telling the story he was too young to remember, but which would become the defining story of his life.

Talk about defining stories. Who among us can hear the name Johnstown without immediately adding the word *flood*? What Chicago is to *Fire* and what San Francisco is to *Earthquake*, Johnstown is to floods. Not once. Not twice. But three times. All during Frank Shomo's lifetime.

The original Johnstown Flood in 1889 killed twice as many people as the Chicago Fire of 1871 and the San Francisco Earthquake of 1906 *combined!* The official number of dead is listed at 2,209, placing it second in mortality among disasters in U.S. history, behind the horrific hurricane in Galveston, Texas, in 1900 that claimed upwards of 6,000 lives.

The cruel irony of the Johnstown tragedy was that nearly as many people died from fire as from water. After twenty-four hours of torrential rainfall, the dam broke on the earthen reservoir on the South Branch of the Conemaugh River. It happened a little after 3:00 in the afternoon on May 31, 1889. The dike collapsed and a wall of water 75 feet high and a half mile wide swept through town, breaking gas mains as it carried away buildings, igniting floating debris trapped beneath bridges, creating an inferno atop the deluge.

It was the biggest story in America since the Civil War. A newspaper reporter from New York wired back a story from Johnstown that began, "God stood on a mountaintop . . ." to which his editor

★ ★

wired back, "Forget flood. Interview God." In Philadelphia, soon-to-be internationally famous reporter Richard Harding Davis wrote dispatches from Johnstown describing the discovery of a prisoner found drowned in his locked cell in the local pokey. A catcher's mask lying in the mud, wrote Harding Davis, looked like it had been "hastily flung off to catch a foul ball."

The infant Frank Shomo was a man in his late forties when the second great flood struck Johnstown on St. Patrick's Day in 1936, killing twenty-five. It had been a cold winter, piling up 14 feet of snow that didn't begin to melt until a storm accompanied by 50-degree weather struck in mid-March. The river swelled to 17 feet above normal.

Then there was the bizarre event of July 20, 1977, when what was supposed to be a passing storm system hovered over Johnstown like a bad check writing. In nine hours the stalled storm dropped almost a foot of rain. Three dams broke. Eighty-five people died. Frank Shomo, then a mere eighty-seven, had to be physically evacuated, protesting all the while that he'd seen worse than this before.

Even as government disaster crews were rushing to Johnstown after the deadly 1977 flood, local entrepreneurs had put a smile on the face of catastrophe. Street-corner hucksters were selling souvenir T-shirts bearing the message "Floods–3, Johnstown–0."

The Johnstown Flood National Memorial is located at the base of what remains of the dam that burst that deadly day in 1889.

Where the Heck Is Kecksburg?
Kecksburg

As the crow flies, the village of Kecksburg is located a mere 57 miles southeast of Mars. So is it any wonder that a UFO landed in the woods near this Westmoreland County farm-country hamlet nearly four decades ago? Obviously a returning Martian aircraft lost its way home to Butler County and made an unscheduled stop before disappearing again. At least that's one theory that has *not* been advanced as an explanation for what happened over the skies of eastern Ohio and western Pennsylvania in the twilight hours of December 9, 1965. Thousands of people claimed to have seen a flaming object streaking southeastward over Pittsburgh. Witnesses said the object made three sudden and deliberate changes in direction before dropping beneath the tree line 2 miles north of the Pennsylvania Turnpike, where hundreds of late-afternoon motorists watched it descend.

"Unidentified Flying Object Falls Near Kecksburg. Army Ropes Off Area," declared the front page of the *Tribune-Review,* the daily newspaper in nearby Greensburg, in the next day's edition. Later editions on December 10, 1965, reported, "Searchers Fail to Find Object." Witnesses reported seeing armed military troops and vehicles sweeping the wooded area where the object had fallen or landed. Volunteer firefighters from Kecksburg and other neighboring towns, responding to a report of an airplane crash, were blocked by state police from approaching the site. Curiosity seekers were waved away at gunpoint by soldiers and threatened with arrest. Before the authorities arrived, one witness, a machinist named Jim Romansky, got close enough to the crash and/or landing site to see a partially buried object. He described it as metallic, bronze-colored, and acorn-shaped, large enough for a man to stand inside. Romansky said the outside of the object appeared to be a single piece of metal without rivets or seams. On the bottom, around what would be the fat part of the acorn, he saw strange markings resembling Egyptian hieroglyphs. (Cue eerie music: Oooo-OOOO-Weeeee-Oooooo . . .)

Later that night another witness watching from the window of his house saw a military-drab-painted flatbed truck with no cargo drive toward the scene. The same truck drove back along the same road with *something* about the size of a Volkswagon Beetle in the cargo bed covered with a tarpaulin. The truck disappeared into the night and so did any official acknowledgment that something had fallen from the sky near Kecksburg. Despite the extraordinary number of eye witnesses (including news media) to a large military presence in the area, the only nonclassified record released by the U.S. government of the events of December 9, 1965, was discovered years later in the files of the air force's Project Blue Book. After a report of the coordinates of the impact site of a skyborne object from a radar station in Oakdale, Pennsylvania, "a three-man team has been dispatched to Acme" (a nearby town used as the post office address for many in the Kecksburg area) "to investigate an object that started a fire." The search team found nothing, according to the file.

So what the heck happened in Kecksburg almost forty years ago? And why have the unanswered questions and the government's refusal to declassify information from that period, during the height of the Cold War, continued to this day? It's not like the story has gone unnoticed all these years. Local talk radio and "UFO-ologists" have kept the story alive in public memory. In 1990 the Kecksburg Unidentified Flying Object Incident was featured on the syndicated TV show *Unsolved Mysteries,* complete with a fabricated prop depicting a 7-foot-tall acorn-shaped bronze object with strange writing around its base. That wire-and-plaster prop is currently on display on a 12-foot-tall wooden tower behind the Kecksburg Volunteer Fire Company on Water Street just off Route 982. The only other permanent reminder that something strange happened in Kecksburg is a street sign identifying township route no. 493 leading toward the UFO landing site as Meteor Road. Of course, no meteor was ever discovered near there, either.

National interest in the Kecksburg incident was raised more recently when in October 2003 Bryant Gumbel hosted a two-hour special on the Sci-Fi channel called *The New Roswell: Kecksburg Exposed.* The special featured a town hall meeting with about fifty residents of the community, some of whom witnessed the events described and others who think it's all a bunch of hooey. It is clear from the TV special, and from the people I spoke to in Kecksburg two days after it aired, that the community is still divided over the truth of what, if anything, occurred. "I was a teenager when that was supposed to have happened," said a fifty-year-old resident, "and if something fell out of the sky, I would have known about it." As for the town meeting televised two nights earlier, he said, "I've lived here all my life and I didn't recognize half the people and half the names in that town meeting—and this is a small community. Everybody knows everybody."

Clearly, however, enough happened on December 9, 1965, that everyday citizens stand by their story and a growing list of sophisticated professionals have added their weight to petitions and lawsuits seeking declassification of government documents pertaining to the Kecksburg incident. President Clinton's former chief of staff, John Podesta, joined the Sci-Fi channel and others in Freedom of Informa-

An acorn-shaped UFO "prop" used in the television show *Unsolved Mysteries* sits atop a 12-foot-high platform outside the Kecksburg Volunteer Fire Company.

★ ★

tion lawsuits seeking release of pertinent information from NASA, the Department of Defense, and the U.S. Army and Air Force.

After more than four decades, the U.S. government is finally acknowledging its failures to release information pertaining to what happened in the skies over Western Pennsylvania that night. In October 2007 a spokesman for NASA admitted that two boxes of documents from 1965 dealing with the Kecksburg incident were missing. In a ruling following a Freedom of Information lawsuit filed in 2003, federal judge Emmet Sullivan ordered NASA to go back and find the missing records and turn them over to the court. "NASA has been stonewalling and now it's required to do the search it didn't do in the first place," said New York journalist Leslie Kean, who filed the Freedom of Information lawsuit. "It's a victory for patriotic people who didn't like being told that they were making things up." As of press time of this edition of *Pennsylvania Curiosities,* the missing NASA files had not been released.

If the unidentified object was Soviet in origin, why would it still be classified? (Stan Gordon, a Greensburg investigator, verified with the Russian space agency that KOS 96, a failed Soviet probe of the planet Venus, reentered the atmosphere over Canada the same day at 3:18 a.m., more than thirteen hours before the Kecksburg sighting.) If it was indeed extraterrestrial in origin, well, Pennsylvania's Roswell is as mysterious and intriguing as what happened in 1947 in what we in the Keystone State should start calling "New Mexico's Kecksburg."

Latrobe Brewing Company? Exit 14 off NJT but Don't Drink and Drive
Latrobe

Latrobe, Pennsylvania, a city of 8,900 residents on the western edge of the Allegheny Mountains, is famous for being the birthplace of Arnold Palmer (1929), the banana split (1904), and Rolling Rock beer (1939). Arnie's Army, the name given to the legions of fans who followed Palmer from hole to hole during his glory years on the PGA tour, had nothing on the loyalty shown over the decades by Rolling Rock enthusiasts who treated the brew as a Pennsylvania icon and the city of Latrobe as its shrine. Rolling Rock wasn't just another Tom, Dick, or Bud of a brew marketed by the giant national beer companies in St. Louis or Milwaukee. No, Rolling Rock was a triumph of mom-and-pop retailing and word-of-mouth marketing. During the famous wedding scene in the Academy Award–winning movie *The Deer Hunter,* Robert De Niro's character, Mike, urges Linda (Meryl Streep) to drink a Rolling Rock because "it's the best beer out there." Now *THAT'S* effective product placement. Rolling Rock was distinctive from other beers from the color of its bottle (green) to the nickname for its seven-ounce bottle (pony) to the label on the bottle (painted on the glass rather than printed on paper) to the mysterious "33" on the back of the bottle (Thirty-three letters in the ingredients? Thirty-three words on the label? The year 1933, in which Prohibition ended?), and most of all to the pledge etched on the back of the bottle and committed to memory by all loyal Rock drinkers: "Rolling Rock—From the glass-lined tanks of Old Latrobe, we tender this premium beer for your enjoyment as a tribute to your good taste. It comes from the mountain springs to you." Ah, Rolling Rock. It was like drinking from a waterfall.

And then, the unthinkable. In the year 2006 the Latrobe Brewing Company, this western Pennsylvania institution, this wholesome symbol of hometown pride and small-town fame, was sold to Anheuser-Busch. On July 31, 2006, the Latrobe brewery on the Loyalhanna Creek in a residential neighborhood on the north side of the railroad tracks was shut down. And the beer that made Pennsylvania famous was now brewed in the industrial meadowlands of North Jersey—in Newark, "For Crying Out Loud," New Jersey. Rolling Rock beer had become just another national brand name, its uniqueness trampled like a pony beneath the huge furry hooves of Clydesdales. And the mountain springwater promised on the label now came straight from the Passaic River. Since Anheuser-Busch can do anything it wants to, the Rolling Rock bottle looks exactly the same as it did when it was brewed in "Old Latrobe" and the "we tender this premium beer" pledge appears word for word on the back of the bottle with a remarkable prefix: "To honor the tradition of this great brand, we quote from the original pledge of quality."

When Molly and I visited Latrobe in the summer of 2007, the brewery was shuttered and all signs of the six-plus decades of Rolling Rock history were gone from the building except for a grimy ghost image of the horse on the Rolling Rock label created by the elements of wind and rain and dirt from a large sign once bolted to the side of the building. Today the old Rolling Rock brewery is the home of the Boston Beer Company, which makes Samuel Adams.

All that remains of the old Rolling Rock Brewery is the grimy ghost image of the Rolling Rock label left after the sign was removed.

Penn State: Love Me like a Rock

Rolling Rock has enjoyed an astounding popularity among Pennsylvania college students over the years. Its legend was cemented among generations of Penn State students and alumni at the famous Rathskeller bar at the corner of Pugh Street and College Avenue in downtown State College, where for years the standard order for an individual was "a coupla Rocks" because they were the seven-ounce ponies rather than the twelve-ounce long-necked "horses."

In what may have been the first documented case of supersizing, in the fall of 1972 during a crowded Penn State home-game football weekend, a customer weary of continually returning to the bar to order "a coupla Rocks" asked if he could buy a case instead. Like Archimedes in his bathtub, Rathskeller owner Dean Smith uttered something that sounded like "Eureka!" And so began the Skeller tradition of selling twenty-four-bottle cases of Rolling Rock beer consumed on-site. Four pals chip in, six ponies per pal, no problem, no mess, and the empties end up back in the case on the table. Brilliant!

Supersizing led to stupendous sizing. In 1983 new owner John O'Connell decided to celebrate the Rathskeller's fiftieth birthday since the end of prohibition in nineteen—that number again—thirty-three. The then-existing *Guinness Book of Records* world record for "most cases of beer sold by a bar in a single day" was 200 cases by a thirsty tavern in Germany. On November 9, 1983, Skeller sudsers outcased the German record holders by a mere 703 cases. By closing time the Penn State champions of the world had polished off 903 cases of Rock. Do the math. That's a case per customer on a day when 903 people stopped by to have a beer, or two, or twenty-four. "Case Day," as the annual event became known, peaked in 1996 when a decade-plus-long record 1,053 cases were sold in a single day. Sometimes too much of a good thing becomes, well, a thousand cases of beer consumed by college students in a single day. The Rathskeller, now called the All-American Rathskeller, no longer sells Rock by the case.

★ ★

Mr. Smith Goes to Loretto
Loretto

Before America's first saint, Bishop John Neumann, ever set foot in
Philadelphia, another immigrant priest had already spent forty years
in western Pennsylvania, where his memory among frontier Catholics
has been raised to near-saint status. One day, perhaps, Father Dem-
etrius Gallitzin, known as the Apostle of the Alleghenies, will join
Saint John Neumann and Saint Katherine Drexel as Pennsylvania's
officially canonized members. As it is now, his memory lives on as a
4,000-acre state park in Cambria County, Prince Gallitzin State Park.

Prince Gallitzin, a member of Russian royalty and son of the czar's
attaché to France and Holland, came to America in the wake of the
French Revolution. He was a recent and devout convert to Catholi-
cism, and he studied for the priesthood in the Diocese of Baltimore,
where he became the second man ordained to the priesthood in
the United States. Preferring to downplay his royal Russian back-
ground, Prince Gallitzin used an Americanized nom de clergy, "Mr.
Rev. Smith." In 1799 Archbishop Carroll of Baltimore asked Mr. Rev.
Smith to travel to western Pennsylvania and establish a parish among
a small group of Catholics living in the mountain wilderness. The
undercover prince built a log church in Loretto, Cambria County,
and ministered to a congregation scattered over hundreds of square
miles. During Gallitzin's lifetime Bishop Kendrick of Philadelphia
described him as "a priest whose pure and humble life excites [Cath-
olics] to the exercise of the evangelical virtues."

By the time he died at the age of seventy, on Easter Sunday,
1840—twelve years before Saint John Neumann was consecrated
Bishop of Philadelphia—five priests were assisting the princely priest
Gallitzin in his missionary work. Loretto, a town of just over 1,000
people, is still considered one of the founding shrines of Catholi-
cism in western Pennsylvania. According to a magazine article about
Prince Gallitzin published by the St. Benedict Center, "the little town
of Loretto, Pennsylvania, which he founded, continues to be one of

the most Catholic towns in America, as evinced by its ten Catholic churches and three monasteries."

A Town Called Mars
Mars

Life in Mars is pretty much the same as life in any other small town in western Pennsylvania. The only difference is that visitors passing through other towns aren't apt to greet locals with "Nanoo, nonoo" or "Take me to your leader." Last fall, the Fightin' Planets of the Mars Area High School football team finished up a disappointing four-and-six season, but native Martians took it in stride. According to Lester Kennedy, who wrote about life in Mars for the town's centennial booklet published in 1973, "Mars is situated 55 miles southwest of Venus (Pa.); 1,875 miles northeast of Mercury (Nev.), and 925 miles north of Jupiter (Fla.). It is approximately 35 million miles, at point of closest approach, from the planet Mars."

More prosaically, Mars is 18 miles north of Pittsburgh and 12 miles southwest of Butler. Except for its uncommon name, Mars is typical of thousands of small towns strewn across the length and breadth of America.

Mars (population 1,713) is a borough not quite a half mile square in the southern part of Butler County. Its claims to fame are its name and an aluminum flying saucer modeled after Warner Brothers cartoon character Marvin the Martian's. The saucer usually sits in the town square on Grand Avenue, although it's small enough for teenage pranksters to move it around town from time to time. There's a blue Pennsylvania town marker in downtown Mars that is inaccurate on two counts. It says, MARS, NAMED AFTER THE STAR OF MARS. FOUNDED 1876. Upon last sighting Mars was a planet, not a star, the fourth rock from the sun. And Mars dates its incorporation as a community to the opening of the Mars post office in 1873 in the home of one Samuel Parks. The origin of the name Mars is also disputed. The minority opinion is that Mrs. Parks was a student of astronomy

What, No Galaxy, Pennsylvania?

There's an Atlas in Northumberland County, which is as good a place as any to start a tour of the world and the near solar system, courtesy of Pennsylvania towns with names like Moon, Mars, and Venus. A traveler crossing the state might scratch his or her head and check the road map: "I didn't know Dallas was in Pennsylvania. And Houston. And Austin. Not to mention Denver, Brooklyn, Milwaukee, Sacramento, Richmond, and Buffalo!"

There's a Frisco, Pennsylvania, but no San Francisco. There's a Bangor and a Salem and a Reno and a Knoxville, but they aren't followed by Maine, Massachusetts, Nevada, or Tennessee. Entire states have a Pennsylvania after their names. There's a California, a Virginia, an Idaho, an Iowa, an Indiana, and even an Oklahoma, which is appropriate because the most famous Oklahoman is buried in the Pennsylvania town that bears his name, Jim Thorpe. There's both a Yukon and an Alaska, Pennsylvania.

Americans of Irish descent can visit Dublin, Belfast, Ulster, Munster, Donegal, Sligo, Waterford, and Derry without ever leaving Pennsylvania. There's even an Irishtown and a Paddytown. German Americans will feel right at home in Germany, Berlin, East Berlin, Hamburg, Nuremburg, and not one but two Germantowns, a Germanville, and a Germania. Homesick Scots can go to either Glasgow or Scotland, with maybe a side trip to Brogue. Italians can tour Milan, Rome, Verona, and Florence, not to mention Little Italy neighborhoods in cities across the state. There's a Frenchville and a Paris too, and if Gallic pride can handle a visit, Pennsylvania also has its own Waterloo.

There's an English Center, Pennsylvania, as well as London, Oxford, Cambridge, Lancaster, York, and Nottingham. Pennsylvania has its Gibraltar and its Corsica and Malta too. There's a Poland and a Warsaw. There's a Moscow and a St. Petersburg. There's a Dalmatia and a Bohemia and a Macedonia and a Moravia. There's Athens and Sparta and even Troy. South of the border but still in the state are Mexico, Lima, and Santiago. To the north (but not that far north) are Finland, Sweden, Ottawa, Halifax, and Newfoundland, Pennsylvania.

The Middle East is well represented in this Middle Atlantic state. There's Egypt and Luxor and Jericho and Palestine and Hebron and Galilee and Bethlehem and Nazareth and Jewtown. There's Bagdad and Tripoli and Crete. Unlike their Middle Eastern namesakes, these communities aren't likely to go to war with each other. But if they did, they could always work out a peace agreement at Geneva, Pennsylvania.

and suggested the name. The majority opinion is that Mars was chosen to honor the political patron responsible for Mr. Parks's winning the post office contract, the Honorable Samuel Marshall. For a brief period in 1877, the town was on the verge of being named Overbrook, because of the opening of a B&O Railroad station bearing that name, but because there was already an Overbrook post office in Philadelphia (also named after a Pennsylvania Railroad train station), the name Mars stuck.

Today, Martians tend to live more comfortably with their alien identities than the citizens of, say, Roswell, New Mexico.

Step On Up to the "Church on the Turnpike"
New Baltimore

The Pennsylvania Turnpike has 512 miles, five tunnels, fifty-five interchanges, twenty-two service plazas, and one Catholic church. In fact, the Pennsylvania Turnpike may be the only limited-access toll road in the country that has steps leading from the shoulder of the highway up an embankment and into a church. You can see the steps on either side of the turnpike at mile marker 129 in New Baltimore between the Bedford and Somerset exits.

So what's up with that? The "Church on the Turnpike," as St. John the Baptist Catholic Church has become known to countless travelers over the years, was founded by German immigrants in 1824. The church building itself, which stands about 100 yards off the south side of the turnpike, was built in 1890. It resembles a miniature European cathedral and was built by hand by artisans from the parish. In 1937 when the right-of-way for the Pennsylvania Turnpike was being surveyed, the route chosen for the new highway cut right through the cemetery of St. John's eighty-acre plot in Somerset County. A deal was struck between the Turnpike Commission and the Trustees of St. John's. The existing graves would be excavated and moved in exchange for access in perpetuity for travelers on the turnpike who wanted to stop at the church. Concrete steps with

★ ★

They call St. John's Catholic Church in New Baltimore the "Church on the Turnpike" for good reason. Travelers on the Pennsylvania Turnpike can stop for Sunday services without taking an exit. There's parking and stairs leading to St. John's on both east- and westbound sides of the turnpike.

metal railings were built up the sides of the embankments on both east- and westbound lanes (the latter steps lead up to the Findley Street overpass).

The deal was struck in good faith and has never been rescinded. The church is frequently visited by travelers pulling over to the shoulder when they see the large lighted cross of St. John's beckoning from the side of the turnpike. The church's message sign with its schedule of masses is turned toward the highway, and according to St. John's pastor, Father Mark Begley, most "off-turnpike" Mass-goers prefer to attend the 6:00 Saturday evening mass or the 10:30 Sunday morning mass. "I get a lot of people who come off the turnpike during the day looking for someone to hear their confession," said Father Begley. "They've been traveling and maybe they've done some things they wish they hadn't done, and they want to confess in a place where they're not known and they'll never be seen again."

Truckers like the lighted cross outside St. John's because it is a landmark midway between the Bedford and Somerset exits. A few years ago, the lights on the cross were broken, and Father Begley said that he received phone calls from passing truckers offering to help pay for new lights for their nighttime beacon. The parish paid for the new lights without the truckers' contributions.

The most unlikely "off-turnpike" support for the church came from Charles "Chick" Curry, a retired IBM computer service specialist who had been driving past St. John's during his trips across the state since the 1950s. What caught Curry's eye was not the steps so much as the clock tower on the church. The hands on the 6-foot clock face never moved. Curry was a clock buff since childhood and had become an accomplished clock maker. One day in 1999 on his way home to Delaware, he finally decided to find out once and for all why the clock didn't work. He pulled over on the turnpike shoulder and climbed the steps to the church, which, to his surprise, was well tended and in good repair. He explained his interest to Father Begley, who showed him the reason the hands never moved. The clock's hands were bolted to the face. There was no time-keeping mechanism inside the clock tower. There never had been.

Curry (a "raised Presbyterian") offered to build a clockworks for the church. He even offered to build a mechanism to ring the church bell on the hour. And he offered to do it for free. "They didn't think I was for real," Curry said of the reaction from St. John's parishioners to his offer. But he was for real. It took him three to four months to design and build a clockworks and bell-ringing mechanism. "It's a ten-pound sledgehammer, actually," he said of the bell clapper. He even cut, shaped, sanded, and varnished new minute and hour hands from redwood to match the nonfunctional steel hands.

After a two-month test of the electrically powered clock in the church's community room, Curry's clockworks were installed in the tower and officially dedicated on October 29, 2000. "It begins striking the hour at exactly eight seconds before the hour," Curry said. "Sometimes I'll call up there and look at my master clock and I'll say, 'You should hear it start chiming in three . . . two . . . one . . . now!' And I'll hear it over the phone."

In Search of Gravity Hill
New Paris

I was on the verge of summoning Leonard Nimoy to help me solve the mystery of Gravity Hill. The mystery wasn't what happens at Gravity Hill (water flows uphill, cars on a downhill slope roll backward) or even why that happens (scientifically speaking, there is no explanation, although optical illusion is the most cited reason), but rather *where* Gravity Hill is in Pennsylvania.

Gravity Hill was one of the first "curiosities" I was urged to find by callers to a Philadelphia radio talk show I was hosting. "It's somewhere in Bucks County," I was told, "up near Yardley." Other callers disagreed. "No, it's near New Hope," said another. "No, it's definitely in Warrington." People knew exactly where it was but they couldn't tell me how to get there. I started calling police stations in the area, figuring that if there was a Gravity Hill in the neighborhood, the cops would know about it. Some did; some didn't. But it was always in the next town over.

I began asking people I'd meet in my travels around the state. "Yeah, there's one of them in Lancaster County," said Larry Homan, a chainsaw sculptor. "Water flows uphill. It's a road in the middle of a cornfield." I never gave up on finding Gravity Hill, wherever it was, but I was beginning to think it was a rural myth. Then, as luck would have it, I came across a brochure for the Bedford County Visitor Bureau touting "Gravity Hill, New Paris, Pa." When I told Dennis Tice, director of the Bedford County Visitor Bureau, how long I'd been looking for Gravity Hill in Bucks County, he deadpanned, "Yeah, we bought it from them and moved it up here." Directions to Gravity Hill are available on the Bedford County Visitor Bureau Web site (www .bedfordcounty.net/Gravityhill/index.htm), but be forewarned, it's not easy to find.

Molly and I were lucky: We found it pretty much on our first try. The directions say to take Route 30 (the Lincoln Highway) to Schellsburg in Bedford County. At the only traffic light in town, make the turn onto Route 96 north toward New Paris (formerly Mudtown) and travel for about 4 miles. You want to turn left onto Bethel Hollow Road (State Route 4016), which is just before a small bridge that is not a bridge so much as a roadway over a culvert. We had to make a U-turn here, once we realized that was the bridge. There's only one way to turn onto Beth Hollow Road, so turn there and follow it for ⁶⁄₁₀ of a mile to a fork in the road, and bear left. Stay on this road for another mile and a half until you come to a stop sign. Bear right and travel several hundred yards until you see the letters GH spray-painted on the road. (You were expecting, maybe, a neon sign saying WEL-COME TO GRAVITY HILL?) Proceed past the first GH about ¹⁄₁₀ of a mile and stop your car. Put it in neutral. And start screaming as you begin to roll up what looks like a downhill slope.

Is this uphill or downhill? Can you tell from the photo?

★ ★

Molly and I found Gravity Hill at about 3:00 on a Thursday afternoon. There was already a minivan with a Virginia license plate, filled with children, stopped in the middle of the road, testing the phenomenon. It's a little creepy being there, actually, because you are in the middle of a rural road with no one nearby. When I got out of the car to take pictures, the Virginia van pulled away, perhaps out of nervousness. I gave Molly the video camera to record our experience, which ended up with both of us yelling at each other because she insisted on shooting in the opposite direction of what I wanted. At one point when we were videotaping the experience, a car pulled up from the other direction and slowed down next to us. I rolled down my window and told the woman driving that "this is the place." She smiled and said, "I know; I grew up around here. When we were teenagers we used to come up here to see if water really would flow uphill." She gave me a mischievous look and added in a whisper, "But we used to do it by peeing."

"Eeeeewwwwwww," said Molly, after the lady drove away. Fortunately, we had come prepared with a bottle of Poland Spring water. Molly manned the camera as I poured the water, which on video is very clearly shown flowing in some direction. You will have to take our word for it that it was uphill.

There are actually two Gravity Hills a short distance from each other. The second one is marked by a telephone pole with the number 69 on it. To me, this Gravity Hill just a few hundred yards down the hill was more powerful than the first. I could actually feel it in my stomach. It felt like a rubber band wanting to pull me back from the direction I was going. Molly didn't feel the rubber band sensation in her stomach, but she was freaked out by how fast our car started rolling backward uphill in neutral on what looked like a downhill slope. "Ohmygod, ohmygod," she kept saying, as I added "Ohmygod, ohmygod," while trying to keep the car on the road as it raced backward. It was truly weird.

★ ★

Gravity Hill is by no means unique to Pennsylvania. In fact, the phenomenon has become fairly well commercialized in other states. They go by different names: Spook Hill in Lake Wells, Florida; Mystery Spot in Santa Cruz, California; the Oregon Vortex in Gold Hill, Oregon; and Gravity Hill in Mooreville, Indiana, to name a few.

There Ain't No Zombies like Pittsburgh Zombies
Pittsburgh

Life as we knew it ended forty years ago in a hillside cemetery outside Evans City, Pennsylvania, where Pittsburgh commercial filmmaker George Romero shot the opening scenes to his classic low-budget horror thriller *Night of the Living Dead*. From the moment Johnny (Russell Streiner) teases his sister Barbra (Judith O'Dea) "They're coming to get you, Barbra. See, there's one of them coming now," while visiting the grave of their father, the reanimated bodies of the undead have been roaming Western Pennsylvania (and the rest of the world) in their insatiable hunger for living human flesh. Romero's 1968 zombie pic spawned more than a dozen sequels, prequels, rip-offs, remakes, and homage spoof comedies, such as 2004's *Shaun of the Dead*, where British slackers battle the undead with vinyl record albums and cricket bats, and *Night of the Living Bread*, an eight-minute short where mutant slices of white bread, muffins, and communion wafers come to life and attack people who ward them off with weapons of mass bread destruction like electric toasters.

For his own part Romero, a New York native who attended Carnegie Mellon University in 1960, stayed true to his Pittsburgh filmmaking roots. He cast local actors in every role. The first zombie seen in *Night of the Living Dead* is William Hinzman from the nearby Allegheny County borough of Coropolis (also birthplace of *Batman* actor Michael Keaton). Hinzman's long angular visage has become the gold standard of undead countenances and has served him well in a motion picture acting career in which he has played deceased flesh eaters as recently as the 2005 comedy classic, *The Drunken*

Dead Guy, where Hinzman appears in the role of "the experienced zombie." In Romero's first well-received sequel, 1978's *Dawn of the Dead*, he returned to the Pittsburgh area—specifically the recently opened indoor mall in suburban Monroeville. The movie starts in a TV station in the city of Philadelphia, then under siege by long dead but still-voting residents of South Philly, later ending on the roof of a zombie-infested mall off Route 22 just east of Pittsburgh.

Day of the Dead, Romero's 1985 sequel, was filmed in the Lawrence County borough of Wampum, Pennsylvania and his third-quel, *Land of the Dead*, brings it all back home to Pennsylvania, even though it was filmed in Toronto. In this version, Pittsburgh is the last city on earth and not a bad city at that, considering, you know, that they're surrounded by zombies. Using—at the time—unknown actors (Dennis Hopper, John Leguizamo), Romero tells a story of Pittsburgh as a triangular island (and this must be where Andy Rooney came up with his cockamamie concept) with rivers on two sides for protection and a zombie-zapping electrical fence guarding the land access from the east. Essentially this was the same geographic advantage that caused the French and English to go to war over Fort Duquesne/ Fort Pitt. Downtown Pittsburgh was a well-defendable point of land. Unfortunately, the postapocalyptic leaders of humanity's last viable outpost were no more enlightened than Pennsylvania politicians have been since the days of robber baron industrialists.

Land of the Dead ends with the zombies taking over Pittsburgh and eating the fat cats in Fiddler's Green. And the unlikely hero, or at least the living dead-man-walking with the most dignity, is a zombie in a gas station mechanic's overalls named Big Daddy. In life Big Daddy is actor Eugene Clark, and he was a college football player drafted by the Pittsburgh Steelers, until the siren call of Hollywood cast him into zombiehood.

I won't give away the ending, but I'll tell you it involves the Monongahela River on the south and the Allegheny River on the north.

★ ★

The Three Rivers Ferry
Pittsburgh

Thousands of people in Pittsburgh take a boat to get to Steelers football games. It's the best way to beat the traffic on game day. For $5.00 you can get a round-trip ticket on the ferry-size water taxis that shuttle back and forth across the Monongahela River from South Side to the stadium complex on the north side of the Allegheny River opposite downtown Pittsburgh.

I took the football ferry packed with Steelers fans to one of the last home games to be played at Three Rivers Stadium in 2000. It was a rainy Sunday in October and the opposition, the then-winless

Go, Steelers! Water taxi, please . . .

Cincinnati Bengals, was as dreary as the weather. But the fans were upbeat, even the Bengals fans, one of who carried a sign that said, I'LL GO ANYWHERE FOR THE BENGALS' FIRST WIN. Three Rivers Stadium was flanked by the construction sites of the two new stadiums being built to accommodate the Steelers and the Pirates. On the ferry ride across the river, I asked a fan what the new Pirates stadium would be called. "They're going to call it PNC Park," he said. "That's because they have windows in the men's rooms and ladies' rooms." It took me a minute, but I got it.

Three Rivers was a saucer-shaped concrete bowl of the same age, style, and fate of Veterans Stadium in Philadelphia. Each city has replaced its single multipurpose stadium with separate baseball and football stadium a short distance from each other. The Steelers' new home, Heinz Field, opened on October 7, 2001, with the Steelers' home opener against, who else, the Cincinnati Bengals. Pittsburgh's Three Rivers area has always been associated with the city's professional sports. Two Pennsylvania historical markers were placed outside Three Rivers Stadium to commemorate America's first professional football game and the first World Series.

The first professional football game was played on November 12, 1892, in nearby Recreation Park between the Allegheny Athletic Association and the Pittsburgh Athletic Association. Allegheny won, with the winning touchdown being scored by William "Pudge" Heffelfinger, who was paid $500 to play. He was the first football player ever to be paid outright, and professional football dates its origin to that game. The first World Series was played at Exposition Park, on the site of Three Rivers Stadium, in October 1903 between the National League Pittsburgh Pirates and the American League champion Boston Pilgrims (later to be called the Red Sox). Games four through seven of the best-of-nine game series were played on the site, featuring Hall of Famers Honus Wagner for Pittsburgh and Cy Young for Boston. The Pilgrims won the first World Series five games to three.

★ ★

Finding Pittsburgh's Vatican
Pittsburgh

You can't get to Troy Hill by accident. You have to know where
you're going or else you won't find it. And you get the feeling that
the residents of this hillside Pittsburgh neighborhood overlooking the
Allegheny River and the Strip District like it that way. It took Molly
and me at least three tries to find Troy Hill, even though it is hiding in
plain sight—much like St. Anthony's Chapel at 1704 Harpster Street,
where there are more first class relics of Catholic saints anywhere
in the world outside of the Vatican. A first class relic is a bone frag-
ment from the remains of a person elevated to sainthood. And there
are thousands of saintly bones on display in ornate reliquaries at St.
Anthony's Chapel, which is only slightly harder to find that Troy Hill
itself.

This century-old chapel is only open to the public from 1 until 4
p.m. on Tuesday, Thursday, Saturday, and Sunday. Molly and I arrived
at one o'clock on the last Thursday in June only to be informed that
Sister Margaret, the nun who gives the guided tour of St. Anthony's
Chapel, was on a trip home to Ireland. Talk about timing. We were
allowed to explore the hushed chapel by ourselves among a handful
of worshipers saying the rosary or kneeling in private prayer. It is a
gorgeous church, reminiscent of a vastly larger European cathedral
tucked away on a small street in a north-side Pittsburgh residential
neighborhood. Here stacked almost floor to ceiling behind the main
altar are physical remains of more than 4,000 saints placed inside
reliquaries, which are boxes that resemble cathedrals themselves. The
side aisles of the chapel are lined with large niches containing life-
sized hand-carved wooden figures depicting the fourteen Stations of
the Cross (and guarded by an alarm system).

How this remarkable sanctuary of saintly remains came to Troy Hill
is the story of one priest and one parish. But mostly one priest. Father
Suitbert G. Mollinger, a Belgian priest from a wealthy family, became
pastor of the Most Holy Name of Jesus Parish in 1875. The parish rec-

★ ★

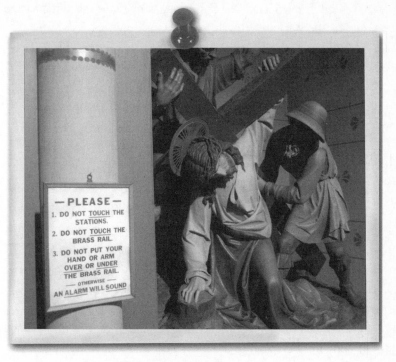

Please do not touch.

tory adjoins the chapel and Holy Name of Jesus Church is across the
street. In the 1880s during a time of much political and cultural unrest
in Germany and Italy, Father Mollinger made several trips to Europe
and acquired thousands of relics from Catholic churches, hundreds of
which included original certificates of authentication dating back to
1714. From a 21st Century perspective, some of the holy relics gathered by Father Mollinger require a leap of faith. For instance there
is one reliquary shaped like a monstrance (an ornate vessel used to
display the Blessed Sacrament or communion wafer), which is said to
contain a sliver of wood from the True Cross (on which Christ was
crucified) as well as relics from Saint John the Baptist, Mary Magde-
lene, Saint Lawrence, Saint Dionysius, Saint Blase, Saint. Stephen (the
first martyr), Saint Anthony of Padua (for whom the chapel is named),

and a shred of the Sacred Winding Sheet (sometimes called the Sacred Shroud of Turin). Other relics include a sliver from the table at the Last Supper and a piece of the veil worn by Mary, mother of Jesus. A pretty impressive collection even for nonbelievers to behold.

When parishioners of the Most Holy Name of Jesus failed to raise money to build a separate chapel for the relics, Father Mollonger financed the construction himself with his inheritance from his wealthy family in Belgium. The enlarged chapel was dedicated in 1892, the same year Father Mollinger died. In his later years the priest became famous as a healer himself, and on display in the chapel were the crutches of hundreds of the faithful who claimed to have been cured by Father Mollinger's hands (some of those crutches can be seen at the St. Anthony Chapel Gift Shop across the street). Upon his death, and because he left no will, Mollinger's family members descended on the chapel and virtually looted it of anything that could be carried away—crystal chandeliers, candelabras ,and a black onyx altar, among them. Subsequently the chapel and what remained of its contents were sold to the Most Holy Name of Jesus Parish for $30,000. St. Anthony's Chapel is only opened to the public twelve hours a week, so perhaps it's best to call first (412-323-9504), if only to make sure Sister Margaret isn't off gallivanting in Ireland.

An Unlikely Pittsburgh Native
Pittsburgh

Pop artist Andy Warhol's celebrated fifteen minutes of fame take up an entire seven floors of an industrial building in downtown Pittsburgh just a few blocks away from the house where he grew up. It's hard to say which is more unlikely, that a character like Warhol is a product of Pittsburgh, or that a city like Pittsburgh would be home to the Andy Warhol Museum if he weren't a hometown boy. The facts are that Warhol lived in Pittsburgh until leaving for New York to continue the art career he had begun while studying painting and design at the Carnegie Institute of Technology.

★ ★

Andy Warhol was an odd chap, to say the least, and his oddness and his talent are on display at a museum devoted to his work on Sandusky Street not far from Pittsburgh's new stadiums. He was a mama's boy, Warhol was, and his mother joined him in New York following his father's death three years after he left Pittsburgh in 1949. Julia Warhola and her husband, Andrej, had immigrated to Pittsburgh from the Carpathian Mountain area of what is now Slovakia. Among the personal items on display in the Andy Warhol Museum are postcards the son sent his mother from his travels around the world. "Hi, Im alright im in Rome now its real nice here. Bye," he wrote in 1956. Other postcards with virtually the same unemotional and ungrammatical message were sent to his mother from other countries.

The answer to that is found in the 500 works of art that are on display, making the Andy Warhol Museum the most comprehensive lone-artist museum in the country. The pop art Campbell's soup can paintings are there, as well as the stylized portraits of Marilyn Monroe, Elvis, and Natalie Wood. The story of Warhol's life in the New York art and music and moviemaking and magazine-publishing scene is told in various exhibits on different floors. His talent is undeniable.

The Andy Warhol Museum, at 117 Sandusky Street, is open Tuesday through Sunday. Call (412) 237-8300, or visit www.warhol.org.

The "unlikely" Andy Warhol Museum in Pittsburgh.

★ ★

CBS Reports That Pittsburgh Is an Island
Pittsburgh

To me, the funniest observation Andy Rooney ever made during his
thousand-year reign as a commentator on *60 Minutes* was when he
noted that a guy with a size seven head and a size seventeen neck
should be able to pull his dress shirt over his head without unbut-
toning the top button. I didn't say it was hilarious, but it was funny.
And that was, like, twenty-five years ago. About a decade or so ago,
it dawned on me that Andy Rooney isn't supposed to be funny; he
isn't supposed to be profound. He's supposed to be some guy rav-
ing away at the next bar stool, or next to you on an airplane, and
you're supposed to be too polite to get up and go to the bathroom.
Rooney has made some ornery, peculiar, and just plain dumb obser-
vations over the years, but on Sunday night October 29, 2006, on *60
Minutes,* Andy Rooney spoke an untruth. In an otherwise harmless
piece about American cities and what he discovered looking at an
atlas, Rooney said, "One of the biggest surprises to me is Pittsburgh. I
didn't know it's on an island, like New York City."

Pittsburgh is not on an island, of course, and if it is on an island,
it's like the island that Beaver, Sunbury, Easton, and Philadelphia are
on. Two rivers meet within the city limits. This does not an island
make, unless, like Manhattan, those two rivers surround the city. That
Andy Rooney *thought* Pittsburgh was an island isn't as disturbing
as the fact that CBS and *60 Minutes* aired his stunningly inaccurate
observation. Remember, impressionable kids watch this show. People
in Ohio watch this show. I called the *Pittsburgh Post-Gazette* after
Rooney's island comment that Sunday night and spoke to the night
city editor Mike Anderson. He had heard about Rooney's Pittsburgh-
as-Tahiti reference but in true working-newspaperman fashion he
replied to my question, "What do you think Rooney was trying to
say?" Anderson replied, "I'm not going to make any money trying to
think of what Andy Rooney was trying to say."

In general Pittsburghers' reaction to Rooney's alternative geography lesson were gentler than mine. "Andy," wrote Markrud44 to the *60 Minutes* Web site with Rooney's commentary (www.cbsnews.com/stories/2006/10/24/60minutes/rooney/main2118518.shtml#ccmm), "you're not the only one who wasn't aware Pittsburgh is an island. I've lived in Pittsburgh my entire life and wasn't aware it is an island either . . . actually it isn't." More than a year after the original air-date, the Web site carries the uncorrected commentary with Pittsburgh still an island.

The Black Babe Ruth
Pittsburgh

If Josh Gibson had been the same race as Babe Ruth, Forbes Field in Pittsburgh might have been called "The House That Gibson Built." But Josh Gibson was a black man playing baseball in the 1930s, the same era as the Babe, which meant that he couldn't play on the same team with white major leaguers. Instead, he played his entire baseball career for two of the greatest teams in Negro League history, the Pittsburgh Crawfords and the Homestead Grays.

Homestead is a steel town just a few miles downriver from Pittsburgh; the Negro League Grays played their home games at Forbes Field in Pittsburgh when the Pirates were out of town. The Grays signed a strapping eighteen-year-old from the North Side named Josh Gibson in July 1930. In that year's Negro League World Series between the Grays and the New York Lincoln Yankees, Gibson hit a home run over the 457-foot wall in left center field at Forbes Field, a feat that would not be repeated until thirty years later, when Mickey Mantle did it during the 1960 World Series. The following week the Negro League World Series shifted to New York, and Gibson became the only player ever to hit a ball out of Yankee Stadium—a shot measured at an impossible 600 feet.

Catcher Josh Gibson was nicknamed the Black Bomber during a sixteen-year career in which he hit 800 home runs while batting over .300. When Gibson jumped over to the rival Pittsburgh Crawfords

Dominick and Eugene Meet Birdy

Two of my favorite movies of all time are set and shot in Philadelphia and Pittsburgh. The Philadelphia movie is *Birdy*. The Pittsburgh movie is *Dominick and Eugene*. They are enough to do a state proud.

I live in West Philadelphia, not far from where they filmed the opening sandlot baseball scenes in *Birdy*, which is a movie about unlikely friends who become brothers. I recognize by intuition the hilly Pittsburgh neighborhood streets traveled by the trash truck in *Dominick and Eugene*, which is about unlikely brothers who become friends and more.

Birdy stars Matthew Modine as the title character who raises pigeons and wants to fly like a bird, and Nicolas Cage as his friend Al, who raises girls' heartbeats and wants to know what Birdy knows about life and aerodynamics that he doesn't. It's hilarious and sad and wonderful and more Philadelphia than most movies ever touch. They've even got the William Penn statue joke in there. "Hey, Birdy, remember when we'd get those old ladies to look up at City Hall tower?" asks Al as the camera shows The Founding Father in all his unintentional randiness (see earlier in the book). Birdy and Al go off to war (in the movie it's Vietnam, in the book it's World War II, in reality it doesn't matter), where Al loses half his face and Birdy loses half his mind, the remaining half being that of a bird. His better half.

Dominick and Eugene stars Tom Hulce and Ray Liotta as the title characters, the former being a beloved but obviously brain-injured municipal trash-truck loader, the latter being his brilliant and loving but obviously stressed-out medical student twin brother. Jamie Lee Curtis is thrown in as a love interest, but it's really a story about brothers coming to grips with losing each other's company after all these years. One shiver-me-timbers moment of dialogue comes after

Dominick's dog has been killed by a car. The trusting and innocent and inconsolable Dominick is praying before the altar of his parish church. After he rises from his knees to leave, a well-meaning parish priest tries to console him with hollow words about a doggie heaven. The now furious Pittsburgh trash man turns tail and stalks halfway up the aisle. Then he turns, glaring first at the priest and then at the crucified figure of Christ above the altar. "If I was God," he says, "I wouldn't let that happen to my boy."

I don't want to give away the ending to either movie (they're on video, people!), but I will tell you the final word of dialogue in *Birdy:* "What?"

★ ★

in 1932, he joined a team with five future Hall of Famers all playing at the same time, something not even the 1927 Yankees can
claim. Besides Gibson future Hall of Famers playing for the Crawfords
included his battery mate Satchel Paige, Oscar Charleston, Judy Johnson, and "Cool Papa" Bell.

Gibson returned to the Grays in 1936 and finished his career in
1946, winning the Negro League batting title for the ninth time in his
final year. The following year, Josh Gibson had a stroke caused by a
brain tumor and died in his Strauss Street home on Pittsburgh's North
Side. When Boston Red Sox slugger Ted Williams was inducted into
the Baseball Hall of Fame in 1966, he said, "I hope that some day
Satchel Paige and Josh Gibson will be voted into the Hall of Fame as
symbols of the great Negro players who are not here only because
they weren't given a chance." That day came in 1972. Josh Gibson
was inducted into Major League Baseball's Hall of Fame despite never
having played for a National or American League team.

Today in Pittsburgh, Josh Gibson's career is marked with a Pennsylvania historical marker at 2217 Bedford Avenue, where his baseball
career started at Ammons Field.

A View with a Pew
Pittsburgh

Pittsburgh is the only city in America where a visitor standing on the
sidewalk admiring the skycrapers can get a stiff neck from looking
down. That's because the best view of the spectacular Pittsburgh
skyline is from aptly named Grandview Avenue in Mount Washington, the hilltop neighborhood directly across the Monongahela River
from downtown Pittsburgh and the famous Golden Triangle. Even
on a cloudy day, the view is impressive; but on a sunny day or a clear
night, the view of the sparkling river city hundreds of feet below
is breathtaking. So impressive is the vista that in May 2003 USA
Weekend magazine ranked the "Nighttime view from Mt. Washington, Pittsburgh" number two on its top-ten list of America's Most

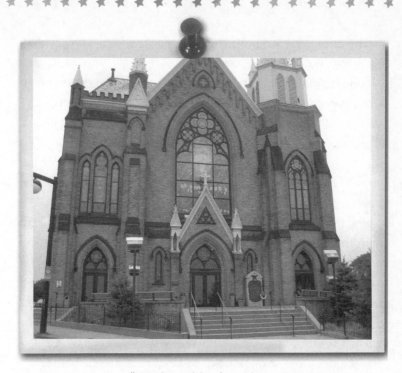

"Keeping spiritual watch over Pittsburgh."

Beautiful Places. Pittsburgh's skyline outranked views of number four Hawaii, number five San Francisco, number eight Key West, and number ten Savannah, Georgia. Not too shabby.

You can't actually get a stiff neck from looking down on downtown from the 1,200-feet-above-sea-level elevation of Mount Washington, but you can be eyeball to eyeball with someone staring back at you from an office window on the fifty-fifth floor of the sixty-four-story U.S. Steel Tower, Pittsburgh's tallest building. Architecturally, to me the standout building in the Pittsburgh skyline is its third tallest, the awesome glass-turreted Pittsburgh Plate Glass building. It is simply stunning, appearing both modern and medieval, like a castle or a keep built from dark glass. Nearby is Fifth Avenue Place, which looks like a power drill in midtransformation to becoming a spaceship. From Grandview Avenue that building's top mast looks like a

✦ ✦

drill bit being clenched by its four pyramid-shaped spires meeting in the center.

Looming in the distance from the hills northeast of downtown is a very important-looking building with a very important-sounding name—the Cathedral of Learning. It was built, as you might expect with a name like that, as a statement about the importance of education. It is ground zero at Pitt, the defining landmark on the spacious University of Pittsburgh campus. It was conceived in the best of times and completed during the worst of times, between 1926 and 1937. During the depths of the Great Depression, Pittsburgh schoolchildren were encouraged to "buy a brick" for a dime to finish construction. When completed, the Cathedral of Learning, at 535 feet, was not only the tallest building in Pittsburgh, but it was a Billy Penn's hat-width away from being the tallest building in Pennsylvania. (Philadelphia City Hall, with its 37-foot-tall bronze statue of William Penn on top, is 13 feet taller.) Gothic is the only way to describe the Cathedral. It looks like it belongs in the dark skyline of the Gotham City depicted in the *Batman* movies. The Cathedral of Learning has 2,529 windows. (Take THAT, Pittsburgh Plate Glass Building!)

The grand view from Grandview Avenue continues. Look to your left past the bridges, to where the Monongahela meets the Allegheny to form a new river called the Ohio. On the far side are the two new professional sports stadiums—one for baseball, one for football—built with taxpayer money. They replaced storied Three Rivers Stadium, home of both the football Steelers and the baseball Pirates during their glorious championship seasons. So panoramic is the view from up there, you are tempted to tell the person next to you, "Hey, I can see your house from up here."

Is it any wonder that they built a church with the best view of all? From the sidewalks and skyscrapers of downtown, the impressive view to the south is dominated by a mountain and defined by the church on top. St. Mary of the Mount Catholic Church at 403 Grandview Avenue is a Pittsburgh landmark, as impressively conceived architecturally as any of the Golden Triangle skyscrapers. From an office-tower window, the panoramic view of the Pittsburgh skyline enjoyed by churchgoers is blocked by other buildings. But every sky-scraper has a clear view of St. Mary of the Mount.

A neighborhood church built with neighborhood funds, St. Mary of the Mount has the best perch in the big city. Dedicated on December 19, 1897, the vaulted gothic church faces downtown Pittsburgh with an enormous spire-shaped window above its front doors. From this mountaintop vantage with the sunlight streaming through this stained-glass window, what other Biblical theme could have been more appropriate to illustrate than the Ascension? The people who live on the steep streets of Mount Washington are proud of their church, proud of their grade school (founded 1909), and proud of St. Mary of the Mount High School, which graduated its first class of seniors in 1918, and which boasts of having the oldest active alumni association in America. Well into its second century, St. Mary of the Mount has joined the twenty-first century by creating a Web site (www.smomp.org) bearing the church's self-described mission: "Keeping spiritual watch over Pittsburgh."

Great View, If You're So Inclined
Pittsburgh

Compact downtown Pittsburgh offers a dramatic skyline when seen from any angle, but perhaps the best and most dramatic view is from the top of Mt. Washington, the Pittsburgh neighborhood that looks down on the skyscrapers rising on the north side of the Monongahela River from its perch on a ridge on the south side. Looking up at the steep slope of Mt. Washington from the opposite shore, the expression "You can't get there from here" leaps to mind. A mountain goat might be able to. But you can too, if you're so inclined. And Pittsburghers have been so inclined for 130 years and counting.

The Duquesne Incline consists of two bus-size wooden structures that resemble Victorian-style private train cars from the late 1800s.

★ ★

The difference is that these cars travel vertically rather than horizontally. You might say that the Pittsburgh inclines were America's first urban elevated railways, but actually they were more like America's first mass-transit elevators. The 400-foot ride on a 30-degree angle to the top of Mt. Washington takes two and a half minutes; the two cars heading in opposite directions pass each other

A ride with a view.

midslope. Large windows—front, back, and side—offer spectacular views not to be missed by anyone untroubled by vertigo. A round-trip ride costs a dollar.

From the top of Mt. Washington, the city of Pittsburgh lays itself open like a huge oyster with a breathtaking pearl gleaming in the middle. To the west of the Allegheny River are the new Pirates and Steelers stadiums. In the middle is a glowing fountain, the centerpiece of Point State Park, where the Monongahela River meets the Allegheny to form the mighty Ohio River. To the west is downtown Pittsburgh, with its impressive skyscrapers, home to more national

✦ ✦

corporate headquarters than its cross-state big brother and rival, Philadelphia. You can take it all in from the observation deck at the top
of the Duquesne Incline. There's also a museum in the waiting room,
telling the story of Pittsburgh's triumphs and travails.

At one time there were fifteen inclines serving the city and its
working-class neighborhoods in the hills surrounding the riverside
mills and factories. But after private automobiles became com-
monplace in the wake of World War II, one by one the inclines shut
down. Only two inclines serve the city today. The Monongahela
Incline, Pittsburgh's first, was built in 1870 and is still in operation
about a mile west of the Duquesne Incline, which was built in 1877.
In 1962 the Duquesne Incline, then operated by the city-owned
transit company, was shut down because it was unprofitable. A year
later the community rallied and took over the operation of the cable
car system under the Society for the Preservation of the Duquesne
Heights Incline. Today it is operated by friendly and enthusiastic volunteers who recognize first-time travelers and ask how they liked
their ride after the return trip. Seventy-five percent of the Duquesne
Incline's riders these days are tourists rather than commuters.

There is one bit of Pittsburgh tradition that lives on among those
with certain romantic inclinations. The Duquesne Incline is still a popular place for young Pittsburgh gentlemen to ask the ladies they love
for their hand in marriage. Who could turn down a young man with
the world at his feet? The hard part—getting an empty car in which
to pop the question—is a lot easier if you have the right password to
let the incline operator know a proposal is in the offing. "If you ask
the right question, you can get a car that's empty except for the two
of you," said David Miller, president of the Duquesne Incline preservation society. "The right question is, 'Fred Smith still work here?'"
And don't ask unless you mean it.

Hail to the Chiefs, Pennsylvania

There's a President, Pennsylvania, not too far from Polk, in Venango County. On your way from President to Polk on Route 62, you have to go through the town of Franklin. You can bypass Franklin on your way from President to Clinton in Fayette County, but you'll come perilously close to the nearby town of Breakneck, which somehow seems appropriate. You can't get from President to Bush or Gore because those towns don't exist, which also seems appropriate.

The President–Clinton trip is one of the President-to-president road trips in Pennsylvania. You can travel from President to Truman in Cameron County and President to Harding in Luzerne County. Of course, you could also resign yourself to drive from President to Nixon in Susquehanna County.

Early American presidents are much better represented. There's the President–Washington trip, followed by President–Adams, President–Jefferson, and President–Madison. Those are the first four presidents in order, and I suppose you could make it five if you added a few hundred miles on the President–Adams trip to include Quincy, located—interestingly—in Franklin County. (The man was *everywhere!*) The President–Monroe trip would be next, followed by President–Jackson way up in Susquehanna County. There is no Van Buren and no Harrison. But the Presidential journeys pick up with President–Tyler, President–Polk, and President–Taylor.

Due to Pennsylvanians' good taste, there is no President–Fillmore trip. Nor is there President–Pierce. Nor, amazingly, President–Buchanan. (James Buchanan was the only Pennsylvanian to be elected president, which makes Pennsylvania sort of the Phillies of presidential politics: one winner in all those years.) President–Lincoln can be driven in an afternoon, so can President–Grant even if you add the side trip to Ulysses in Potter County.

The Hard Hat Padre

Shanksville

I met Al Mascherino at a lonely country crossroads far from anything of significance except history. It was the intersection of a road leading to nowhere and a road leading to a tiny town of 235 residents who were living happily and anonymously until the world discovered a town called Shanksville on September 11, 2001. In an ungodly roar followed by what some neighbors thought was an earthquake, the brilliant blue sky north of town turned first to fire and then to black smoke as Shanksville and the world learned of the terrible fate of United Airlines Flight 93.

Al Mascherino saw the plane minutes before impact at 10:06 that Tuesday morning. He was heading toward Pittsburgh on the Pennsylvania Turnpike when he saw the plane to his left, too large and too low in the sky not to be noticed. On the radio there was news about a terrorist attack on the World Trade Center. He thought it was an anniversary broadcast about the 1993 bombing of the towers. Then his cell phone rang and he learned how close the terrorist attack on America had come to home. Like many of his countrymen, he knew he had to do something. But what?

It is fitting that I met him at a crossroads, because the Reverend Alphonse Mascherino, sixty, is a man of the cross. He grew up in Downingtown, graduated from Bishop Shanahan High School, and in 1976 was ordained a Catholic priest in the Diocese of Altoona-Johnstown. The events of September 11 led him to this crossroads, where he has established the UAL Flt 93 Memorial Chapel, a nondenominational place of worship dedicated to "the Heroes of Flight 93 and the memory of all those who perished on September 11, 2001." Within a month of the tragedy, Mascherino purchased a hundred-year-old white clapboard building that had been used as a warehouse after seventy years of service as the Mizpah Lutheran Church. Such wonderful plans he had for a chapel. Plans, but no money. He had to sell a collection of antique coins to meet the down payment, let alone buy lumber. So he worked alone on the chapel and shared his dream with all who would listen. A construction trade magazine dubbed him the Hard-Hat Padre. "What you see here all came together in ten days," he said. Local companies signed on with material and labor in order to meet Padre Al's goal of dedicating the chapel on the first anniversary of 9/11.

Under a brilliant blue sky, the Flight 93 chapel gleams almost impossibly white with red, white, and blue (purple, really) flowers lining the pathway. Inside, there is a room to the right with wall plaques bearing photos and brief biographies of the forty-two passengers and crew members who perished. On the rear wall above the choir loft is a stained-glass window with the Star of David in the middle and the Ten Commandments and a menorah on either side above the word *Zion*. The century-old antique window was donated by a Jewish congregation from a historic synagogue in nearby Greensburg, Pennsylvania. Hanging from the middle of the ceiling is a lamp of perpetual remembrance crafted and donated by a Somerset artist. Outside on a bell tower is a thousand-pound steel bell cast in 1860. The bell was another donation, and Padre Al has dubbed it the Thunder Bell, "the voice of Flight 93." The bell symbolizes the sound of the impact of the plane rolling through the hills and valleys, the voices of the heroes who fought back against the terrorists. The bell tolls once each day, at exactly 10:06 a.m. Next to the bell tower is a 14-foot-tall Memorial Torch of Liberty, the work of Somerset craftsman David Weimer. The 1,400-pound sculpture is made of titanium steel, the same metal as in the fuselage of the Flight 93 aircraft. The torch is symbolically linked with the torch on the Statue of Liberty.

When Molly and I visited the chapel in June of 2007, Padre Al proudly showed us some of the recent additions to the growing number of tributes to the heroes of 9/11. In the grassy lawn behind the chapel is a polished black marble octagon memorial monument showing the names and faces of the seven United Airlines crew members who died aboard Flight 93. The monument, crowned with a

bronze replica of Flight 93, a Boeing 757, was presented by Newark
United Airlines flight attendants on September 11, 2006. Nearby in
the grass was an I-beam from one of the World Trade Center buildings, recovered by ironworkers at Ground Zero. The metal has been
cut into the shape UA93, with cutouts reading "WTC" in the *U*,
"911" and "PA" in the *A*, and "VA" in the 9 with the hole in the
top of the number 9 shaped like the five-sided Pentagon. Padre Al
had just purchased the adjoining property with a one-story house
so as many as twelve visitors can spend the night. Molly and I were
the first guests to stay over, and that night in the surreal darkness of
the sparsely populated Pennsylvania farmland, a shaft of light from a
powerful beacon beneath the bell tower sent a message hundreds of
feet into the heavens. The beacon can be seen from miles away on
the south side of the Pennsylvania Turnpike between the Bedford and
Somerset exits. Padre Al said one night a big rig pulled up in front of
the chapel. The trucker said he had seen that beacon for months, and
he finally decided to get off the turnpike and track down its source,
sort of like a wise man from the East following the star of Shanksville.

Padre Al patiently tells visitors the meaning of each and every
detail of the memorial chapel he designed. On September 11, 2003,
twenty family members of the Flight 93 hero/victims came to the
chapel for a second anniversary memorial service. They thanked the
people of Shanksville and America for honoring their loved ones. The
Thunder Bell tolled forty times.

There have been consequences for Padre Al's commitment to the
chapel. Because the padre insisted that the chapel be nondenominational, the Roman Catholic bishop of Altoona severed ties with
him. A diocese spokesman said, "The chapel is Father Mascherino's
personal project . . . to be (permitted) by the diocese to work in the
chapel. That cannot be." (For more information, visit www.flt93
memorialchapel.org.)

The chapel is located at the intersection of Stutzmantown Road
and Coleman Station Road.

★ ★

Temporary Memorial to Flight 93 at the Impact Site

Shanksville

The grassy hillside in Stoneybrook Township where Flight 93 crashed and the temporary memorial site several hundred yards away have the feel of a holy place, windswept, silent, and eternal. Something great and tragic has happened here. In the distance giant dragline earth excavators sit silhouetted against the horizon, a reminder of when this played-out strip mine looked less like a meadow and more like an ugly black scar on the earth. The actual crash site is fenced off near a tree line at the south end of the reclaimed meadow. A

The temporary UAL Flt 93 memorial honors those who mounted the first American counterattack on the terrorists responsible for the hijackings on September 11, 2001.

tiny American flag marks the impact site where forty Americans died while fighting back against terrorists.

Volunteers staff the temporary memorial site from 10:00 a.m. until 6:00 p.m. during spring, summer, and fall and from 10:00 a.m. until 4:00 p.m. during the dark months of winter. They will show visitors photographs of the crash site immediately after 9/11. And perhaps most chilling are the transcripts in a loose-leaf binder of the final minutes of the cockpit flight recorder on Flight 93—then utter silence.

The temporary memorial, which will be replaced by a permanent memorial to Flight 93 scheduled to open on the tenth anniversary of 9/11 in 2011, is dominated by a 40-foot-long fence, on which visitors from around the country and the world have placed messages and mementoes. A marble monument with the words *Let's Roll,* spoken by passenger Todd Beamer before the passengers' revolt, was sent by a man in Guatemala. There are benches with the names of the passengers and crew who died on Flight 93. And there are private memorials with poems like this one: "Perhaps they are not the stars but rather openings in heaven where the love of our lost ones pours through and shines down upon us to let us know they are happy."

America's County, USA
Somerset County

There are sixty-seven counties in Pennsylvania, sixty-eight if you count America's County. "America's County" is the name registered with the U.S. Patent and Trademark Office by the Chamber of Commerce of the former Somerset County in the Laurel Highlands of western Pennsylvania. The Chamber of Commerce announced the name change in July 2003, the first anniversary of the rescue of nine miners from the flooded Quecreek Mine.

Some chutzpah, you might say. What makes Somerset County any more "America's County" than Adams County, where the Battle of Gettysburg was fought? Or Chester County, where an ill-clad Continental Army suffered the winter of 1777 at Valley Forge?

★ ★

Or Philadelphia County, the state's only city-county, where the Declaration of Independence and the U.S. Constitution were born?

Somerset County is merely one of several southern Pennsylvania border counties hard on the Mason-Dixon Line where north met south, east met west, and history was made. Is Somerset more American than neighboring Fayette County, site of Fort Necessity National Battlefield, where in 1754 a twenty-two-year-old British colonel named George Washington fought and lost the first battle of the French and Indian War? Pennsylvania is one big America's County. What makes Somerset so special?

Three words: *That was then.*

During the first decade of the twenty-first century, Somerset County has had compelling reasons to justify its prideful slogan. Somerset County's previous claim to fame had been the Somerset exit on the Pennsylvania Turnpike. But then, in the span of less than a year, this thinly populated, rural, and largely unnoticed county was visited by two events that riveted the attention of America and much of the world: the first was a tragedy, the second a triumph, and each symbolizing something important, something essential about everyday heroes in America.

In July 2002, television viewers around the country shed tears of relief when then Pennsylvania governor Mark Schweicker appeared on TV after a three-day drama that no one had seriously expected would end happily at the Quecreek Coal Mine. "All nine are alive," the governor announced. Ten months earlier and exactly 8 miles away, the passengers of United Airlines Flight 93 died in a fiery crash upon impact into an inactive strip mine owned by the same coal company that owns Quecreek.

Eight miles and ten months separated these events. People in Somerset were still reeling from the heartbreak of September 11, after sudden death dropped out of the sky and into their backyard, when the next summer they learned that nine of their own were trapped hundreds of feet underground in a mine shaft: nine local residents, in all likelihood doomed. Such loss they'd suffered before. They were familiar with miners who never returned from work. But after September 11, somehow it didn't seem fair. Was it an accident of geography—or because of it—that sleepy Somerset County had been singled out?

And then a miracle. Working without reliable maps and little more than a hunch, rescuers drilled frantically and struck the air pocket where the miners had sought refuge. Elation turned to despair when the drill bit broke on the larger man-size rescue shaft being drilled. Below ground by the fading light of their miner's lamps, nine men wrote final words of love to their families, then placed them in plastic bags buttoned inside their pockets. And then they bid farewell to each other and tethered themselves together with rope so that if their bodies were swept away by the flood, at least they would be found—if they were ever found—together. And then . . . the second drill bit arrived! The frenzy among rescuers aboveground grew even as the men below grew quieter and quieter. And finally, late on a Saturday night, national news interrupted TV programs all around America. "All nine alive."

I'll admit, I cried like a baby. I sniffled in front of my family, and then I excused myself to the bathroom where I let it all out. I cried from happiness and cried from shame because I had written the miners off for dead in my heart. And then they were alive again. It was a miracle, wasn't it? But how? Why? A year later during the first-anniversary ceremonies at the site of the Quecreek rescue shaft, a former state official gave voice to a common feeling. Planes don't crash in Somerset County, but coal miners do die. "It was like the angels of Flight 93 were watching over this place," said David Hess, the state secretary of environmental protection during the rescue. "It was almost like they said, 'Not these men. Not here. Not again.'"

America's County, Pennsylvania. I don't know what I expected to find when I drove from Philadelphia to Somerset County, 225 miles due west on the Lincoln Highway. What I wasn't expecting were windmills. Six of them. Huge, white, modern windmills just south of Route 31 on a hilltop the same distance away from Quecreek as the Flight 93 impact site. Since the year 2000, I learned, America's County has built fourteen windmills generating enough electricity to power 2,500 homes for a year. I'd never seen a windmill at work before. They look like little boys flailing their arms at bullies. Whoosh, whoosh, whoosh, touching nothing but air. But still they turn because they have to. What is a windmill without wind? What is a hero without courage?

Trivia

During our travels through western Pennsylvania, my daughter, Molly, and I saw several ornate and well-constructed multidwelling birdhouses, but nothing to compare to this aerial Taj Mahal on Main Street in Somerset, a living and currently occupied memorial to J. Warren Jacobs, the original builder of the famous Purple Martin House. Jacobs (1868–1947) was a carpenter and amateur ornithologist who designed the first of these bird condos for purple martins, acrobatic swallows that eat insects plucked out of the air and even drink on the fly by skimming over ponds, lakes, or rivers with an open beak (now I get it . . . *swallows!*). There's an annual Purple Martin Festival at the end of June in the Mason-Dixon Historical Park near Mt. Morris in Greene County (the southwestern-most county in Pennsylvania), home of the Jacobs Birdhouse Company in Waynesburg, Warren Jacobs's hometown where he built the first such structure in 1912.

A Memorial to a Very Happy Ending

Somerset County

It is almost impossible to overstate the nature of the miracle that took place deep beneath the earth of Bill and Lori Arnold's dairy farm about 6 miles north of Somerset, Pennsylvania. During three days in late July in 2002, the Arnolds' farm became the rescue site for the Quecreek miners, the nine who emerged alive and whole against all odds. That event changed the Arnolds' lives as much as any of the families touched by angels that day. Since then, while working full-time as dairy farmers, the Arnolds created the nonprofit Quecreek Mine Rescue Foundation to operate a museum and memorial on the site of the rescue on their property just 100 yards off Route 985.

The memorial is marked by rusting hulks of rescue equipment, including a large cylindrical airlock designed with the help of the navy that was never actually use. Also at the sight you can see the actual rescue shaft where the miners emerged, as well as the 6-inch air shaft drilled within the first hours to provide the miners with breathable air. Inside the barnlike education center/museum is the actual rescue capsule, the bright yellow tubular metal cage that was lowered hundreds of feet and returned with living miners. The most striking feature at the center of the memorial site is a 7-foot bronze statue of a coal miner, apparently on his lunch break, reading a book. So much dignity and expressiveness can be found in this statue of a middle-aged miner reading by the beam of the light on his hard hat, a thick book cradled in hard, veined hands, his pickax resting on a rock next to his knee, his right arm resting on his metal lunch pail as comfortably and naturally as if he were sitting in an easy chair. If you climb up and look over his shoulder, you can see the words of the page the miner is reading: "They who work the mines and they who read great books are but one."

The proud miner statue brings poignancy and humanity to what is otherwise a display of industrial equipment. The Arnolds have

★ ★

plans to add thirty-one bronze figures around the site to capture the moment of the rescue.

Now more than five years later, Pennsylvania understands more fully the extraordinary good fortune that visited this site in July 2002. The 2006 incident at Sago Mine in West Virginia and the 2007 incident at Crandall Mine in Utah showed America just how devastating these catastrophies can be.

The Quecreek Mine Rescue Site is open seven days a week, year-round during daylight hours. Programs at the education center/museum take place Tuesday through Saturday, 11:00 a.m. until 5:00 p.m., from April 1 until November 1. Call ahead for information (814) 445-4876, and check out their Web site at www.quecreek.org for directions and the most current update.

"They who work the mines and they who read great books are but one."

3

Northeast

NEPA, as Northeast *Pennsylvania is sometimes called, mostly by people who don't live there, is coal country. Hard coal country. Anthracite.
Unfortunately, the coal industry hasn't been hot in Pennsylvania since
corruption and greed led to the Knox Mine Disaster in 1959. As tragic
as the final chapters of the coal industry have been, the capital city of
NEPA, Scranton, has achieved an almost cult status among fans of the
NBC hit comedy TV show* The Office, *about the travails of a paper company in a paperless society.*

*Northeast Pennsylvania extends from the New York border on the
north and east through the Endless Mountains to the still wild Delaware River, which continues as the border with New York southward
until Port Jervis, where New Jersey meets New York. Pennsylvania never
actually touches New Jersey except by bridge, which residents of both
states seem to like. On the Delaware the Northeast ends at Easton,
home of Crayola crayons, pronounced "crowns" by many on both sides
of the river.*

*Befitting coal country, the largest pothole in the world can be found
in Archbald. Perhaps the strangest story about a town in the Northeast
is that of French Azilum in Bradford County, which was founded in
1793 as a refuge for French Royalty seeking to escape the reign of terror during the French Revolution. The largest building in the settlement
was reserved for the queen, Marie Antoinette, who never lived to see,
or enjoy a dessert, in Pennsylvania.*

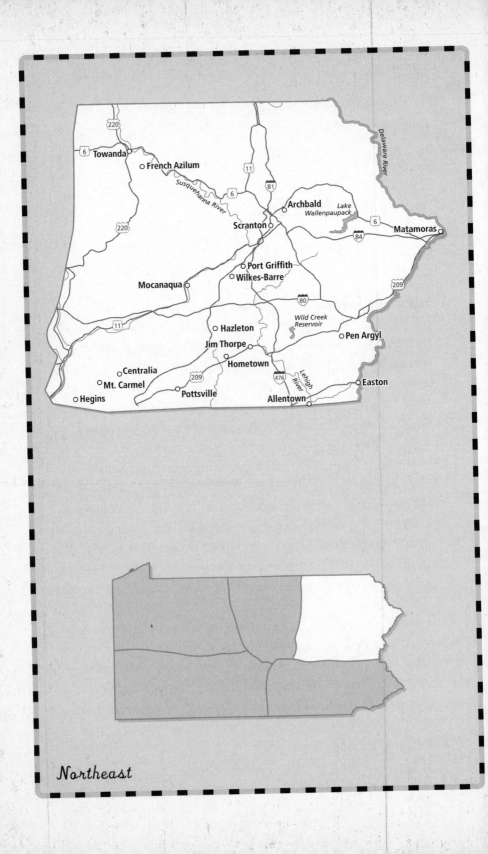

Northeast

The World's Largest Pothole
Archbald

Pennsylvania has an official state bird (the ruffed grouse), an official state dog (Great Dane), an official state flower (mountain laurel), and an official state insect (the firefly). But did you know that Pennsylvania has commemorated something else so thoroughly indigenous to the Keystone State that cars bearing Firestone tires are turned away at the state line?

I speak of Pennsylvania's official state pothole. Contrary to the personal experience of locals, the official state pothole cannot be found in the passing lane of the westbound Schuylkill Expressway. No, Pennsylvania's official state pothole can be found just off Route 6 in Lackawanna County between Scranton and Carbondale in the borough of Archbald. It is the only pothole to have a state park named after it.

You thought you knew potholes? Here's Pennsylvania's Official State Pothole.

But this is no ordinary pothole—it's a glacial pothole. During the ice age, glacial meltwater carrying sand and gravel and rock particles fell like a waterfall hundreds of feet through crevasses in the Laurentide Continental Glacier, forming a pothole in the bedrock beneath. When the glacier finally receded, trees and other vegetation grew on

★ ★

top of it so that you'd never know there was a pothole there in the first place—sort of like nature's asphalt.

The Archbald Pothole would have remained hidden from humans forever, perhaps, if it hadn't been situated in the most heavily mined anthracite region in northeast Pennsylvania. In 1884 a coal miner named Patrick Mahon set off an explosive charge while extending a tunnel, when suddenly tons of water and rock came tumbling down, setting off a panic in the mine. After removing between 800 and 1,000 tons of stones rubbed round by the glacier, mine inspectors discovered that the miner had opened up the bottom of a pothole about 38 feet from the surface.

In 1887 a fence was built around the perimeter of the pothole and the walls were shored up to prevent collapse as the fame of the pothole spread throughout the geological community, which dubbed Archbald as "a world-class glacial pothole." In 1914 the widow of the landowner turned over a one-acre plot containing the pothole to the Lackawanna Historical Society. In 1940 the county added 150 acres to the site as a park and later turned the site over to the State of Pennsylvania. The Archbald Pothole State Park was officially dedicated in 1964.

Today the Archbald Pothole is a major tourist attraction, unlike the Schuylkill Expressway westbound pothole, the Route 611 southbound pothole, and the Route 309 northbound pothole, all of which continue to attract a fair share of motorist attention because, unlike Archbald, these potholes are actually getting bigger.

Fire in the Hole

Centralia

It started, some say, as a trash fire in a landfill located in one of the abandoned coal mines that honeycomb this valley between Big Mountain and Mahanoy Mountain on the edge of Pennsylvania's Western-Middle anthracite field. It was Memorial Day weekend in 1962 when the fire underground was first noticed. It's been burning

★ ★

A stop sign on a street leading to nowhere almost mocks the fate of Centralia, where houses once stood on both sides of this now-empty street.

ever since, like a subterranean forest fire with an inexhaustible supply of fuel. The town above, Centralia, has become a symbol of mankind's futile efforts to bandage the wounds the earth has suffered to serve humanity's needs and greed.

Even in its heyday, Centralia was never much of a town, except for the people who called it home. It sat isolated at the end of a lonely stretch of Route 42 through Columbia County. Its nearest neighbors were Ashland in Schuylkill County and Mt. Carmel in Northumberland County. The only reason you would have heard of Centralia, if you've heard of it at all, is because it's been on fire since John F. Kennedy was president.

A visit to Centralia is a visit to a ghost town, except there is no town. There are streets and sidewalks, curbs and stop signs, but most of the buildings are gone. What was once downtown Centralia is now an empty intersection. A wooden bench at a former bus stop mocks the absence of people and a town. On the bench is the name *Centralia* and its zip code 17927, both of which no longer exist. Across the street are lawn chairs set up under some trees and a sign that says WE LOVE CENTRALIA. The seats are empty. The only public building still standing, ironically, is the firehouse with its yellow fire engine polished and ready to respond to fires the crew can still fight in homes that don't exist. There are perhaps half a dozen occupied houses remaining in what was once a town of 1,100 people. Those few scattered homes are owned by people too proud, too old, or too ornery to leave. Where an entire rowhouse block once stood, now there are single houses, their weak side walls braced by five brick columns resembling outside chimneys.

If you explore the side streets nearest St. Ignatius Cemetery on the south end of Centralia on a summer afternoon like I did, you will find your way blocked by dense underbrush growing over the paved street. Just before the place where nature reclaims what man has left behind, you will see the eerie outline of a human body spray-painted on the macadam like a symbol at a police homicide scene. From there you can see the smoke rising from an open pit uphill at the edge of the fenced-in cemetery, where the fire below continues its spread. Soon the bodies of the long departed will be forced to join the living departed. Even the dead must flee the underground furnace. The pit itself is suitable for a study by Dante, the first circle, perhaps, of the inferno below. A smoking crater is surrounded by flattened trees that were choked by poison smoke long before they fell like twigs before the holocaust beneath them. It's a disturbing reminder of how much human beings have taken from the earth below Pennsylvania, and how little human beings can do when the earth decides to take it back.

At first, the state and the federal government tried to fight the fire by depriving it of oxygen. But the fire was too resourceful, the earth too seamed with cracks as well as veins of combustible coal. Deadly gases began seeping into basements. People got sick. The government tried to vent the gases, but the fire kept moving, silently, inexorably, to new areas.

Finally, the government began condemning properties and paying to relocate people. According to the Pennsylvania Department of Environmental Protection, close to $40 million was spent fighting the spread of the fire and paying Centralians to move. There were 1,100 people who called Centralia home in 1962. By the year 2000 the number was fewer than twenty. There's no longer a post office in Centralia. The only public building listed in the phone book is the Centralia Fire Department (570-875-0687), but if you call, don't be surprised if there is no answer.

Centralia is not easy to get to and harder to find once you're almost there. Traffic is redirected off Route 61 between Ashland and Mt. Carmel. The town is not officially off-limits, but there are signs warning of noxious gases. It's not a tourist attraction, but it is a sad Pennsylvania curiosity.

Where the Tongues Forked

Easton

Easton was the scene of two thoroughly despicable treaties negotiated with the Native American Lenni Lenape tribes and the English colonists. In fact, the expression "white man speaks with forked tongue" could well have originated in the Easton treaty known as the Walking Purchase. William Penn was an honorable man in his dealings with the natives, but when he returned to England and turned over the administration to his son, Thomas, the Penn name was tarnished. In 1737 Thomas Penn produced a "lost" treaty negotiated by his father with the Delaware tribe for as much land as a man could walk off in a day and a half. The Indians under Chief Lappawinsoe were leery about the legitimacy of the document but, they reasoned, how much land can a man walk off in thirty-six hours?

What Chief Lappawinsoe didn't know was that the Penns had cleared a trail through the wilderness before the day of the walk, which started from Wrightstown in Bucks County. Not only that, but three of the fastest runners in the colony had been hired to pace off the land in a relay team. By the end of the day-and-a-half "walk," the runners had traveled more than 50 miles and the land within totaled 1,200 square miles, an area almost the size of Rhode Island, which includes most of Pike, Monroe, Lehigh, and Northhampton Counties. The Indians knew they had been robbed. Chief Lappawinsoe complained that the white men "should have walked a few miles and then sat down and smoked a pipe, and now and then have shot a squirrel, and not have kept up the Run, Run all day." But he felt honor bound to abide by the treaty, which was the beginning of the Delaware's westward migration that eventually took them as far as Oklahoma.

The next Easton treaty took place in 1757, following a period of open warfare on the settlers by the Delawares, who by then were clearly aware of how hugely they had been swindled. This time the negotiations were handled by Chief Teedyuscung, and the dirty trick played by the colonial negotiators was to ply the chief with firewater. "It must shock you to hear that pains have been made to make the King [Teedyuscung] drunk every night since the business began," wrote Charles Thomson, a twenty-eight-year-old schoolteacher from Philadelphia who acted as Chief Teedyuscung's personal secretary during the treaty negotiations. "On Saturday, under pretense of rejoicing for the victory gained by the King of Prussia, and the arrival of the fleet, a bonfire was ordered to be made and liquor given to the Indians to induce them to dance," Thomson wrote to a friend. "For fear they should get sober on Sunday and be fit the next day to enter on business, under pretense that the Mohawks had requested it, another bonfire was ordered to be made and more liquor given them."

With Thomson watching his back, Teedyuscung was not swindled in that treaty. Thomson faithfully recorded the chief's words and in gratitude he was given the Lenni Lenape name *Wegh-Wu-Law-Mo-End,* which meant Man Who Talks the Truth. "It's as true as if Charles Thomson's name is on it" became a popular expression throughout the United States until the Revolutionary period.

The French Connection
French Azilum

If Marie Antoinette had only said, "You've got a friend in Pennsylvania" instead of "Let them eat cake," who knows what would have happened in Bradford County? If the deposed queen of France had made it to the refuge prepared for her and other French nobles in Pennsylvania, perhaps the village of French Azilum would have been called "Paris on the Susquehanna." French loyalists arrived in northeastern Pennsylvania in the fall of 1793 to settle the village on the shores of the Susquehanna about 10 miles south of Towanda. As it was, Marie Antoinette and King Louis XVI lost their heads during the French Revolution before they could join other fleeing French nobility in America.

The settlers were assisted in their venture by wealthy Philadelphians Robert Morris and French-born Stephen Girard, and the village of Azilum was laid out in a gridiron pattern with 413 half-acre plots surrounding a two-acre market square. By the following spring thirty rough log-cabin structures had been erected by French settlers, many of them refugees from the slave revolt on the island of Santo Domingo (Haiti). The largest of the structures was La Grande Maison, a massive two-story log structure measuring 80 by 60 feet with numerous small windows and eight fireplaces. This was supposed to have been the deposed queen's residence, but after her execution it was used as a public hall where visiting French dignitaries such as the devious foreign minister Talleyrand and the future French king Louis-Philippe were entertained.

Following the Reign of Terror and the normalization of the domestic situation in France and Haiti, many of the French loyalists, unused to the rough life of frontier America, returned home or to the Caribbean or to established southern cities such as Charleston and New Orleans. That, combined with the bankruptcy of American patron Robert Morris and the invitation by Napoleon Bonaparte for the return of French exiles, led to the end of Azilum as a functioning French town in Pennsylvania by 1803. There were fifty buildings left behind, including several small shops, a schoolhouse, a theater, and a chapel. None of the original structures remains, although a reconstruction of a 1790s log cabin is on the town's site, as well as the lovely whitewashed LaPorte house, built in 1836 by the son of

Marie Antoinette never lived to see it, but this is the view from the Marie Antoinette Scenic View of French Azilum on the far side of the Susquehanna River in Bradford County.

one of the original French settlers. The French influence did not vanish completely from northeastern Pennsylvania following the failure of the Azilum colony. Among the French refugee families who remained to settle in the area are the LaPortes, Homets, LeFevres, Brevosts, and D'Autremonts, none of whom, at last sighting, has lost their heads.

The French Azilum Historic Site is now operated by the Pennsylvania Museum and Historical Commission, but the vista of what the area looks like can be seen from the Marie Antoinette Lookout on Route 6 on the east side of the Susquehanna River near Standing Stone Road. (French Azilum, R.R. 2, Box 266, Towanda, Pennsylvania 18848. Call 570-265-3376 or visit www.frenchazilum.com.)

Pigeons from Hegins
Hegins

In the narrow valley between the ridge line of Mahantango Mountain to the north and Broad Mountain to the south, where Route 25 meets Route 125, sits the town of Hegins. This quiet Schuylkill County community once captured the attention of the world every Labor Day, because at the end of each summer, the good citizens of Hegins went on a killing spree. All for a good cause, of course.

The occasion was the annual Fred Coleman Memorial Shoot, sort of a skeet-shooting competition in which live birds were used instead of clay pigeons. Fred Coleman was something of a legend among Pennsylvania coal towns at the turn of the twentieth century, when shooting live pigeons out of the air was a popular pastime among men who made their living underground. In 1934 the first annual occurrence of what was to be called the Fred Coleman Memorial Shoot took place at Hegins Park. Fifty years later thousands of spectators gathered each Labor Day weekend to watch dozens and dozens of men and (by now) women with shotguns compete to see who could blast the most birds out of the sky. Proceeds went to charity.

Contestants stood at a firing line 20 yards away from where pigeons were released one at a time from little boxes placed in the

★ ★

middle of the playing-field-turned-shooting-range. After each vol-
ley the dead birds would be gathered up by "trapper boys," the
equivalent of "ball boys" in tennis, who would run onto the killing
field and pick up the grisly remains. More often than not, the birds
were not killed outright, and the trapper boys would chase down the
flapping wounded pigeons and stomp on them or wring their necks
before tossing them into a refuse barrel with the rest of the dead and
dying—thousands of them.

In Pennsylvania, where schools close in many rural counties on
the first day of deer-hunting season, shooting animals is more than
a sport, more than a family tradition—it is a birthright. To many the
idea of shooting pest birds like pigeons is no more barbaric than
shooting rats and other vermin. Besides, shooting live pigeons was
more sporting than shooting clay pigeons because the live birds are
so panicky and unpredictable when they take flight.

And so the good citizens of Hegins were shocked—*shocked!*—
when the first animal rights protestor types showed up at the fifty-
first annual Fred Coleman Memorial Shoot in 1985. And by the turn
of the twenty-first century, the Hegins pigeon shoot was as dead as
Fred Coleman himself. During the years in between, Hegins, a town
few people in Pennsylvania had ever heard of before, became notori-
ous around the world because of the persistence, organization, and
media savvy of the animal rights protestors.

Traditionally Labor Day is a slow news weekend. Newspapers and
TV stations that would not ordinarily send reporters and photogra-
phers to cover an animal rights protest could plan on dramatic doings
in tiny Hegins. City folk were appalled by the slaughter, of course.
And the "outside agitators" played like a violin the parochial passions
of the townspeople. As publicity grew each year, counterprotestors,
often fueled by alcohol, would gather to mock and antagonize the
animal rights activists. In 1996, when a Fund for Animals volunteer
videotaped the event to provide proof of cruelty to the birds, a coun-
terprotestor, or perhaps merely a drunk, obliged by biting the head

off a live pigeon on camera. The man was arrested and the photographic evidence helped convict him.

In 1997 seven anticruelty protestors were arrested after successfully blocking traffic on Route 25 for ten hours by linking their arms through plastic sleeves embedded in ten-gallon containers filled with concrete. Special equipment was needed to cut through the concrete without injuring the protestors. Pro-shoot T-shirts for sale at the Hegins event read, "It's not about pigeons. It's about freedom." And so it went. Animal rights groups from as far away as England and Russia joined in describing the Hegins pigeon shoot as "the world's cruelest event." Ku Klux Klan members showed up one year to demonstrate—unwanted and unappreciated—solidarity with the American values represented by the pigeon shooters. What had been a small-town party had turned into an international cause celebre and a Pennsylvania embarrassment.

What finished off the pigeon shoot finally was a ruling by the Pennsylvania Supreme Court that did not outlaw the event outright but upheld the right of SPCA humane officers to make arrests in cases where pigeons were treated cruelly before or after they were shot, in other words, virtually at any time during the proceedings. Writing for the majority in a July 1999 decision, Pennsylvania Supreme Court chief justice John P. Flaherty described the pigeon shoot as "cruel and moronic." Organizers canceled the pigeon shoot that same year, the last of the twentieth century. After sixty-six years the Fred Coleman Memorial Shoot in Hegins, Pennsylvania, had become history.

Pennsylvania, This Is Your Hometown
Hometown

In 1984 Bruce Springsteen's hit album *Born in the USA* included a haunting ballad called "My Hometown." Things didn't turn out so great for the Hometown in Springsteen's song, which became a metaphor for troubled times facing thousands of communities across the country.

★ ★

"My Hometown" could have been the soundtrack for most of Pennsylvania's coal- and steel-manufacturing towns in the closing decades of the twentieth century. In fact, in the 1982 "Allentown" with a similar theme, singer Billy Joel named names but we won't here. After the song and video became a huge hit and something of an embarrassment to political and business leaders of Pennsylvania's fourth-largest city, Joel revealed that he had chosen to name the song after Allentown, which is neither a coal nor a steel town, because he liked the no-nonsense sound of the name—Allentown. Still, the lyrics resonated locally, as well as nationally, with young

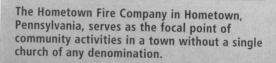

The Hometown Fire Company in Hometown, Pennsylvania, serves as the focal point of community activities in a town without a single church of any denomination.

people discovering that the American dream doesn't come with a guarantee.

In the two decades since songs like "My Hometown" and "Allentown" captured the bewildered sense of betrayal at the disappearance of traditional industrial jobs, young people have learned their lessons. Sons and daughters no longer expect, nor do they necessarily want, to follow their fathers into the mines or their mothers onto factory floors. What hasn't changed is the penchant Pennsylvanians have for staying put. Among the fifty United States, Pennsylvania leads the nation in a telling statistic. According to the 2000 census, when compared with the population of any other state, a greater proportion of Americans born in Pennsylvania still live in Pennsylvania. Put another way, if you are a native Pennsylvanian, chances are you live in or near your hometown.

George Pinkey is a classic example. For more than sixty years, he has lived in the same town where he once attended elementary school grades one through four in a one-room schoolhouse. His earliest memory here was of sitting on his father's shoulders watching an effigy of Adolf Hitler pass by during a "welcome home" parade for GIs returning from World War II. What separates Pinkey from most Pennsylvanians who have lived their entire lives in the same place is that his hometown *is* Hometown. "I've been in all fifty states," Pinkey says, "but I've never been in another Hometown."

Neither have I. In fact, I had never been in any hometown but my own until I discovered Hometown, Pennsylvania, on my way to Centralia, a Pennsylvania hometown that is no more. Hometown, Pennsylvania (population 1,500), is a hilltop community of pleasant homes located 2 miles north of the borough of Tamaqua and about 8 miles south of the city of Hazleton on Route 309. Unlike neighboring communities in the heart of Pennsylvania's anthracite-mining region, Hometown looks more like a one-stoplight suburban bedroom community outside Philadelphia or Pittsburgh. There is no "there" there, no downtown with sidewalks, no bench on the courthouse

★ ★

lawn. There is the Beacon Diner, a landmark, and the Hometown Farmer's Market, an even bigger landmark that operates only one day a week (Wednesday 8:00 a.m. to 8:00 p.m.) and attracts customers from 100 miles away. Hometown is, in fact, a thoroughly unremarkable town except for its remarkably unremarkable name.

I guess when you live in a place called Hometown, you get used to hearing people say the name without meaning the place where you live, the same way someone named Jones doesn't take it personally when people talk about "keeping up with the Joneses." I couldn't get a rise out of most Hometowners I spoke to when I asked for anecdotes, amusing or otherwise, about listing their hometown address as, well, you know. I was directed toward George Pinkey, a former township supervisor, as the hometown historian of Hometown and the surrounding coal region. He has few kind words for the big mining companies that abandoned their operations, leaving scarred earth and unemployment in their wake. "When they were done with us in the 1950s, we were like a sucked orange," Pinkey said. "What saved Hometown, ironically, was that there was no coal here. All around us, but not under here."

Hometown was founded in 1828 by a Philadelphia businessman trying to make a buck from the coal-mining industry by growing food that fed the mines' horses and mules. These animals never saw the light of day again after they entered the mines. They eventually died underground after pulling countless cars loaded with anthracite. When coal was king, Hometown was a farming community. "I think there's a doctoral thesis somewhere about how many pounds of hay and cabbage and corn it took to produce a ton of coal," says Pinkey. After World War II, when the mines began to close, the farms were sold to developers who built houses and cul-de-sacs and roads that dead-ended for no apparent reason. Hometown became a suburban bedroom community for larger neighbors with fading downtowns. In the process Rush Township, of which Hometown is a part, has become the second-wealthiest municipality in Schuylkill County.

Curiously, or perhaps tellingly, there is not a single church of any denomination in Hometown. On Sunday churchgoers go to their other hometown churches in Tamaqua or Hazleton or Mahanoy City. And afterward on every other Sunday between Labor Day and Memorial Day, upward of 200 people attend the all-you-can-eat breakfast at the Hometown Fire Company hall. Says Pinkey, "The volunteer fire company is the closest thing we have to a community-wide social organization." Not exactly a church, but still, all you can eat.

The Handprint on the Prison Wall
Jim Thorpe

Sure, I knew the Irish had it rough, I knew they were exploited by the coal mines, and I knew the company store owned their bodies and souls. But until I saw the gallows with the four ropes and the handprint on the prison wall, I guess I never saw how rough.

Midway up the hill on West Broadway in picturesque Jim Thorpe—the Switzerland of Pennsylvania, according to the welcoming signs—is the Old Jail Museum, formerly the Carbon County Prison, built in 1871 and designed by Edward Haviland, whose famous father gave us and the world the first state penitentiary on Fairmount Avenue in Philadelphia. It was here on June 21, 1877, that four so-called Molly Maguires were strangled to death (one took seventeen minutes to die) from the same scaffold after a shameful trial orchestrated by the president of the Philadelphia and Reading Railroad and prosecuted by his private attorneys based on evidence provided by his private police force.

Twenty Mollies in all would hang. They were Irish immigrants guilty of protesting conditions in the coal mines, where a man could earn 49 cents for mining a ton of coal and receive a bill for supplies at the end of the day. "Bobtail checks" they called them. Tons loaded minus supplies provided equaled $0.00. Then in 1875 they cut the miners' pay by 10 percent.

After surviving a seven-month strike, the owners rewarded the returning miners by cutting their pay another 10 percent. Desperate

How Jim Thorpe Came to Pennsylvania

In the light of day on a September afternoon, the town of Jim Thorpe glows with a rust red from the Carbon County courthouse. The building was built with stone quarried from the mountain called Mauch Chunk ("Bear Mountain" to the original inhabitants, who called themselves Lenni Lenape, which in their tongue meant "original inhabitants"). The town itself was called Mauch Chunk until 1954, when the body of the greatest American athlete, Jim Thorpe, was interred there in exchange for its original name.

No small irony there—an Indian name changed to honor an Indian with a European name. On May 28, 1888, in what was still called Indian Territory, now called Oklahoma, a nine-and-a-half-pound baby boy was born to a member of the Thunder Clan of the Sac and Fox tribe. He was born at sunrise. His mother named him *Wa-tho-huck,* meaning "Bright Path." His father, Hiram Thorpe, a direct descendent of Chief Black Hawk and an accomplished athlete in every sport he endeavored, named his son James.

The story of Jim Thorpe, All-American, is better known to most people through the movie by that name, starring Burt Lancaster. But Jim Thorpe was a real person and his athletic exploits led him to be named the best athlete of the first half of the twentieth century in a poll by sportswriters in 1950. Thorpe broke into the American consciousness in 1907 when he came to Pennsylvania's famous Carlisle Indian Institute and made it even more famous by playing football under the coach who would himself become a legend, Glenn "Pop" Warner. Playing in a game against national football power, the Army team, Thorpe scored on the opening kickoff, which was called back due to a penalty. On the ensuing kickoff Thorpe ran for another touchdown on Carlisle's way to a twenty-seven-to-six victory. "He was able to do everything anyone else could do but he could do it better," said army cadet Dwight D. Eisenhower, who Thorpe put out of the game with a crushing tackle that ended Ike's football career. "There was no one like him in the world."

In 1912 Thorpe won two gold medals at the Stockholm Olympics in the decathlon and pentathlon. He met King Gustav V of Sweden, who shook Thorpe's hand and said, "You, sir, are the greatest athlete in the world." That is the quote that appears on Jim Thorpe's tomb, located a couple of miles outside of downtown Jim Thorpe on North Street (Route 903). Thorpe played professional baseball for the Giants, Reds, and Braves. He was the highest-paid player in the National Football League, of which he served as president

Final resting place for "the greatest athlete in the world."

(con't.)

from 1920 until 1926. He could do everything on a football field, including kick. On a return to Carlisle in 1941 at the age of fifty two, Thorpe stood in the middle of the field and drop-kicked a football over the goal. He then turned and placekicked a field goal over the other end zone—wearing street shoes.

When he died in 1953, a newspaper editor in Carbon County seized upon the idea of bringing Jim Thorpe's body to the towns of Mauch Chunk and East Mauch Chunk, which would merge and change their names to Jim Thorpe. Thorpe's widow agreed to move his body to Pennsylvania, and in 1954, one hundred years after the founding of East Mauch Chunk, the athlete's body was buried there. The Jim Thorpe Memorial has been augmented in recent years with a sculpture garden and metal placards telling stories from his life.

men do desperate things. There were murders on both sides. Only the Mollies met the gallows.

On the wall of Cell No. 17 of the Old Jail, like a modern-day Shroud of Turin, is a handprint said to belong to one of the Mollies before his execution. He rubbed his hand on the dirt of the floor and held it against the wall until the four fingers and the thumb were clearly outlined. It will remain for the next century, he told his guards in 1877, as a symbol of injustice. They shrugged their shoulders and got on with the business of death. Afterward, they returned to the cell and tried to wash the handprint off the wall, but it wouldn't come off. They wiped it and washed it. Then they painted over it. Then they dug out the plaster and replastered the spot. But always the handprint returned, as real as conscience and just as inexplicable.

In 1975 the *National Enquirer* hired a college professor to perform a spectographic analysis of the handprint to determine its origin and what it consisted of. The professor's report indicated that there was nothing there—no grime, no perspiration, no pigmentation, no noth-

Cell No. 17 of the Old Jail, where the handprint of a miner unjustly sent to his death over a hundred years ago can still be seen on the cell wall.

ing. According to the analysis the handprint doesn't exist. But it's there.

The Old Jail Museum itself is open for tours only on weekends. In the dungeon I visited beneath the prison, there was no electricity and only one toilet in sixteen cells used for solitary confinement. Others used buckets emptied only when the prisoner was released. The most startling aspect about the tour is the realization that people were actually serving time here until recent years. The cells for solitary confinement were used until 1980, and the prison remained open until 1995. (Old Jail Museum; call 570-325-5259.)

Little Bear Woman

Mocanaqua

Just downstream from the borough of Shickshinny in Luzerne County, on the east side of the Susquehanna River directly across from Dog-town, lies the tiny village of Mocanaqua, the Indian name for the most famous Pennsylvanian you've never heard of. Her name was Frances Slocum, and she was among the ill-fated clan of Connecticut Yankees that settled in the Wyoming Valley of northeastern Pennsylvania in the 1760s. (In fact, what is now the city of Scranton was called Slocum's Hollow.) The family found themselves the lightning rods for hostility from Indians, British Redcoats, and especially native Pennsylvanians who thought that the colonists from the Nutmeg State were nuts to come all the way from New England and declare this area part of Connecticut. This led to the Yankee-Pennamite Wars, which were interrupted by the Revolutionary War, which in this part of Pennsylvania is remembered forever for a disastrous engagement between the American garrison at Forty Fort and the combined British-Indian forces that became known as the Wyoming Massacre.

Jonathan and Ruth Slocum were Quaker farmers, nonviolent and fair minded, who had a good relationship with the native tribes of the area. Even after the Wyoming Massacre in July 1778, in which upwards of 300 men, women, and children were slaughtered by the Indian allies of the British, the Slocum family felt secure in their homestead in what is now Wilkes-Barre. In the middle of a November day in 1778, while the adults and older siblings of the Slocum clan were off working in distant parts of the farm, a raiding party of three Delaware Indians entered the Slocum cabin and made off with five-year-old Frances, leaving a brother and sister behind.

Frances Slocum was never seen again, at least not for almost fifty years. In 1835 a fur trader by the name of George W. Ewing was doing business with the Miami tribe near Fort Wayne, Indiana, when he noticed an old woman with white features. In her native Miami tongue, he asked her questions and learned that she was born white, the child of Quakers in Pennsylvania named Slocum. Since being taken from her home by the Delawares, she had lived with the Miamis, raised by a loving father and mother who had lost their daughter of about the same age. They named her Mocanaqua, which means "little bear woman." She married twice; her second husband, Shepoconah, became a powerful chief among the Miamis. They had children and moved to Indiana with the tribe.

Touched by her story, Ewing wrote a letter to the postmaster in Lancaster, Pennsylvania, telling the tale and asking him to publicize the story, seeking to find surviving members of the Slocum family. Two years later, Frances Slocum was reunited with her younger brother and sister, who had never lost hope of finding her. She chose to remain with her family of fifty years, but a few years later, she used her status as a white woman and Indian mother to establish legitimacy for the claims of the Miamis to land in Indiana. Her story, "The Lost Child of Wyoming," had become famous. In a treaty signed by President Zachary Taylor in 1838, the land occupied by the Miamis in Indiana was granted (temporarily) to the tribe because of the claim by Frances Slocum's Indian-fathered daughter, Ozahshinqua. Among white Americans, Frances Slocum became known as "White Rose of the Miamis," and upon her death in 1847, a monument was built along the Mississinewa River in Indiana.

In Pennsylvania her name lives on along the banks of the Susquehanna River as a town named Mocanaqua, "little bear woman." For the Native American language–impaired, there is also the 1,035-acre Frances Slocum State Park, 10 miles northwest of her Wilkes-Barre birthplace.

The Blonde Bombshell
Pen Argyl

Jayne Mansfield was a Bryn Mawr girl. Literally. She was born in Bryn Mawr Hospital on April 19, 1933. By the time she died in a late-night car crash on the road from Biloxi, Mississippi, to New Orleans,

Why, Oh Why, Wyoming?

The state of Wyoming is named after Pennsylvania's Wyoming Valley. Why, one would wonder, would a territory carved out of the then-territories of Dakota, Utah, and Idaho in 1868, and eventually granted statehood in 1890, be named for a relatively unknown valley 2,000 miles away? All of those territorial names were Indian in origin, but Wyoming is an eastern American Indian name, the language equivalent of giving a French province a Russian name. In Algonquin the word *wyoming* means either "large prairie place" or "mountains and valleys alternating" depending on whether you are using the French translation or the Russian.

The name Wyoming was famous in nineteenth-century America because of an eighteenth-century American massacre made more lyrical, if not more famous, by a Scottish poet named Thomas Campbell. In 1809 Campbell wrote an epic poem, "Gertrude of Wyoming," about a Revolutionary War battle on Pennsylvania soil that, I'm sure, most Pennsylvanians have never heard of. (I base that on the fact that I had never heard of it, and I'm the Pennsylvania guy writing this book.) In the 1800s Gertrude of Wyoming was as famous a name as Monica Lewinsky and for pretty much the same reasons—she was a famous victim everyone knew about, and nobody wanted to be in her shoes—although more people admired Gertrude. She was the fictional heroine of a horrific ordeal. During the Revolutionary War the Wyoming Massacre outside Wilkes-Barre was the British equivalent of the My Lai Massacre during the war in Vietnam.

On July 3, 1778, a force of 400 keen but poorly trained Pennsylvania citizen militia, most too young or too old to be proper soldiers, advanced under General Zebulon Butler from a fortified position to meet the forces of British general John Butler, a distant relative, and his Iroquois allies under Chief Sayenqueraghta. It was a scene out of a movie. Think of the massacre of the British and Americans by the Indians in the Daniel Day Lewis version of *Last of the Mohicans.*

The continentals were drawn into a trap. While advancing on a line of apparently retreating British soldiers after a brief engagement, the Americans were attacked on both flanks by hundreds of Iroquois warriors crouching in the high grass. The untrained farmer soldiers panicked. Some fought. Some ran. They all died. Men were roasted alive in sight of the American fort where the remaining garrison huddled with the women and children. At midnight under firelight, an old white woman, who had been captured by the Iroquois as a child and later married to a chief, walked in a circle and personally executed between sixteen and twenty American soldiers with a tomahawk. She was known as Queen Esther and said to be the daughter of a Frenchman named Montour, as in Montour County.

When the soldiers were sacrificed, the Iroquois turned their attention to the women and children and remaining men fleeing Forty Fort. Gertrude of Wyoming was one of them. The event became the story that became the poem that became the metaphor for America's brave resistance and eventual triumph over British tyranny and Native American savagery on the frontier. At least, that was how it was seen in 1868 when Wyoming got its name. But then again, consider the options. Would you want to live in a state named Gertrude?

> And tranced in giddy horror Gertrude swoon'd;
> Yet, while she clasps him lifeless to her zone,
> Say, burst they, borrow'd from her father's wound,
> These drops?—Oh, God! the life-blood is her own!

Louisiana, on June 29, 1967, she'd spent most of her life away from her home state. But she is buried in Fairview Cemetery outside Pen Argyl in Northhampton County, where her mother's family still lives. Jayne Mansfield was the poor man's Norma Jean, a not-quite Marilyn Monroe. She was famous mostly for two things, which she showed off at every opportunity.

Mansfield arrived in Hollywood in the mid-1950s and got her first job after writing "40-22-34" on a card she left in a producer's office. Never a star but always an attraction, Jayne Mansfield once said, "I decided early in life that the first thing to do was to become famous—I'd worry about acting later." Jayne lived up (or down) to her ambitions. While trying to break into the movies, she won a series of beauty contests with names like Miss Negligee, Miss Nylon Sweater, Miss Geiger Counter, and Miss Tomato. She appeared in a legitimate hit movie, *Will Success Spoil Rock Hunter?*, but mostly she is remembered as a heaving bosom in various low-budget foreign movies like *The Loves of Hercules* starring her muscleman husband, Mickey Hargitay.

In 1964 when the Beatles arrived in the United States on their first tour, they were asked which American celebrity they would most like to meet. The lads chose Jayne Mansfield. Upon meeting them, she asked the mop-topped John Lennon if his hair was real. He replied by looking at her breasts and asking, "Are those real?"

In the end, Jayne Mansfield's career in Hollywood was all but over. She was appearing at a supper club in Biloxi when she died in a car crash, in which—contrary to widely held belief—she was not decapitated. A blonde bouffant wig she was wearing was thrown from the vehicle, which started the rumors. Like the swimming pool outside her Sunset Boulevard home and the bed inside it, Jayne Mansfield's tombstone is in the shape of a heart. The inscription beneath her name reads, WE LIVE TO LOVE YOU MORE EACH DAY. (Fairview Cemetery, Middletown Road just outside of Pen Argyl.)

The Day the Earth Ate the River
Port Griffith

If Don McLean wrote an epic song about the Pennsylvania coal industry along the lines of "American Pie," the date January 22, 1959,
would be remembered as "the day the music died." That was the
day the earth swallowed the river and old King Coal drowned.

It happened in Port Griffith, one of the towns "up the line" as
they say in Wilkes-Barre, meaning the Wyoming Valley communities along the Susquehanna River north of it and south of Scranton,
where the same towns become "down the line." There were eighty-
one miners at work that day in the Knox Coal Company's two mine
shafts, one of them a nearly exhausted dig in the Pittston Vein,
which ran alongside and underneath the Susquehanna River. Soon
it became an underground branch of the Susquehanna. At 11:20
a.m., the river broke through the roof of the mine, sending a virtual
Niagara Falls into not only the Knox mine but into all the other mines
that honeycombed the valley. Most of the miners escaped, but twelve
were swept away.

The hole in the river formed a giant whirlpool that sucked 2.7 million gallons of water per minute into the mines. Attempts were made
to plug the hole with fifty-ton coal cars, called gondolas, that were
dumped into the river. Sixty gondolas were sucked into the whirlpool
and vanished like toys down the bathtub drain. It took another 400
coal cars plus 25,000 cubic yards of earth, rock, and boulders before
the hole in the river stopped gulping after three days. During that
time more than 10 billion gallons of water poured into the mines.
The Knox Mine Disaster, as it has been known ever since, marked the
end of deep anthracite mining in the region. It was Pennsylvania's
wreck of the *Edmund Fitzgerald,* and like Lake Superior, the Susquehanna never gave up her dead. The bodies of the twelve miners were
never found.

In the aftermath the web of greed and corruption that caused the
Knox Mine Disaster was uncovered. State mine inspectors turned the

★ ★

other way as Knox Mine officials ordered their miners to dig shafts more than 125 feet past the "stop line" beneath the Susquehanna. When the river burst through, only 6 feet separated the mine roof from the riverbed. One of the founders of the Knox Mine, John Sciandra, was the boss of the northeastern Pennsylvania organized crime family. A secret partner in the Knox Mine was an official with the United Mine Workers Union. The level of corruption by government inspectors, the betrayal by union leaders, and the criminal greed that drove it all were exposed in the trials of ten people indicted in the aftermath of the Knox Mine Disaster. However, only three served jail time.

In front of St. Joseph's Church in Port Griffith stands a tombstone engraved with the names of the twelve men who perished in the Knox Mine Disaster. Every January 22, a memorial service is held at the church not only for the twelve dead miners, but also for the death of the coal industry. In the wake of the mine flooding, 7,500 jobs were lost in towns up and down the line.

Hot New Beer Is America's Oldest
Pottsville

One of Pennsylvania's most popular beers was an overnight success, comparatively speaking. A decade or so must seem like the day before yesterday to a company that's been brewing beer for more than 170 years. Before there was a Bud for you or a Schaeffer to sing about, before Miller even had life, let alone a high life, there was a Yuengling Brewery in Pottsville. Founded in 1829 by David G. Yuengling, the family-owned business is America's oldest brewery and was so designated by the National Registry of Historic Places during the Bicentennial celebration in 1976.

To have survived all that time, the Yuengling Brewery had to overcome a hurdle that put most of its competition out of business for good: the Eighteenth Amendment to the Constitution, better known as Prohibition, which became law in 1919. Yuengling responded by switching over to the production of an almost nonalcoholic brew called near beer. In 1920 the company opened a dairy next to the brewery. Somehow, the company survived until 1933 when Prohibition was repealed. To celebrate the victory of "wets" over "dries" at the polls, Yuengling produced its first real beer in more than a decade and called it Winner. (A truckload of Winner beer was shipped to new president Franklin D. Roosevelt as a welcome to the White House.)

For most beer drinkers outside of central Pennsylvania, Yuengling remained the answer to a trivia question (What is America's oldest . . . ?) until the fifth generation of Yuenglings transformed it from a beloved regional beer into a nationally known brand name. Richard L. Yuengling purchased the company from his father and uncle in 1985 and immediately began marketing the product to younger customers. The result has been a 400 percent increase in sales. Yuengling's Black and Tan—half porter, half lager—was an immediate hit among urban sophisticates in Philadelphia and Baltimore. Soon Yuengling lager had become a staple in bars where just a year before people didn't know how to pronounce it (for the record, it's *YING-ling*). To this day, the order of "lager" will get you a bottle of Yuengling in most bars.

In 1998 Yuengling brewery began the largest expansion in its seventeen-decade history with the construction of a new brewery in Tampa, Florida, of all places. The original brewery at Fifth and Mahantongo Streets in Pottsville is still the greatest, however, and tours are conducted twice a day Monday through Friday and three times a day on Saturday during the summer months. For more information call (570) 622-4141 or visit www.yuengling.com.

The Best NFL Team You Never Heard Of
Pottsville

During the third quarter of a long and lousy Monday night football game on October 13, 2003, the St. Louis Rams scored a rare safety on their way to a thirty-six-point shutout over the Atlanta Falcons. The two-point safety made the score nineteen to zero, and there

★ ★

being little else of interest to discuss in the contest on the field, the ABC statistics crew put together a graphic showing the five NFL teams that had allowed the most safeties in a single season. Finishing third on the all-time list, with four safeties during the 1927 season, were the Pottsville Maroons. ABC commentator John Madden, who knows a little football, looked at the graphic and said, "Pottsville? Where's that?" After a moment Madden's broadcasting boothmate Al Michaels replied, "Pennsylvania, I think." You could almost hear the scratching of heads on national TV. Finally some director gave them the answer over their headsets, but Madden didn't pretend he knew it all along. "I'm embarrassed," he said. "I should know this." And perhaps he should have known, considering that during his playing days Madden was an offensive lineman for the Philadelphia Eagles, the closest NFL city to Pottsville.

What Madden and Michaels didn't tell Monday-night-football viewers was that the Pottsville Maroons were not only a member of the National Football League; the team from tiny Pottsville with homegrown players from Coal Country was an NFL powerhouse. In fact, Pennsylvania's "other" NFL championship-winning team was denied its place in the record books on a technicality. The Maroons should join fellow Keystone State NFL championship teams like the four-time Steelers (1974, 1975, 1978, 1979), three-time Eagles (1948, 1949, 1960), and the 1926 Frankford Yellow Jackets, which was the NFL franchise in Philadelphia before the Eagles were founded. On December 6, 1925, the Pottsville Maroons defeated the Chicago Cardinals, in Chicago, by a score of twenty-one to seven to win the NFL championship. No one disputes that the Maroons from Pottsville (population 16,000) won the match against the Cardinals from Chicago (population 16,000-plus-five-million).

But the rightful champions got hosed by the NFL rules committee in a ruling that stripped the Maroons of the title. The dispute—in a nutshell—is over the NFL's decision to suspend Pottsville at the end of the 1925 season for agreeing to play an exhibition game against

Notre Dame University the week *after* the Chicago Cardinals game. The issue was not the opponent but the venue, Shibe Park (later Connie Mack Stadium) in Philadelphia. League rules at the time forbade one team from encroaching on another team's core fan base (or in today's terminology, "media market"). The owner of the Frankford Yellow Jackets—which won the championship a year later—protested to the league that those mighty Maroons from Pottsville were muscling in on the Yellow Jackets' humble hive of fans. The subsequent suspension led to the Cardinals being declared the NFL champions in a postseason awards ceremony in which the Cardinals' owner refused to accept the championship trophy. This has never prevented the Cardinals from listing their 1925 NFL Championship on the team's resume in whatever city the Cardinals happen to have called home over the last eight decades (Chicago, St. Louis, Phoenix, wherever . . .!).

However, for Pottsville, this was their last shot at the Bigs. Never again would a Pottsville sports team, professional or amateur, win a national title. And this was *the* National Football League, and it was the championship game, and Pottsville did beat Chicago straight up. So why doesn't Pottsville at least get an asterisk in the record books, if not a championship trophy?

As you might imagine, this issue is of keenest interest to sports fans from the city of Pottsville, the county seat of Schuylkill County and formerly a literary capital back when novelist John O'Hara wrote tales of its intrigues and class distinctions for a nation still interested in places like Pottsville. Today an NFL team called the Maroons from a coal town the size of Pottsville seems as impossible to justify as an NFL franchise named for the meat-packing industry in some small midwestern factory town like, say, Green Bay, Wisconsin. And yet the Maroons were as real as the Green Bay Packers (who lost thirty-one to zero to the Maroons in the 1925 Thanksgiving Day game played in Pottsville—Brett Favre was the backup quarterback that day). A few years later the Maroons, like the Cardinals, moved to another city.

★ ★

Unlike the Cardinals the Maroons name and the franchise died in Boston in 1930.

And so recognition of the Pottsville NFL championship lies, for want of a better word, marooned by NFL history books. Pennsylvania's Historical and Museum Commission has marked the Maroons' achievement with a lawyerly worded blue and yellow historical marker in downtown Pottsville. It reads, "In 1925 the Maroons compiled a record widely believed as the league's best. They climaxed their season by defeating Notre Dame in a well-publicized pro-vs.-college match in Philadelphia—but were denied the league championship in a controversial league decision."

Notre Dame fielded the Four Horsemen that day beneath a steel-gray December sky in 1925. The pros from Pottsville beat the fabled backfield from South Bend 9–7 in an exhibition game that cost them the national title. The following season the Maroons outscored their opponents by a remarkable 409 to 31 points, including seventeen shutouts over a twenty-game schedule and still managed to finish third in the NFL standings behind the Frankford Yellow Jackets and the Chicago Bears.

Hollywood Gives Scranton a Thumbs-Up
Scranton

If you love Pennsylvania, you've got to love what happened in Scranton during the last weekend in October 2007. Despite two days of almost constant rain on Friday and Saturday, the capital city of NEPA (Northeastern Pennsylvania) won the hearts and minds of Hollywood during the three-day Office-Con, a gathering of cast, writers, producers, and thousands of fans of the NBC hit comedy *The Office,* which is set, even if not actually shot, in Scranton, Pennsylvania. The almost funereal weather didn't hinder the enthusiasm of the estimated 5,000 fans from all over the country and world whose devotion to the quirky comedy about the office employees of the fictitious Dunder Mifflin Paper Company had brought them from as far away as Australia

✦ ✦

to have a chance to mingle with the cast. And fans were delighted to be there with or without all the show's stars at what will undoubtedly become an annual event. And when the skies cleared into brilliant sunshine around 4:00 p.m. Saturday afternoon, it was like the buoyant karma of the gathering had won the battle with nature. From the hilltop campus of the University of Scranton, where the Office Convention was headquartered, downtown Scranton seemed to gleam in a halo of golds and russets from the tree-crowded hillsides.

Did you get the memo?
Paper is **NOT** dead!

It looked every bit as beautiful as *The Office* executive producer Greg Daniels described it during a crowded press conference where he became perhaps the first person, with a straight face anyway, to compare hardscrabble Scranton with the mythical Emerald City. "As we drove into Scranton for the first time, it was like arriving in Oz after reading about it all those years," Daniels said. "The surrounding area is so much more beautiful than the dusty brown lots in Van Nuys (California) where we create our show."

The Office has made famous an old saying that a Scranton cop told me dates back to the days of vaudeville: "There ain't no party like a Scranton party, 'cause a Scranton party never ends." And *The Office* cast partied like it was still 1999. They sang karaoke late at

★ ★

night, they jammed onstage with the local band, the Scrantones, Philly-born Kate Flannery (who plays Meredith) joined the band to sing along to the "Pennsylvania Polka," and Ed Helms (who plays Andy) summed up the cast's experience: "It's like we're the Beatles in Scranton." And in a way this quirky TV comedy series is doing for Scranton what the Beatles did for Liverpool and what Rocky did for Philadelphia. It's making a hometown suddenly feel special in the eyes of the world for being what it's always been—itself.

Deep below Scranton
Scranton

Tony Donofrio has an upstate Pennsylvania voice that could crack slate, even here, 250 feet underground in the Lackawanna Coal Mine outside Scranton. Tony is our tour guide and his voice does not require amplification. It is a high-pitched, high-speed voice with wide-nasal midwestern *A* sounds, perfect for a bunch of beefy guys sitting around a table in Chicago toasting "Da Bears!" Tony has been a coal miner since 1964, when the coal industry in this part of Pennsylvania was already on its last legs. You can tell he'd rather be digging coal than giving tours, but you can also tell that he takes pride in giving tours to people who shake their heads at the thought of human beings spending their working lives in perpetual darkness and danger. "It's not for everybody," says Tony of the miner's life; twenty people in the tour group nod.

The tour takes about an hour, more than enough time to convince even hardy souls that working life aboveground has its sweeter pleasures. For instance, there are no monkey veins in most surface jobs. Monkey veins are seams of coal so narrow that miners must crawl on their hands and knees or squat-walk like lesser primates. Assignment to a monkey vein was awarded by the labor union law of natural selection based upon seniority. The more seniority, the less monkey walking. Most of the Lackawanna Coal Mine tour is through roomy and well-lighted chambers, but at some point during the tour, Tony or one of his cohorts will kill the lights just long enough to demonstrate the claustrophobic effects of an optical condition known as pitch black.

"Hear that?" asks Tony, banging an iron rod onto the tunnel roof overhead. "That's solid. That's the sound a miner wants to hear. Now hear this?" he asks, demonstrating the sound a miner doesn't want to hear overhead, a muffled dull *thunk* rather than the solid *ping* of iron on rock. Thunk means something's wrong, a cavity no dentist can fill.

The story of the Lackawanna Coal Mine is the story of Scranton. The city took its current name in 1851 from the founders of the

That hand sticking up is supposed to be a miner trapped in a cave. Tour guide Tony Donofrio can push a button that makes the hand move, scaring the bejabbers out of visitors to the Lackawanna Coal Mine tour.

Lackawanna Iron and Coal Company, established in 1840. George W. and Seldon Scranton discovered that the black diamond heat of burning anthracite did wonderful hardening things to nails and, later, rails. The expression "hard as nails" may have been around for a long time, but Scranton made nails harder, stronger. By 1900 1 out of 6 miles of railroad tracks laid in the United States was forged steel from Scranton.

★ ★

The owners of the region's coal mines felt they were the stewards of God's abundant gifts underground. They were, in their own words, "Christian men to whom God in His infinite wisdom had given control of the property interests in this country!" A young man named Henry Ford wanted to build an automobile manufacturing plant in Scranton, but the coal barons at play in the fields of the Lord felt such employment opportunities would only confuse their childlike workers, not to mention cut into profits by creating a competitive wage situation among prospective employees. Ford looked elsewhere, and Scranton looks back in regret, or perhaps relief, that it did not become Pennsylvania's Detroit.

After all, being Pennsylvania's Scranton was difficult enough. In 1897 union-minded miners in Lattimer outside of Hazleton protested wages and conditions and were answered with a hail of bullets from sheriff's deputies that killed nineteen outright and wounded another forty-nine. The Lattimer Massacre led to the rise of a young labor leader named John L. Mitchell, who was elected president of the United Mine Workers union two years later at the age of twenty-nine. Mitchell, whose statue stands in front of the Lackawanna County courthouse in Scranton, led the mine workers in a bitter and passionate and seemingly never-ending strike in 1902. It was the longest strike in labor history until that time—165 days or twenty-three weeks or five-and-a-half months—requiring the personal involvement of President Theodore Roosevelt to settle it. It transformed the labor-management landscape, prompting laws to protect the rights of working men and their families.

The need for such laws is apparent here, 1,200 feet downhill from the opening of the Lackawanna Coal Mine. That's where we meet a child, actually a mannequin of a child, who could be seven years old but looks younger. The little boy is called a nipper. His job was to open and close doors to allow coal cars to pass and ventilation to circulate. "This nipper," said Tony, "had this much light to work with for eight, ten hours a day." Think of a Zippo lighter illuminating a subway concourse. That's how much light his coal oil headlamp could muster. Even by 1908, four years after the strike, one out of four mine workers was a boy between the ages of seven and sixteen.

The skies above Scranton foundries glowed twenty-four hours a day until the Pennsylvania iron ore gave out. Coal was king for another generation, but peak production came in 1917 during the First World War. Nothing has been the same since the Knox Mine Disaster of 1959. But one thing is true in Scranton, Wilkes-Barre, Hazleton, Shamokin, and wherever else God's self-appointed stewards harvested the wealth below the earth—childhood is no longer as dark as it once was. (Lackawanna Coal Mine is open daily 10:00 a.m. to 4:30 p.m. April through November. For more info visit www .theminegame.com.)

The War between the States
Wilkes-Barre

At about the same time that Charles Mason and Jeremiah Dixon arrived in Philadelphia to begin the survey that would settle the boundary dispute between Pennsylvania and Maryland in 1763, settlers from Connecticut began arriving in the Wyoming Valley of northeast Pennsylvania. Not only did they claim that the land belonged to them; they claimed that the land was part of the colony of Connecticut. Now, it's understandable that there could be some rival claims to the same land by adjoining colonies such as Pennsylvania and Maryland, especially when there are no natural boundaries like rivers to mark where one state ends and another begins. But how the heck do settlers from Connecticut leapfrog over New York, land in Pennsylvania, and call it home?

Needless to say, there was a king involved. In fact, it was the same King Charles II who in 1681 granted William Penn the land in the New World that would become Pennsylvania. Unfortunately, nineteen years earlier in 1662, King Charles II had granted portions of northeastern Pennsylvania to the colony of Connecticut. Like the border dispute with

★ ★

Maryland, the land feud between Pennsylvania and Connecticut sim-
mered for almost a century before being resolved. Unlike the dispute
with Maryland, which was settled with the border survey that became
famous as the Mason-Dixon line, the issue of Connecticut Yankees in
Pennsylvania was resolved the old-fashioned way, in a series of bloody
but historically obscure battles called the Yankee-Pennamite Wars.

Pennamite was the Biblical-sounding name (think Philistines) that
the proper colonists from Connecticut called their Pennsylvania neighbors. In 1762 the first Connecticut settlers arrived in the area around
Wilkes-Barre. A year later the Yankees were driven out of the region
by the Lenni Lenape in a massacre sparked by the murder of their
Chief Teedyuscung, which they blamed on the new settlers. When
the Yankees returned in 1769, they found that their Pennamite rivals
had taken over their lands and built a fort to defend their hold on the
land. Thus began the first Yankee-Pennamite War (1769–1771).

The Yankees, like their American League baseball team namesake,
were pushy overachievers who attracted the immediate dislike of
everyone they encountered. The word *Yankee* originated as a deroga-
tory term used by the Dutch already settled in New Amsterdam (later
New York) to describe the newly arrived English settlers in Connecticut.
The American equivalent to Yankee would be "Johnny-come-lately,"
although the literal Dutch *Jan Kaas* means "John Cheese." These Connecticut Yankees not only claimed ownership of already-settled land in
Pennsylvania, but they also claimed that King Charles II gave them title
to the north-south band of land as wide as today's Connecticut and
extending all the way to the Pacific Ocean. Pennsylvania's acting governor, Richard Penn, grandson of founder William Penn, wrote a letter
describing the invasion of the colony by the Yankees as an "insolent
outrage by a set of men who had long bid defiance to the laws of the
country." Then he came as close as a Quaker can come to ordering his
colonists to take up arms to repel the invaders. They did.

There were two or three wars, depending on which historian you
believe. All agree that the combatants took time out to join forces

Trivia

Name Games: The Good, the Bad, and the Ugly

How would you like to grow up in a town called Drab? Or Drain Lick? Or Grimesville? All these are actual names of towns in Pennsylvania. So are Brave and Paradise and Fearnot. Pennsylvania is as full of town names that inspire—Independence, Challenge, Enterprise, Freedom, Energy—as it is town names that, well, don't inspire: Blandburg, Needmore, Slabtown, Slate Lick, Burnt Cabins, Scalp Level, Spraggs. For every Prosperity, there is a Grindstone. For every Hearts Content, there is an Ickesburg. For every Friendsville, there is a Lickingville. For every Crown, there is a Crumb.

Pennsylvania is rich in names like Diamond, Chrome, Gold, and Pearl. It is also saddled with town names like Hungry Hollow, Gravel Lick, Rife, and Seldom Seen. There's Savage, Rough and Ready, Stalker, and Thumptown. There's Shaft and Taxville.

Pennsylvania has town names that seem to be linked by emotion, if not geography. Does Desire lead to Panic? Does Defiance result in Force? Are Fairchance and Fairplay in the same athletic conference? Are Frugality and Economy the result of Effort? Do you have to go through Grimville to find Jollytown? Is Husband a destination for unmarried women from Hope? Do they Ache when they find their Hero is with a Lover? Can they Admire him when they find out she's really from Hooker? Is Progress possible without Endeavor? Is Decorum compatible with Candor? It's all something you have to Hunker down and Muse about, perhaps at one of the Two Taverns.

Pennsylvania has a King and a Queen. It has a Tippecanoe and a Tyler too. It has a Forest as well as a Gump. But for some reason the town of Vim lacks a matching Vigor.

against the British during the Revolutionary War. Hostilities recommenced after the Continental Congress court of arbitration ruled in 1782 that the Wyoming Valley belonged to Pennsylvania. But the Connecticut settlers wouldn't leave, and in 1784 the Pennamite forces burned the Yankee stronghold of Wilkes-Barre. Connecticut and Vermont sent reinforcements to fight the Pennamites. It was truly a war between the states. What a mess.

The entire issue wasn't settled until 1799, when the Pennsylvania Legislature passed the Compromise Act to settle the claims of Connecticut. In the end the Connecticut influence in Pennsylvania includes the towns of Wilkes-Barre, Plymouth, Kingston, Pittston, Hanover, and Forty Fort (named after the Connecticut plan to establish townships that could support and protect forty families). The Yankee-Pennamite Wars were more like skirmishes between rival militias, and the total casualties numbered in the hundreds rather than thousands, but who knew that Pennsylvania and Connecticut actually fought a war against each other? Pennsylvania won, of course. Otherwise we'd all be speaking Yankee.

North Central

Democratic political strategist *James Carville, who managed successful campaigns for Bob Casey for Pennsylvania governor and Harris Wofford for U.S. Senator from Pennsylvania and Bill Clinton for president, famously described Pennsylvania as being "Philadelphia and Pittsburgh with Alabama in between." By that he meant, well, you know what he meant. Geographically this politically conservative "in between" area is represented by a big T-shaped section across the northern tier of counties and down the center of the state. That has proven to be true in most elections. But if there is a conservative rural "heart of Dixie" in the Keystone State, it can be found in North Central Pennsylvania. Not that that's a bad thing. Especially if you happen to be a deer. Because despite the per capita percentage of hunters in Pennsylvania compared to any other state, deer outnumber the humans in heavily forested sections of North Central.*

The boundaries of North Central Pennsylvania include all or parts of Potter, Tioga, Lycoming, Clinton, Centre, and Cameron Counties from the New York border to State College. It is an area 50 times the size of Philadelphia with one-fifth as many people. It was the center of Pennsylvania's lumber industry in the mid-1800s, and its largest river town, Williamsport, with 29 sawmills, boasted of having more millionaires per capita than any other city in America. You can hear the story at the Pennsylvania Lumber Museum off scenic Route 6 in Galeton in Potter County, which calls itself "God's Country." By 1920 the forests of North Central were stripped bare and the loggers simply moved on, leaving it to the state and national governments to begin the conservation efforts that have restored the green to Penn's Woods.

CHAPTER 4

213

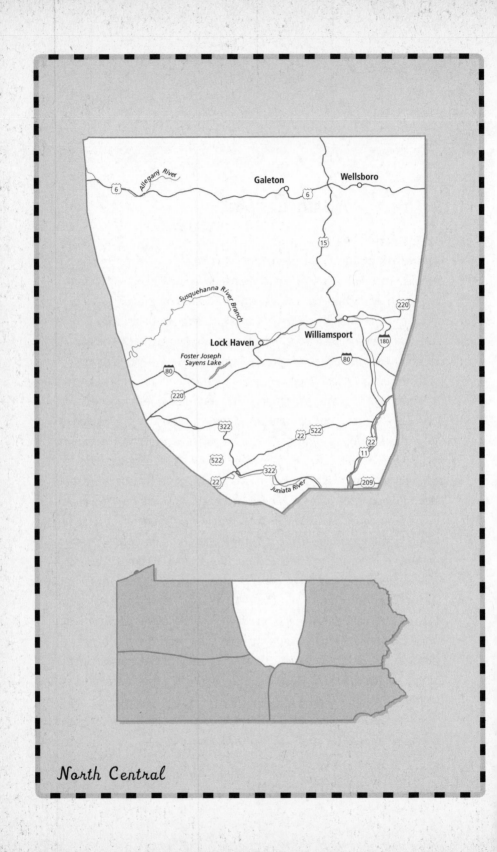

North Central

When Lumber Was King in Pennsylvania
Galeton

It has been written that when William Penn landed in Pennsylvania in 1682, his colony was so thickly forested that a squirrel could run from Philadelphia to Pittsburgh without once setting its feet on the ground. So it's really no leap of imagination to understand how one of Pennsylvania's first and greatest businesses was the lumber industry. Most of the original forest that

More deer than people live in sparsely populated Potter County (16,000 people over 1,100 square miles), which calls itself "God's Country."

once carpeted the commonwealth has been cut down at least once. In fact, Pennsylvania's huge state forest system was born in the first half of the twentieth century from lumbered-out mountains left barren by the lumber companies that had swept through and moved on in search of more trees. Imagine the leafy rolling mountains we see today throughout central and northern Pennsylvania without a single living tree to bend in the wind.

Much of the growth of mature trees in Pennsylvania is the legacy of the Civilian Conservation Corps (CCC), one of the so-called alphabet-soup agencies set up by the federal government during the Great Depression to put millions of unemployed men to work. Between 1933 and 1942 the CCC planted 200 million new trees in the nation's forests, and Pennsylvania has living proof of those efforts. The story of the CCC is among those told at the Pennsylvania Lumber Museum on Route 6 in Potter County, not far from Galeton, where one of the

★ ★

largest sawmills in the world was located when lumber was king in Pennsylvania. The Lumber Museum tells the story of the "woodhicks," the seasonal lumberjacks who worked from November until April in the lumber camps that dotted the forested landscape of Pennsylvania.

Woodhicks worked from 5:00 a.m. until lights out at 9:00 p.m. six days a week. They lived in bunkhouses in camps of sixty men and worked through the cold and snow, cutting down trees and hauling the lumber to train cars traveling on tracks laid by the lumbermen. It was hard work performed by hard men who lived in close quarters and rarely bathed. They hung their wet socks and long johns on clotheslines strung near the bunkhouse woodstoves and, as the self-guided tour booklet notes, "the stench of steaming clothes added to body odors is left to your imagination." Also left to the imagination was the lumber industry in Pennsylvania, which one hundred years ago produced the majority of the white pine and hemlock boards used by builders and cabinet makers in the United States.

For more information call the museum at (814) 435-2652 or visit www.lumbermuseum.com.

Home of the Growler
Lock Haven

Lock Haven, contrary to popular perception, was not named because the town's residents leave their doors unlocked. Even today, that could be said of more Pennsylvania towns than would care to admit it. Others suggest that Lock Haven got its name from its founder, Jerry Church, who was a loon and should have been "locked away" because he lived in a tree house when everyone else had their feet set firmly on the ground. This, of course, is a gross exaggeration. Jerry Church didn't live in a tree house. He had his law offices in a tree house 11 feet off the ground overlooking the Susquehanna River. He felt it was cheaper than advertising for clients.

Subsequent generations would recognize Jerry Church's eccentricity for the genius it was. While the rest of Lock Haven was underwa-

★ ★

ter from regular Susquehanna River floods, Jerry Church's feet would have been dry from his law office perch even during Hurricane Agnes in 1972, after which a dike was built through downtown.

Whatever you do at the Texas Lunch restaurant in Lock Haven, don't order a hoagie.

At any rate it was Jerry Church, lawyer and land speculator, who founded Lock Haven in 1832, giving it a name that was bound to attract canal boats operating along the west branch of the Susquehanna in Clinton County. The canals in Lock Haven connected the Susquehanna with Bald Eagle Creek. Church had to quit school at the age of fourteen after attempting to kiss his teacher. He worked for two years after that making shingles and then quit, noting in his memoirs that hard work did not agree with him and hurt his feelings.

With Jerry Church as a founder, Lock Haven was bound to have some eccentric institutions, and one of them is Texas Lunch, the all-night diner that is known for growlers the way South Philly is known for hoagies.

The growler, so named because your stomach supposedly growls after eating one, is basically a chili dog with a special recipe. The original Greek owners of the restaurant called their special sandwich a Texas hot dog; they discouraged use of the nickname by charging an extra 25 cents to any customer ordering a growler rather than a

Rivals Since Birth

Pennsylvania has always had a certain attitude—I refuse to call it an inferiority complex, it's more like a healthy revulsion—toward New York. Well, lah-dee-dah, so what if your big city just surpassed our big city to become the biggest city in America in 1800? We Pennsylvanians, with our Quaker tolerance, German steadfastness, and frontier spirit, barely noticed. And that Erie Canal that linked the Great Lakes with the Atlantic Ocean through New York Harbor in 1825 and guaranteed New York's commercial dominance over Philadelphia, we couldn't help but notice that. And when New York went on to become the most powerful, successful, glamorous, and influential city in America and the world, well, wasn't that nice for New York?

Of course, for Pennsylvania it was like swallowing sulfuric acid and then being asked if we'd care for another drink. Those damn Yankees! We've loved to hate them for 200 years. Where we Pennsylvanians were pleased to snuggle into the heart of America by calling ourselves the "Keystone State," our northern neighbors declared their modest aspirations by declaring New York the "Empire State." They were like rich in-laws who described your best expensive china as "quaint." The emotional difference between New York, the state, and New York, the city, is lost on most Pennsylvanians, except for those who live in harmony, most of the time, with their nearby New Yorker brethren who dwell in caves and huts and such along the 320-mile border separating the least populated regions in both states. Whether by accident or divine design, there are more deer than people found in the six northern-tier Pennsylvania counties that form the straight edge along the topographically invisible line defining New York's southern boundary. Even at the business end of the border on the east, where the Delaware River emphatically divides the two states, the mighty rival metropolises staring across the water at each other are Matamoras, Pennsylvania, and Port Jervis, New York, hardly a showdown between the Eagles and the Giants.

Historically, Pennsylvania's pride has been bruised by New York's size— both the city and the state. New York State is only 4,000 square miles bigger than Pennsylvania (49,576 to 45,333), and New York's population advantage of five million can be explained in a song. "You take Manhattan, the Bronx and Staten Island, too . . . " and what's left of New York City is still bigger than Philadelphia. Fortunately, since the beginning both states had neighboring New Jersey to pick on like a younger brother.

These natural-gas-fueled street lamps burn twenty-four hours a day in Wellsboro, the Tioga County seat.

The face New Jersey shows Philadelphia is Camden, New Jersey's poorest city. The face New Jersey turns to New York City is Hoboken. The poor Garden State never had a chance to impress its larger, prettier, more important neighbors. Benjamin Franklin described New Jersey's civic predicament—"like a barrel being tapped at both ends"—as being stuck between Philadelphia, then the largest city in America, and the already thriving seaport of New York. Hence were born the first Jersey jokes.

The rivalry between New York and Pennsylvania is not so much one sided as it is more deeply felt by inhabitants on the western shore of the Delaware. And Pennsylvania hates admitting that! These days the battle of pride between the states is passionately joined by New Yorkers only when important issues are on the line, such as the outcome of a Sixers-Knicks or Penguins-Islanders or Steelers-Jets or Flyers-Rangers or Pirates-Mets game. Need I mention how Pennsylvanians feel about the Y-word?

Texas hot dog. The current owners have embraced the name, and waitresses wear T-shirts identifying Lock Haven's Texas Lunch as "Home of the Growler." The restaurant is at 204 East Main Street. Call (570) 748-3522.

Little League Baseball
Williamsport

Among Pennsylvania's many exports to the world—a constitutional republic, the Slinky, steel, anthracite, Frankie Avalon, and Crayola crayons—perhaps the most successful has been Little League Baseball. Some thirty million people around the world have played Little League since it was invented in 1939 by a lumberyard clerk from Williamsport, named Carl Stotz. Among them is the current president of

Williamsport, Pennsylvania, the birthplace of Little League Baseball—
one of the state's most successful exports.

the United States, George W. Bush, who played catcher for the Little League team in Midland, Texas. (Al Gore didn't.) Bush is the first president to have played Little League; his father has the distinction of being the first Little League volunteer coach to become president of the United States.

Little League has been a hit around the world since Carl Stotz solicited sponsorship from local businesses to start a youth baseball league. It was Stotz who drew the dimensions of the Little League baseball diamond to be two-thirds the size of the regular baseball field (60 feet from base to base rather than 90, and 40 feet from the pitcher's mound to home plate rather than 60 feet, 6 inches).

In 1939 there were three Little League teams sponsored by Williamsport area companies: Lycoming Dairy, Lundy Lumber, and Jumbo Pretzel. By 1999 the game invented in a Susquehanna River town was being played in Burkina-Faso, an African country with a population less than Pennsylvania's and the one-hundredth nation to join the Little League. Today there are more than 20,000 Little League programs operating worldwide.

The original home of Little League stands on West Fourth Street in Williamsport, across the street from the Pittsburgh Pirates' minor-league baseball club, the Crosscutters, named in honor of Williamsport's famed history in the state's lumber industry. It was on this field that the first twelve Little League World Series were played, from 1947 through 1958.

Since then the World Series has been played across the river in the Howard J. Lamade Stadium in South Williamsport, adjacent to the Peter J. McGovern Little League Museum. Carl Stotz, the founder and first commissioner, was forced out of his position in 1956 when he filed suit in federal court seeking to prevent the expansion of the league. Clearly, he never envisioned the worldwide organization nor the live network TV coverage of the Little League World Series that has accompanied the championship game since 1960.

The Millionaires of Williamsport

The mascot of my alma mater, Lower Merion High School, is a bulldog. I suppose that had something to do with tenaciousness and "Grrrrr" and all that, but as far as I know, Lower Merion Township wasn't infested with bulldogs at any key period in its development. The same cannot be said of Williamsport and millionaires. At one time in the mid-1800s, Williamsport was home to more millionaires per capita than any other town in the United States. The wealth was literally flowing down the Susquehanna River from the lumber trade born of the thick forests of central Pennsylvania. I have visited other Pennsylvania towns that make the same millionaires-per-capita claim, specifically Jim Thorpe (then Mauch Chunk), but only Williamsport has institutionalized the title by naming its high school teams "The Millionaires."

As you might imagine, a Millionaire mascot should look like a millionaire, and Williamsport's does. Think of the guy on the Monopoly box when he was fifteen years old. No need for a monocle, but decked out in top hat, white gloves, and cane, perhaps with a black cape on a windy day.

The main room on the first floor of the Little League museum resembles a baseball playing field, complete with white baselines painted on the floor and a home plate with a mannequin catcher and umpire standing behind it. The room literally shrieks "Play ball!" but a sign at the front door advises visitors, NO BATS OR GLOVES ALLOWED IN THE MUSEUM. The exhibits behind glass show every Little League World Series Championship team photo since 1947. That year's Williamsport all-star team wore mismatched uniforms from a local VFW, Sears, Hossers, and 40 & 8 business sponsors. The 1948 Champions from nearby Lock Haven all wore uniforms sponsored by Keds. In 1957 Monterrey, Mexico, became the first of several foreign teams to win the Little League World Series and the first team to repeat the following year.

The Little League Hall of Excellence is a separate room showing large photographs of Little League alumni who have gone on to make a name for themselves in sports and other endeavors. They include major-league all-stars Mike Schmidt and Tom Seaver, former NBA star and U.S. senator Bill Bradley, movie star Tom Selleck, author and columnist George Will, and humorist Dave Barry.

While I was visiting South Williamsport, construction was under way for an expansion of the stadium complex (a record 41,200 people crowded into Lamade Stadium to see the 1998 championship game won by Toms River, New Jersey, over Kashima, Japan). Today the expanded stadium can accommodate 10,000 in seats around the infield with room for 30,000 more people on the hillside beyond the outfield fences. If you make it to see the Little League August Classic, make sure to take a trip across the Susquehanna River to West Fourth Street in Williamsport to see the little field where Carl Stotz started it all.

5

Northwest

Northwest Pennsylvania is the story of oil. Everyone knows the story of how oil was "discovered" in Pennsylvania in 1859 by Edwin Drake, who drilled the first well near Titusville. It was his drilling technique that made history, if not money for Drake, who died, in the preferred term of the day, "penniless." The biggest boom and bust happened at the town of Pithole, whose population jumped to 15,000 then down to 261 in just a few years.

In the Northwest wooden oil derricks covered hillsides as densely as the trees that used to stand there from Lake Erie and the New York border on the north to the Ohio state line on the west. Oil is still being produced in the Northwest from thousands and thousands of wells throughout the region. And the towns without oil wells are growing groundhogs. Well at least one is. Punxsutawney in Jefferson County has become internationally famous as the Groundhog Day capital of the world. Even before the major hit movie starring Bill Murray, Punxsutawney was known as the place to be on February 2. Since 2004 the official spokesrodent for the Pennsylvania Lottery has been Gus, "the second most famous groundhog in Pennsylvania." Meanwhile, I can guarantee that the most disturbing natural phenomenon that you can witness on the shores of a body of water shared by Pennsylvania and Ohio takes place on the Pennsylvania side of the Pymatuning Reservoir in a town called Linesville, where the sign at the city limits reads, WELCOME TO LINESVILLE. FOUNDED 1824. WHERE THE DUCKS WALK ON THE FISH. You have to see it to believe it. And once you've seen it, you won't.

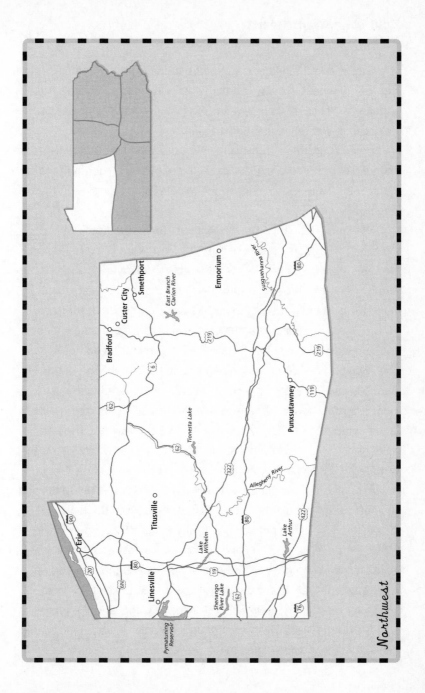

Pymatuning Reservoir

Linesville

Shenango River Lake

Titusville

Lake Wilhelm

Erie

90

20

6N

80

19

62

76

62

322

80

Lake Arthur

Allegheny River

Punxsutawney

119

422

Tionesta Lake

62

6

Bradford

Custer City

Smethport

East Branch Clarion River

Emporium

Susquehanna River

219

219

80

Northwest

Cold Town, Warm Hearts
Bradford

It's August and the heater is turned on in the house where I'm writing this. The heat is always on here—January or July, it makes no difference—because as hot as it can get during the day, it can get colder than you'd imagine here at night.

"Here" is upstate Pennsylvania. It's so upstate that Buffalo is closer than Pittsburgh and Canada is closer than a foreign country has a right to be. I am not so much in the middle of nowhere as on the edge of nowhere.

"Nowhere" would be the next-biggest town, Bradford, which only the jurisdictional reality of the New York state line 2 miles north prevents from being part of the vast Seneca Indian reservation. Therefore I am on the edge of Bradford, shivering during the late summer in the village of Lewis Run in McKean County. Bradford (COOL TOWN, WARM HEARTS reads the sign on the side of an oil refinery tank in the middle of town) has the teeth-chattering distinction of being the AccuWeather-certified coldest place in the state. "The Icebox of Pennsylvania," Bradford has been called, a title shared with neighboring upstate towns of Kane and St. Mary's, each of which claims to be colder than the other. Lewis Run runs even cooler. This I am told inside the Lewis Run home of L. A. "Larry" Rotheraine, a warm-blooded Philadelphia boy gone cold country.

There aren't many people where Rotheraine lives now—something like forty-eight people per square mile, compared to the big city downstate where the population density is 11,745 per square mile. What there are per square mile are mountains, lots and lots of mountains, those rolling green Pennsylvania tree humps that rise and fall endlessly in these parts and much of the rest of the state. But for whatever reason the mountains in McKean County and the prevailing winds from the northwest create uniquely cooler atmospheric conditions. Already in mid-August the leaves are turning on some trees.

✦ ✦

"Seven years ago our first frost came on August 21," Rotheraine said, oddly, almost like it's a good thing.

Rotheraine watches for frost the way a card counter watches for face cards in Atlantic City. That's because this big-city boy is the most successful gardener in McKean County and perhaps in the state of Pennsylvania. For the last fourteen years, Rotheraine has been the master gardener at Evergreen Elm Inc., a provider of services to men- tally challenged adults in Bradford, where Rotheraine teaches and encourages groups and individuals as they help him work an extraor- dinary garden covering a mere two-thirds of an acre. One Saturday night I watched as Rotheraine and three of his eager protégés col- lected their prizewinning vegetables on the last day of the weeklong McKean County Fair.

"Who's got their long johns on?" asked the radio personality introducing the featured country-western band on the main stage, while Rotheraine and his veteran prizewinning assistants toured the midway on a night when temperatures would drop into the low forties. If McKean County is the icebox of Pennsylvania, then Rotheraine's garden is the vegetable bin. That night Evergreen Elm gardeners had entered thirty different vegetables and won thirty ribbons—twenty-two blue, five red, and three white. At the 2003 McKean County Fair, Rotheraine and his clients actually lost . . . well, finished second, anyway, in one vegetable competition. They won the top prize awarded in every other category. (Yawn.) They've been virtually sweeping the top prizes at the fair for so long that Ever- green Elm decided to limit its entries just so someone else could get a chance to win the blue.

What's Rotheraine's secret? It's called biodynamic gardening, a compost-intensive process pioneered by the influential and controver- sial scientist-writer Dr. Rudolf Steiner (1861–1925), whose spiritual- istic concepts of planting and growing vegetables sound like voodoo to traditional agriculturalists. But the proof is in the ribbons and,

★ ★

more impressively, in the yield. Evergreen Elm's garden produces three to four times the average yield for onions, cabbages, beets, carrots, peppers, squash, and other vegetables. The cherry tomatoes can yield as much as forty times the average; a single plant can grow to 15 feet and produce 2,000 tomatoes a year.

I don't pretend to understand how he does it, but I will go on record as saying that the best tomato I ever ate was out of Evergreen Elm's garden. It was like I finally tasted a real tomato for the first time, meaty, flavorful, and juicy without being drippy. But then, I pour ketchup on my scrambled eggs. A more distinguished and discriminating

Master gardener Larry Rotheraine stands next to one of his remarkable cherry tomato plants that yield 2,000 tomatoes per season.

judgment comes from Diarmuid Murphy, executive chef at Glendorn, an exclusive 1,280-acre estate near Bradford that caters to guests with gourmet palates. After the young Irishman's appointment to the top food preparation post in 2002, he was invited by Rotheraine to the Evergreen Elm garden for a tour and vegetable tasting. Ever since, Glendorn's Murphy has purchased as much of the garden's produce as Evergreen Elm is willing to sell. "Across the board, these vegetables blow away every vegetable I've ever tasted," said Murphy, shortly after returning from a James Beard Foundation dinner in Oklahoma. Evergreen Elm's biodynamic vegetables had been the talk of the table among the fine-food professionals at this dinner.

★ ★

It all makes you wonder what Rotheraine could do in a warmer climate where the frost doesn't paint the pumpkins until Halloween. "I could grow more in a warmer climate, but I couldn't get the quality of seeds I get from this cold," Rotheraine said of what he calls his Highlands Star Seeds. "Besides, I love it here. This is my home now. These people are my family." For L. A. Rotheraine, home is where the heat isn't. For more information visit www.rotheraine.com.

Trivia

The Most Famous Town That Doesn't Exist

Since the international success of the movie *Saving Private Ryan*, Pennsylvania has become a symbol of the home of the citizen soldier. Who can forget the final scene of a now old and gray James Francis Ryan standing at attention and saluting in front of a white cross at the American military cemetery in Normandy? The camera then pushes in to show the name on the cross, CAPT. JOHN MILLER, PENNSYLVANIA.

In the movie the American soldiers under his command have bets on what Captain Miller (played by Tom Hanks) did in civilian life and where he lived. In one of the most gripping scenes in the movie, he reveals that he's an English teacher at Thomas Alva Edison High School in Addley, Pennsylvania.

In fact, there is no Addley, Pennsylvania. It was a name made up by *Saving Private Ryan* screenwriter Robert Rodat, who grew up in New Hampshire.

★ ★

Zippo Dee Doo Dah
Bradford

At one time or another in your life, you've probably owned a Zippo lighter. Your Zippo may have had a design, decoration, commemorative decal, or advertisement on the front of it (mine has gears and the Harley-Davidson Motorcycles logo), but I guarantee that yours had the same thing written on the bottom as mine does: ZIPPO, BRADFORD, PA.

Bradford has been the home to Zippo lighters since the beginning, and the beginning was a summer night in 1932 during a dinner dance at the Bradford Country Club where well-to-do Bradfordians, most of whom were in the oil business, gathered to complain about business during those darkest early days of the Great Depression.

A forty-seven-year-old oilman named George Blaisdell had almost been wiped out by falling crude oil prices, and to escape the depressing talk, he stepped out onto the balcony for a smoke. There stood Dick Dresser, an elegantly dressed young man from a wealthy family, trying to light his cigarette with some kind of cheap-looking foreign lighter. When the little wheel on the top of the lighter struck the flint and sparked the wick into flame, a lightbulb went on in Blaisdell's head. What if he could manufacture a better windproof lighter that could be used in one hand? Zippo dee doo dah!

The first Zippo lighters were boxier in shape, a half inch taller and a quarter inch wider than current models, but that's about the only difference. In the first month Blaisdell's company produced eighty-two units designed to sell for $1.95 each. Total sales that first month were $69.15. Blaisdell needed something else, something unique to attract attention to his product. He came up with what he called a "forever guarantee," a lifetime replacement or repair warranty that continues to this day.

Today you can view returned Zippo lighters being received and repaired and shipped off by the virtually all-female crew of employees at the Zippo Repair Clinic at the Zippo Lighter Museum in Bradford. One display case at the museum contains a variety of mangled lighters that have been returned over the years. The list of the causes beneath the damaged lighters includes garbage disposal, bulldozer, power mower, ice crusher, and cocker spaniel.

To get to the Zippo museum, visitors must first walk through the Zippo gift shop, where lighters that once cost $1.95 now retail for $35.95. There are Zippos with World Wrestling Federation stars like

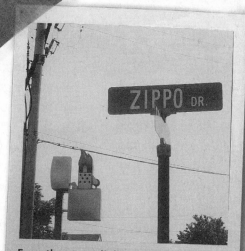

Even the street lights look like Zippo lighters in Bradford.

Stone Cold Steve Austin and the Undertaker. There are Jeep, Ford, and Chevy Zippos. There are Elvis, Beatles, and Kiss Zippos. There's even a *Titanic* Zippo, one of thousands of specialty collectible models manufactured over the years. Outside the Zippo Visitors Center, the streetlights in the parking area and along Zippo Drive are shaped like flaming Zippo lighters.

Incidentally, Blaisdell, who died in 1978 at the age of ninety-three, chose the name Zippo because he was delighted by the sound of a new invention by another Pennsylvania manufacturing company. The Talon Company had revolutionized the clothing industry with a new type of easy-to-use-with-one-hand metal fastener. They called it the zipper. (For more information call the Zippo Visitors Information Center at 814–368–2700 or check out www.zippo.com.)

Oil's Well That Ends Well

Custer City

The question was worth $125,000. "In what state was the first oil well drilled?" asked Regis Philbin. *"(A)* California, *(B)* Oklahoma, *(C)* Pennsylvania, or *(D)* Texas." The contestant on *Who Wants to Be a Millionaire* used one of his lifelines, a call to a friend, to be sure of the answer that anyone from Oil City to Wellsboro could come up with in a heartbeat. It was up in Titusville in Crawford County that Colonel Edwin Drake discovered oil on August 27, 1859, by drilling a well 69 feet into the ground that produced twenty barrels of crude oil a day. It was the first time that oil had been obtained in substantial quantities, and it set off a mad rush of drilling and speculating that turned Oil Creek into "The Valley That Changed the World." The Pennsylvania oil rush was *Who Wants to Be a Millionaire* for keeps, but Drake went broke due to competition and falling oil prices. When he made his discovery, oil was selling for $20 a barrel. By 1861 you could buy a barrel of oil for a dime.

"Oil is just now on a boom. Everybody talks oil, and the visitor must talk oil or endure the unconcealed pity of all around him," wrote Colonel A. K. McClure in the *Philadelphia Times* after a visit to Bradford in May 1883. "The houses as a rule are pitched together like a winter camp, with here and there a solid brick edifice to mock the makeshift structures around it. The oil exchange is a beautiful building, and looks as if it was expected that oil gambling would continue, even after the day of doom, regardless of the shifting of oil centers." McClure described the kind of Black Gold Fever that fueled the mad bidding on oil futures at the exchange, the same type of dime-for-a-dollar "buying on margin" speculation that led to the stock market crash of 1929. "They sold oil by the million of barrels, without a speck in sight, and with only a small percentage of margin money to give substance to the hazard. Five million barrels, and even more, are sold in a day, and speculators make one day to lose the next." After oil was discovered in Bradford in McKean County

★ ★

There are 90,000 (NINETY THOUSAND!) oil wells in McKean County alone. This is the kind of staggering statistic memorialized at the Penn-Brad Historical Oil Well Park.

in 1872 at the imposing depth of 1,200 feet, the greatest oil field in American history went into operation. The Bradford Oil District included all of McKean County and part of neighboring Cattaraugus County, New York. In 1878 the Bradford field produced 6.5 million barrels of oil, 42 percent of the total oil production in the United States. By 1883 Bradford was producing 23 million barrels of oil each year, an incredible 83 percent of American oil production.

Not only was Pennsylvania crude oil plentiful; it was special. The "miracle molecule" found only in Pennsylvania Grade crude oil makes it the best lubricating oil in the world. Unlike asphalt-based oil found everywhere from Texas to Saudi Arabia, Pennsylvania crude is paraffin based. This makes it waxier than other crude oil, a difference you can see. Pennsylvania crude isn't black; it's greenish amber in hue, almost the color of tea.

You can see it for yourself at the Penn-Brad Historical Oil Well Park and Museum located on Route 219 between Bradford and Custer City, not far from where the first oil well in the area was sunk. The 72-foot-tall wooden derrick is an exact replica of the 1890s standard rigs that dotted the surrounding countryside and mountains like trees by the hundreds. What you'll learn at the Penn-Brad Oil Well Park and Museum is that oil wells weren't drilled so much as pounded into the ground. The drill bit was a solid iron cylinder more than 6 inches in diameter and 7 feet in length, weighing up to 800 pounds. Behind the drill would be a 42-foot-long cylinder called a stem, which weighed 2,800 pounds. The bit and stem would be lifted and dropped by a 4½-inch-thick "bull rope," which was lifted and lowered by a wooden beam on a pivot. The beam was moved up and down by a flywheel driven by a steam engine and in later years by a four-cylinder internal combustion engine called a Buffalo Drilling Engine.

It's all very ingenious and Rube Goldberg–looking, but it did the job. The sharpened drill bit would drop, pulverizing the bedrock. The tiny bits were then scooped up into a hollow 30-foot-long wrought iron cylinder called a bailer. When the bailer was full, it would be lifted out of the hole by the bull rope and its contents would be inspected and discarded. The drilling was done in twelve-hour shifts by two-man crews who were paid by the foot. When the contents of the bailer revealed slurry, oil mixed with rock, they had reached the oil sand located between two layers of bedrock. The drilling would continue until the next layer of bedrock was hit, letting the drillers know exactly how deep the oil sand reached. Then it was the shooter's turn.

Shooters had the most dangerous job of all. They drove mule-drawn wagons filled with nitroglycerine and dynamite, the tools

Some Schools Get Snow Days

I met an old-timer at the Penn-Brad Historical Oil Well Park and Museum who told me the following story:

Back in the early 1900s when shooters, the men who "shot" oil wells by detonating nitroglycerine deep underground, still carried their combustibles in mule-drawn wagons, there were occasional accidents. An accident was generally fatal to the shooter, his mules, and any other living creatures within a quarter mile of the explosion. Shooters had to travel over rough ground every day in their dynamite- and nitro-filled wagons, and Custer City was in the middle of the activity.

The old-timer attended the white-clapboard one-room schoolhouse in Custer City, and at least twice a year, the windows of the school would be blown out by the concussion of a shooter's wagon blowing up. When the windows blew out, school was dismissed, but not only because of the drafty conditions. The schoolchildren then became members of a search party looking for any remains of the shooter, which could be scattered for miles. The children would find bloody bits of clothing hanging from trees and chunks of flesh (some human, some mule) lying on the ground. The children would gather these pieces, which would be buried, man and animal, in the same coffin.

James Bryner, founder of the Penn-Brad Oil Well Park and Museum, told me that he'd never heard that story. "We've got more than a hundred elderly volunteers who work here from time to time," he said, "and some of them are prone to exaggeration." There were shooter accidents, that's for sure. Bryner said that as recently as 1968, a shooter's truck exploded on the side of the road, leaving a crater in the highway 20 feet wide and 5 feet deep.

★ ★

of their trade. Two gallons of nitroglycerine, enough to level a city block, would be lowered into the drill hole and then dynamite would be packed on top of that. The dynamite and nitro would be detonated by a heavy iron weight called a go-devil that would be dropped down the well hole. Needless to say, go-devils were good for one time only. The explosion 1,600 feet under the ground would create a porous crater maybe 6 feet in diameter, and into this crater would seep crude oil being squeezed from the surrounding oil sand by millions of tons of pressure. A pumping jack would be installed at the top of the well and crude oil would begin to flow.

Oil wells are now drilled by portable rotary drills, six or seven of which are still in operation by independent contractors in McKean County. Since 1871 a total of 90,000 oil wells have been drilled in the Bradford Oil District. The Penn-Brad Historical Oil Well Park and Museum is open from Memorial Day to Labor Day or by appointment. Call (814) 368-5574.

D-I-V-O-R-C-E Spells Cameron County
Emporium

If you look at the Pennsylvania Statistical Abstract (and I recommend that you do, it's *fascinating* reading), you'll find Pennsylvania broken down by numbers. For instance, 6.2 Pennsylvanians per thousand get married each year, and 3.3 per thousand get divorced (usually not the same people). Some counties' divorce rates are lower than the state average. Delaware County, for instance, has a divorce rate of 1.5 per thousand, the lowest in the state. Philadelphia is second lowest, with a divorce rate of 2.1.

Most counties fall into the mid-twos, with only Greene and Wyoming Counties cracking the fours, with divorce rates of 4.2 and 4.3, respectively. Then we come to tiny (by population) Cameron County in north central Pennsylvania. According to the state statistics for the year 1995, the most recent available, Cameron County has a divorce rate of 874 people per thousand.

★ ★

That's not a typo. Cameron County is the "Divorce Capital of Pennsylvania" and business is booming. "We're a lot higher than we were then," said Cameron County prothonotary David J. Reed, referring to the 1995 divorce statistics. "We handled more than 8,000 divorces in the year 2000." That would be 8,000 divorces in a county with a population of 5,800 for a divorce rate of more than 1,600 per thousand! That's a heap of marital discord.

The divorce business is so brisk that when you call the prothonotary's office (that's where divorce papers must be filed) at the county courthouse in Emporium, the recording gives you a menu of seven choices, the first two of which are divorce related.

This has nothing to do with the rocky state of matrimony in Cameron County. It's because what Elkton is to Maryland, what Las Vegas is to Nevada, Emporium is to Pennsylvania, except people come to Emporium to get divorced instead of married.

Unlike Elkton or Las Vegas, couples don't actually have to come to Emporium to end their marriages. Only the paperwork is necessary.

It all started in the early 1980s after Pennsylvania adopted a no-fault divorce law. Mike Davis, a lawyer in Pittsburgh, wanted to cash in on the new opportunity by offering a "simple, uncontested" divorce in the fastest time. The problem was that the courts in Allegheny County were clogged, and a petition for divorce could take weeks, even months. So the enterprising lawyer started approaching the courthouses in less-populated counties to see if they would process the divorces. First Davis approached Potter County (population 16,717) and Potter County told him to take a hike. (Potter County calls itself God's Country. Imagine the signs: WELCOME TO GOD'S COUNTRY, THE DIVORCE CAPITAL OF PENNSYLVANIA.) So Davis came to Emporium in neighboring Cameron County, and you might say, it was a marriage made in heaven.

Each week, hundreds of divorce petitions from all over Pennsylvania pour into the Cameron County Prothonotary Office, where they are processed and then signed by a visiting judge from Elk County.

The court filing fees are a major source of income for the county. In fact, the divorce-court fee income is almost half of what Cameron County reaps in property taxes. Of course, Cameron County isn't exactly advertising the fact that it has become the "Divorce Capital" of Pennsylvania. "I'd say it's a surprise to most people around here when they hear about it," says David Brown, publisher of the *Cameron County Echo,* the weekly newspaper. "It's pretty much a well-kept secret." That's what makes reading the *Pennsylvania Statistical Abstract* so fascinating! You never know what you'll find.

Hannibal Lecter, Meet Mad Anthony
Erie

During my travels around Pennsylvania, I found that listening to books on tape was a good way of avoiding local radio stations, both good and bad. The trouble with listening to radio on long trips through unfamiliar territory is that the worst stations tend to have the most powerful signals. And as soon as you find a station you like, you drive out of range, or a mountain interferes so that you're alternating between two stations, both of which are lousy.

I've listened to all kinds of books on tape—novels, histories, biographies—but during my trip to Erie, I happened to be listening to Thomas Harris's sequel to *Silence of the Lambs.* Hannibal turned out to be the perfect companion on a stop at the Erie Historical Museum, where I found a kettle that had been used to boil the meat off the bones of Revolutionary War hero "Mad Anthony" Wayne. Wayne wasn't mad when he found himself in a stew pot on the shores of Lake Erie. In fact, he'd been dead thirteen years when his body was exhumed at the request of his son Isaac, who wanted his father's skeletal remains shipped home for burial at St. David's Church in Radnor, about 15 miles west of Philadelphia.

Well, sir, "Mad Anthony" Wayne was ornery in life and he proved to be just as uncooperative in death. Wayne died on December 15, 1796, two years after one of his greatest military victories, this time leading U.S. troops against hostile Indian tribes trying to stop westward expansion. The Battle of Fallen Timbers near Toledo, Ohio, in 1794 was another in a disastrous series of defeats suffered by Native Americans trying to hold on to their land. General Wayne's victory opened up the Northwest Territory to Euro-American settlers. Wayne was commanding the American troops manning the garrisons in the new territory (including Fort Wayne, Indiana) at the time of his death. He was buried in a plain pine coffin in Erie, the largest town in the region.

Which brings us back to that kettle. When Wayne's body was unearthed more than a decade after his death, it was so perfectly preserved that it looked like he could have gone out to dinner that night. Because the trip to Philadelphia was almost 400 miles over rough roads, and because his son Isaac had arrived to claim the body in a small sulky, there was no way to transport the entire body. So the great general's carcass was butchered, with great respect, of course. His flesh was removed from the bones, and the bones were boiled white in the kettle on display in the Erie Historical Museum, next to the fava beans and a nice bottle of Chianti.

The museum, at 356 West Sixth Street, is open year-round Tuesday through Friday from 10:00 a.m. to 5:00 p.m., Saturday and Sunday from 1:00 to 5:00 p.m. Admission charged.

What's Up with Erie?

Erie

Pennsylvania's water boundary with Canada extends for 36 miles along Lake Erie at the northwestern tip of the commonwealth. At its greatest width this little wedge of land reaches 16 miles north of Pennsylvania's otherwise straight-edge boundary with New York. The wedge tapers like an axe blade to the southwest until it meets the Ohio state line almost exactly where New York's southern boundary would extend. In fact, if it weren't for this little northern appendage of land that meets one of the Great Lakes, the western boundaries of Pennsylvania would be perfectly rectangular.

★ ★

Originally, five states claimed ownership of the wedge of land called the Erie Triangle, including New York, Virginia, Connecticut, and Massachusetts, all basing their claims on land grants from the king of England. Following the Revolution, the five states were persuaded to turn ownership of the land over to the new federal government of the United States, and in 1788 Pennsylvania offered to buy the land for 75 cents an acre. Andrew Ellicott, who would later become famous for surveying the street plan for Washington, D.C., surveyed the land to be purchased and reported a total of 202,187 acres. On April 23, 1792, Pennsylvania paid the federal government $151,640.25 for the lakefront property, which may have been the best real estate deal of the eighteenth century.

Trivia

Where's Le Boef?

Erie takes its name from an Indian tribe that lived on the shores of the Great Lake until they were displaced by the Senecas in 1654. Erie County is the only part of Pennsylvania that shares a border with two states (New York and Ohio) and a foreign country (Canada). The French were the first white settlers and they named the nearby creek Le Boef (beef, in English) because of the large herds of bison found in the area. Even today, just south of the city of Erie, a commercial bison (beefalo?) herd can be seen to the west of Interstate 79. The English, who won the land from the French in warfare, renamed the waterway French Creek, obviously in anticipation of a joke inspired by a TV commercial 250 years later: "Where's Le Boef?"

A Man Named Cornplanter
Erie

Pennsylvania owes a debt of thanks to a remarkable Indian leader named Cornplanter for its Canadian lakefront coastline. Cornplanter was a chief of the Senecas, one of the six Indian nations in the Iroquois Confederacy during the American Revolution. Cornplanter's mother was a pure-blooded Seneca and his father was a white trader, probably Dutch, named O'Beale or Abell. Despite his mixed heritage Cornplanter became chief of his people. They controlled the land in western New York and Pennsylvania, roughly the triangular area between Buffalo, Pittsburgh, and Cleveland.

The Seneca fought with the British during the American Revolution, and in 1779 General George Washington ordered a scorched-earth campaign against the Indian tribes of New York, partly in response to the Wyoming Massacre the year before in Wilkes-Barre. Washington ordered General John Sullivan to march north from Easton and link up with two other Continental Army brigades and then descend upon the Iroquois. The Father of Our Country ordered the "total destruction and devastation" of Indian villages and farms so "that the country may not merely be overrun but destroyed." "Our future security," Washington wrote to Sullivan, would depend on "terror." No peace negotiating, Washington ordered his commander, before "the total ruin of their settlements was effected."

Sullivan's Campaign, although a great success during the Revolution, is today little known and yet long remembered by the Indians. "Town Destroyer" was the name the Seneca gave Washington, whose name when spoken caused children to run to their mothers. Despite this, Cornplanter, the vanquished chief, learned to love his enemy.

In 1784, following the Revolution, the Six Nations of the Iroquois Federation signed a treaty with the new nation they called the Thirteen Fires at Fort Stanwix, New York. Six years later Cornplanter came to the nation's capital in Philadelphia to tell his story. His words, through a translator, were eloquent, measured, and heartbreaking.

★ ★

"Listen to me, Fathers of the Thirteen Fires, the Fathers of the Quaker State, O'Beale or Cornplanter, returns thanks to God for the pleasure he has in meeting you this . . . Fathers, six years ago I had the pleasure of making peace with you, and at that time a hole was dug in the Earth, and all contentions between my nation and you ceased and were buried there.

"At that treaty . . . three friends from the Quaker State came to me and treated with me for purchase of a large tract of land upon the Northern boundary of Pennsylvania, extending from Tioga to Lake Erie for the use of their warriors. I agreed to sale of same and sold it to them for four thousand dollars. I begged of them to take pity on my nation and not buy it forever. They said they would purchase it forever, but that they would give me one thousand dollars in goods when the leaves were ready to fall. . . . In former days, when you were young and weak, I used to call you brother, but now I call you father. Father, I hope you will take pity on your children, for now I inform you that I'll die on your side. Now, father, I hope you will make my bed strong."

What happened next in Cornplanter's story does not cover the Fathers of the Quaker State in glory. After negotiating rights to hunt and fish in the new lands acquired by Pennsylvania (actually a tract of land almost twice the size of the current Erie County wedge), Cornplanter and 170 men, women, and children walked to Fort Pitt (Pittsburgh) to take possession of the thousand dollars worth of "prime goods" promised for the autumn. Cornplanter's people were robbed, shot at, and cheated during the long journey. "Fathers, upon my arrival I saw the goods which I had been informed of. . . . One hundred of the blankets were all moth eaten and good for nothing. . . . Feeling myself much hurt upon the occasion, I wrote a letter to you, Fathers of the Quaker State, complaining of the injury, but never received an answer."

Cornplanter's list of grievances, his dignity and eloquence, moved all who heard him. President George Washington, "Town Destroyer,"

treated Cornplanter with affection and respect, enlisting his friend-
ship in further negotiations with native peoples. The Fathers of the
Quaker State, in the form of the Pennsylvania State Legislature,
awarded Cornplanter lands along the upper Allegheny River in what
is now Allegheny National Forest. Cornplanter died there in 1836 at
the age of 101.

Don't Give Up the Ships
Erie

What Gettysburg was to the Civil War, what Valley Forge was to the
Revolutionary War, Erie was to the War of 1812: a Pennsylvania symbol of American resolve and a turning point in war. The borough of
Erie was a small lakeside town of 500 people. Its shipbuilding industry
shifted into high gear when the United States declared war on Great
Britain, then the greatest naval power in the world. By the summer
of 1813, Erie dry docks had completed six vessels for the war effort,
and on September 10, 1813, a squadron of nine American warships
under the command of Commodore Oliver Hazard Perry met the
mighty British in the most famous naval battle of the war fought on
an inland sea. During the Battle of Lake Erie, Perry's flagship, the
Lawrence, was brutally battered by British cannons. Eighty percent of
Perry's sailors were dead or wounded when he shifted his command
to the smaller *Niagara,* taking with him the *Lawrence's* battle flag.
The flag bore the dying words of Captain James Lawrence, who had
died in battle three months earlier: "Don't give up the ship!"

Aboard the *Niagara,* Perry quickly turned defeat into victory. Fifteen minutes after giving up his flagship, Perry forced the British
commander to surrender. In his report Perry penned words nearly as
famous as Lawrence's dying command. He wrote, "We have met the
enemy and they are ours."

The city of Erie never did give up the ship. Or ships. Although the
Niagara was decommissioned and scuttled offshore in 1820, its hulk
was raised in 1913 on the one-hundredth anniversary of the Battle of

Lake Erie. Painstaking restoration took more than thirty years to complete, but by the 1980s the *Niagara* was beyond saving and it was finally dismantled. An exact replica was built and the new *Niagara* was launched from Erie on September 10, 1988. Today the U.S. Brig *Niagara* is one of Erie's biggest attractions, at dock or in full sail. The *Niagara* has been designated the Official Flagship of the Commonwealth of Pennsylvania; Erie is the Flagship City.

Meanwhile, a replica of the real hero ship of the epic battle, the *Lawrence*, was also reconstructed by the Pennsylvania Historical and Museum Commission and then, during a controlled experiment at a gunnery range, fired upon with cannon from the *Niagara* to replicate the actual damage caused by 24- and 32-pound cannonballs. The damaged midsection of the *Lawrence* replica is on display at the Erie Maritime Museum at 150 East Front Street. Phone (814) 452-BRIG (2744) or see it at www.brigniagra.org.

These Fish Were Made for Walking
Linesville

WELCOME TO LINESVILLE reads the sign outside this Crawford County town near the Ohio state line, WHERE THE DUCKS WALK ON THE FISH. More than one visitor has quacked up after reading that sign, but there's nothing fishy about it. Or should I say, it's very fishy? Chances are you'll see more fish in five minutes at Linesville than during a full day at the National Aquarium. The difference is that the fish at Linesville come to see people as much as people come to see them.

Just outside of town is the spillway that separates the Pymatuning Reservoir into two bodies of water, and it is along the spillway that people gather to feed the fish and the fish gather to be fed. It is, quite frankly, the darnedest thing you've ever seen. Hundreds . . . no, thousands . . . no, *gazillions* of fish swarm to the concrete edge of the spillway waiting for people to toss bread into the water. The bread is devoured in a feeding frenzy by huge-mouthed carp as big as a man's forearm fighting one another for every morsel. An entire

Hold on tight to young children when feeding the fish at Pymatuning Reservoir near Linesville, "where the ducks walk on the fish."

loaf of bread is gone in seconds, like a cow among piranha. It's more than a little spooky. The fish literally come out of the water and climb over each other's backs like a churning carpet of carp. Forget the ducks—a *human* could walk on the fish. Besides, all the ducks I observed remained on the edges, away from the fray.

I bought two loaves of day-old "fish bread" from the convenient souvenir concession stand next to the spillway parking lot, and everywhere I tossed the bread, the cagey carp seemed to anticipate it like a dog chasing a stick. They gathered in thick clumps 6 feet below the spillway railing, their mouths undulating like huge toothless Os getting larger then smaller then larger again. My advice: Hold your children tight when they feed the fish.

A couple of hundred yards away from the spillway is the Pymatuning Visitor Center, run by the Pennsylvania Game Commission. Inside you'll find lots of information about raccoons and deer and other wildlife, but nothing about Pymatuning's biggest tourist attraction. When I asked a uniformed Game Commission guard about the carp, he grumbled, "Ah, you'll have to ask the Department of Fish." Then he added, "They're the biggest welfare recipients in Crawford County."

He's not far from wrong. It's hard to say which came first, the people or the fish. But certainly the fish only come in large numbers because of the people bearing bread. The carp go away when the people do during the winter, and they return with the people in the spring.

The Pymatuning Reservoir was built as a public works project during the Depression. Its 17,088 acres make it the largest body of water in Pennsylvania, even though almost half of it is in Ohio. The word *Pymatuning* is of Indian origin meaning "dwelling place of the crooked-mouth man." In modern American English this might translate simply as "the White House."

Has Punxsutawney Gone Hollywood?

Punxsutawney

> Once again the eyes of the nation have turned here to this tiny village in western Pennsylvania, blah, blah, blah, blah, blah.— Phil Connors (Bill Murray) in the 1993 movie *Groundhog Day*

Much has changed in Punxsutawney, Pennsylvania, since the first time I visited on February 2, 1983. Twenty-five years ago Groundhog Day in Punxsutawney was a strictly local event with perhaps a few invited out-of-town guests. The wire service reports on what the groundhog did or didn't see spread to newspapers around the world. But the event itself was more of a mom-and-pop holiday. The first time I traveled to Punxsutawney as a Philadelphia newspaper columnist to attend the sunrise ceremony at Gobbler's Knob, a clearing about 3 miles outside downtown, a crowd of maybe 200 people gathered to see if Punxsutawney Phil, the prognosticating groundhog, would see his shadow and therefore predict an early spring. Among those present was a high school exchange student from Montevideo, Uruguay. I asked her if they had any similarly unique ethnic customs where she came from. She replied, "No, we do not have winter in my country." The Groundhog Day custom was imported by German immigrants, who celebrated February 2 at Candlemas, a Christian holiday, the date of which coincides with a pagan "return of light" festival, much like Christmas coincides with pagan winter solstice rites. I leave to your imagination the answer to the question of whether the Christian or pagan significance of February 2 was successfully imported. However, I will point out that these superstitious German farmers believed that a groundhog could predict the length of winter based on his shadow. Whatever, Punxsutawney, Pennsylvania, has become the American capital of this groundhog weather cult, probably because their groundhog wears a hat.

When Molly and I arrived in Punxsutawney in the summer of 2007, the first thing we noticed was a 12-foot-tall wooden cutout of a groundhog in a top hat standing—almost comically—at the end of a runaway-truck ramp at the bottom of a long hill on Route 119 leading into town. This was the first of dozens of Punxsutawney Phils we saw—images painted on the sides of buildings, carved from logs, painted on the front of T-shirts, and printed on postcards, along with statues, billboards, gimcracks, knickknacks, and geegaws. Punxsutawney Phil was no longer a local secret, or Groundhog Day a seasonal occasion to celebrate. Punxsutawney Phil was now a major industry. And it was all because of a day that would not end in Punxsutawney, Pennsylvania, and a top-grossing movie made about that day in 1993 starring Bill Murray. The success of the movie *Groundhog Day* turned tiny Punxsutawney (population 6,200) into the one-day mid-winter-break Ft. Lauderdale for college students in the years that followed its release. Depending on the day of the week Groundhog Day fell (Wednesday, Thursday, and Friday were best), the mostly college-age crowds that descended on Gobbler's Knob approached 50,000 at their peak. The continued success of the *Groundhog Day* movie on videotape and DVD meant that Punxsutawney would remain something that most people in town had never imagined before—a genuine tourist destination. And what could attract groundhog-happy tourists to a particular business or cultural institution better than a larger-than-life-size fiberglass sculpture of Punxsutawney Phil.

Molly and Phil pose for the third edition of *Pennsylvania Curiosities*.

★ ★

These sculptures, called "Phantastic Phils," are 3 feet tall, 3½ feet wide, and delightful. To me the Phil template in these sculptures more closely resembles Rocky "the flying squirrel" from the *Rocky and Bullwinkle* cartoon show—a happy bucktoothed character, usually with his right hand on his hip and his left hand waving, but every Phantastic Phil is different. There's the greenbacks painted "One Dollar Phil" in front of the bank. There's the coal miner "Philtuminous: The Heritage Hog" in front of a furniture store. There's a kilt-clad, bagpipe playing "Presby MacPhil" in front of the Punxsutawney Presbyterian Church. There's a pharmacist "Phil My Prescription, Please" Phil in front of a drugstore. There's even a bellhop "Phil'd with Service" Phil in front of the Pantall Hotel, where Bill Murray stayed when he visited Punxsutawny before filming started on *Groundhog Day* (which was actually shot in the town of Woodstock, Illinois). In fact, there are so many Phantastic Phil sculptures around town (thirty-two at last count) some residents began to complain to the chamber of commerce: "You've got to stop before there are more Phantastic Phils than people in Punxsutawney."

You can see the real live Phil (who must be well over 120 years old since "officially" there has only been one Phil and the first recorded Punxsutawney groundhog ceremony took place in 1886) in a glass enclosure inside the Groundhog Zoo on the first floor of the Punxsutawney Library off Barclay Square downtown. On the day we visited, Phil was not his usual charming self, preferring instead to sleep behind a rock away from the direct late-afternoon sunlight streaming into his enclosure. I chatted up the two librarians on duty about the impact the movie *Groundhog Day* has had on Punxsutawney. One of them confided, "That was the most boring movie I ever sat through. I fell asleep." Spoken by someone who lives it every day.

To see it for yourself, check www.groundhog.org and www.punxsutawneyphil.com/.

It's Erie, Ain't It?

Erie sports fans are trapped between two foreign powers—the Buffalo Bills and the Cleveland Indians—and their loyalties to Pennsylvania teams are suspect. Erie is such a foreign outpost in the minds of most Pennsylvanians that you almost expect someone from Erie to say, "How aboot a beer, eh?" like their across-the-lake Canadian brethren.

U.S. secretary of homeland security Tom Ridge was the first Pennsylvania governor to hail from Erie, and he charmed the rest of Pennsylvania with self-deprecating jokes about his hometown's relative obscurity. After he announced he was running for governor, Ridge described himself as "the guy nobody has ever heard of from the place nobody has ever been."

America's First Christmas Store
Smethport

How America's First Christmas Store came to be in Smethport in McKean County is a story of ingenuity during the Great Depression. It was 1932 and business at Johnson's Pharmacy in downtown Smethport was slow. Proprietor Leonard Brynolf Johnson had time on his hands, so he started working on his hobby during work hours. Johnson would take pieces of wood, cut them into shapes, and then paint them as lawn ornaments. He'd make Santas and reindeer and angels and Nativity scenes, and he'd leave samples of his work on display in the store. Soon customers were asking him to make them Christmas ornaments along with their prescriptions. In 1935 Doc Johnson put up his first permanent year-round Christmas ornament display, and so was born America's First Christmas Store, even though it was still called Johnson's Pharmacy until the 1950s.

As long as Johnson owned it, America's First Christmas Store had a pharmacy attached. The store expanded to take in two other storefronts and an alleyway at the intersection of Main and Mechanic Streets. The alleyway makes for a very narrow room packed with Christmas ornaments. Today the pharmacy is long gone and America's First Christmas Store is owned by Greg and Dee Buchanan. It attracts collectibles shoppers from around the world. "Most of our business is from travelers along Route 6," says Dee Buchanan. "During hunting season we do a lot of business with the wives of hunters while they're off hunting."

Inside America's First Christmas Store in Smethport, the county seat of McKean County.

★ ★

You won't find anything in America's First Christmas Store that you can't find in other stores during Christmas season, but you'll find it all year-round. One of the occupational hazards, according to Dee, is that "the staff tends to lose the Christmas spirit because they're surrounded by it all the time." Imagine nonstop Christmas carols from January to July. "The Beach Boys have a great Christmas CD and so does Jimmy Buffett," Dee says, adding, "But I find Elvis really depressing. 'I'll have a blue Christmas without you'?"

Part of the cachet of buying a gift here is a tag identifying the gift as coming from America's First Christmas Store. "We get a lot of people who just come for the name on the tags," says Dee. As far as the distinction of being the first year-round Christmas store, Dee Buchanan says, "At this point, no one has disputed the title." Only a Scrooge would do that. America's First Christmas Store, at 101 West Main Street, is open Monday through Sunday 10:00 a.m. to 4:30 p.m. October through December and Tuesday through Saturday 11:00 a.m. to 4:30 p.m. the rest of the year. Call (814) 887-5792.

index

index

index

about the author

Clark DeLeon is a typical native Pennsylvanian, which makes him a curiosity in states with more mobile populations. DeLeon has traveled the world, but he has never lived more than 15 miles from his birthplace in Philadelphia. For twenty years he wrote "The Scene," a daily column in the *Philadelphia Inquirer*'s Metro section. A winner of national and statewide journalism awards, DeLeon's work has also appeared in national publications such as *National Geographic, TV Guide,* and *US* magazines. He currently writes a column for *Metro,* Philadelphia's newest daily newspaper. DeLeon, who became a grandfather in September 2003, lives in West Philadelphia with Sara, his wife of thirty-three years, and Molly, the youngest of their three children.

Clark DeLeon with daughter and traveling companion Molly, next to the famous "gum tree" where strollers dispose of their chewing gum on South Street in Philadelphia.
Photo by Denise DeLeon.